Blueprints for a Collaborative Classroom

DEVELOPMENTAL STUDIES CENTER

Developmental Studies Center
2000 Embarcadero, Suite 305
Oakland, CA 94606-5300
(800) 666-7270 / (510) 533-0213
FAX (510) 464-3670

Funding to support the development, piloting, and dissemination
of Developmental Studies Center programs has been generously
provided by the following:

The Annenberg Foundation, Inc.
Anonymous Donor
Center for Substance Abuse Prevention,
    Substance Abuse and Mental Health Services Agency,
    U.S. Department of Health and Human Services
The Danforth Foundation
The Ford Foundation
Evelyn and Walter Haas, Jr. Fund
Clarence E. Heller Charitable Foundation
The William and Flora Hewlett Foundation
The Robert Wood Johnson Foundation
The Walter S. Johnson Foundation
Ewing Marion Kauffman Foundation
W.K. Kellogg Foundation
John S. and James L. Knight Foundation
Lilly Endowment, Inc.
The John D. and Catherine T. MacArthur Foundation
A.L. Mailman Family Foundation, Inc.
Charles Stewart Mott Foundation

National Institute on Drug Abuse
National Science Foundation
Nippon Life Insurance Foundation
The Pew Charitable Trusts
The Rockefeller Foundation
Louise and Claude Rosenberg, Jr.
The San Francisco Foundation
Shinnyo-En Foundation
The Spencer Foundation
Spunk Fund, Inc.
Stuart Foundations
Surdna Foundation, Inc.
DeWitt Wallace–Reader's Digest Fund, Inc.
Wells Fargo Bank

Contents

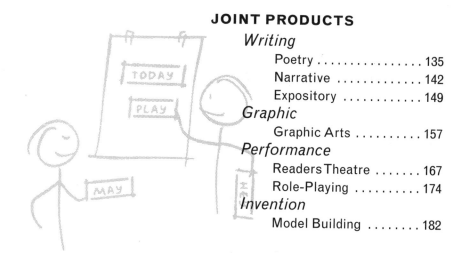

Team-Building Index

Use several of these getting-to-know-you, or team-building, activities early in the year, when students switch to new partner or groups, and periodically to maintain a sense of classroom community throughout the year.

Fly on the Wall Index

These brief vignettes provide a glimpse into classrooms where children and teachers are putting collaborative learning to work. In some cases children's names have been changed, but the words are definitely their own!

Preface

THE HUNDREDS of ideas in this book have been inspired and shaped by the hundreds of people who have worked with us at the Child Development Project (CDP) over the years—teachers, administrators, parents, and children who have created caring communities of learners in their schools and classrooms. A comprehensive school-change effort, CDP has collaborated with elementary schools across the country to help them become increasingly inclusive, stimulating, supportive places to learn—places where children care about learning and care about each other.

The importance of such caring learning communities has been documented in research conducted by CDP's parent organization, the Developmental Studies Center (DSC), and others, showing that when students experience their schools and classrooms as caring communities—places where they feel they have some influence or control over their own behavior and where others care about and are responsive to their needs—they are also more likely to

- like school,
- trust and respect their teachers,
- enjoy challenging learning activities,
- be concerned about and help others, and
- resolve conflicts fairly and without force.

While the approach to collaborative learning described in this book is a powerful way to help students experience themselves as members of a caring learning community, it is only part of DSC's overall approach and programs that foster caring and integrate children's intellectual, social, and ethical development (see page 188 for details about more resources). At DSC we conduct research, create materials, and collaborate with schools and districts to deepen children's commitment to values such as kindness, helpfulness, personal responsibility, and respect for others and to help children develop their capacities to think deeply and critically so they can continue learning throughout their lives.

Acknowledgments

Of all the teachers who have inspired us over the years, several have made explicit contributions to this book by letting us hang out in their classrooms—sometimes for days on end—and collect the Fly on the Wall vignettes in the pages that follow. Janet Ellman, whose fourth grade appears in several vignettes, facilitated a wonderful four-month social studies unit with that class, and her students became a fascinating cast of characters to us (we also visited Janet when she taught a combination second-third grade). Marlene Storey is one of the first teachers we worked with, many years ago, and after seeing her first-graders interview each other we institutionalized the practice of partner interviews. Maureen Jackson gracefully builds collaboration into the life of her combination first-second grade, making it possible for students to help and be helped throughout the day. Laurel Cress is another teacher who began building collaborative learning into her classroom years ago, convinced of its power to promote mutual respect among the children in her bilingual classroom. When Becky O'Bryan's fourth- and fifth-graders work collaboratively, they hold the same high standards for themselves and each other that she holds for them. In Michele Frisch's kindergarten, children master collaboration with lots of role-plays, including how to share a "coconut" (walnut) one child has brought to school. And Laura Ecken has made collaboration the operating principle in her grade two-three class because of her strong commitment to an inclusive classroom community. Renee Andrews Millam's kindergarten, while not represented with a vignette, has also been a source of much inspiration. We feel extremely fortunate to know and have worked with these teachers.

The ideas and activities in this book have evolved over the course of fifteen years of interactive work between classroom teachers and DSC staff members (especially the CDP staff developers), whose insights have contributed to this book; notably among them we would like to thank Sylvia Kendzior and Stefan Dasho. Carolyn Hildebrandt, Peter Shwartz, and Linda Kroll all contributed to the writing of early drafts of formats, activities, or sections of this book. Lynn Murphy shepherded the book project through its evolution, Beverly McGuire was the copy editor, Emily Bezar provided desktop publishing assistance, and Visual Strategies designed the cover.

This book could not have been written without Marilyn Watson's conceptualization of the "CDP approach" to collaborative learning and her many, many ideas for putting it into practice. But the book you are holding exists because two people sat down and wrote it. Cindy Litman mined the draft materials that accumulated over the years, visited classrooms, talked with teachers, tried out new ideas, and shaped and generated the activities, hints, and suggestions that make this book such a rich resource. Anne Goddard worked with and added to Cindy's lively draft to fashion a book that is well organized and a pleasure to read—clear, inviting, and intelligent. One other person has made a particularly important contribution to this book: Allan Ferguson designed the book's friendly layout, was its indefatigable desktop publisher, and made the playful line drawings that are its signature.

Blueprints for a Collaborative Classroom

Introduction

WHAT IS *the Blueprints Approach?*

Collaborative groups that lead to collaborative classrooms

For collaborative learning to do its job, it can't simply be about assigning groups and activities. Putting students into partnerships and groups carries with it a responsibility to see that students learn to respect (and not disrespect) each other as group members, that they all find ways to contribute and learn, and that the sum total of collaborative group work be a collaborative classroom. We don't think this can happen if groups compete, if children are assigned arbitrary roles rather than negotiate their own roles, or if the kinds of activities students do in groups are not sufficiently varied for different children's different abilities to shine. That's why in the blueprints that follow we spend as much ink on how to prepare students for group work as on specific activities. It's why we pay attention to motivation and suggest ways to get students interested in the learning task before they ever begin it. It's the reason we highlight possible sticking points in students' social interactions, so that you can help them anticipate possible solutions. And it's why these blueprints are designed for so many different ways for children to express curiosity and joy.

Learning from years of classroom experience

This book draws on years of working with teachers across the country to build caring classroom learning communities. Collaborative learning is one of several ways these teachers help students learn to value and respect one another. Perhaps the single most important thing we have learned over the course of this work is to find ways to honor children's intrinsic motivation to learn and to want to fit into their social group. All of the blueprints and activities in this book are designed with this goal in mind—to provide the structures that will allow children to succeed as self-motivated learners and as contributors to the group well-being.

Flexible formats for teachers

In writing this book, we made some strategic decisions about the amount of structure to provide. We wanted to be immediately useful, so rather than write at length about how to do this kind of collaborative learning, we built how-to's into each blueprint. And rather than fill our pages with detailed activities that would necessarily be limited to a particular topic at a particular grade level, we chose *formats* as a way to provide a comprehensive set of structures that can be adapted to many applications—across the curriculum and across the elementary grades.

The beauty of these blueprints is that the format stays consistent even as the content changes. Blueprints offer flexible support—formats that can be used over and over, and adapted, amended, or expanded to suit your content needs at any time.

The sample activities for blueprints help you put the formats into practice immediately. For any given blueprint, try activities from those suggested or let them spark ideas of your own. In many of the blueprints you will also find listings of resource materials full of additional activity ideas that you can fit into the blueprint formats.

Dependable formats for students

For students, each blueprint format is a little like a set of extended ground rules—dependable steps that make the work go more smoothly. This means that as students become familiar with the steps in a given blueprint, as they become more practiced and competent, they can take increasing responsibility for guiding their own learning. When students aren't worrying about logistics, they have more energy for the content of their learning and the quality of their interactions. Blueprints make it easy for students to concentrate on *what* they are doing, not the directions for doing it.

Three-stage activities that build in motivation, responsibility, and reflection

Blueprint activities proceed in three stages. First, you introduce the activity and engage students in its learning and social goals or challenges. Second, students work in partners or groups and you observe, intervening only if necessary. And third, you lead students in reflecting on what they learned—about the topic and about working together. These three stages of any blueprint activity build in motivation and preparation, allow students to take responsibility for their learning and group work, and help deepen students' understanding of what they have learned and experienced.

WHAT LEARNING PRINCIPLES ARE INCORPORATED?

Blueprints are based on a key set of assumptions about how children learn and develop. These assumptions, or principles, are drawn from the best available research and theory in education and psychology, and each has also been borne out in classrooms across the country—again and again.

Children's social development and academic growth are intertwined and are best fostered in interactive learning situations.

From birth, children continuously try to make sense of what is going on around them—they are in a constant state of interactive relationship with their surroundings, including people, objects, actions, ideas, and feelings. Thus, learning is actually very much a social process, and social growth and intellectual development occur together—not always at the same moment, but certainly hand in hand. Blueprints channel the natural urge of children to interact by enabling them to interact with a purpose.

Children need assistance learning how to apply values in daily life.

Blueprints highlight strategies for helping children succeed socially as well as academically. In some cases this means you will model or role-play particular behaviors before students get started. And in every case it means asking students to think in advance about some of the social challenges that their group work may entail. Blueprints also ask you to help students reflect on their social as well as academic learning at the end of any activity.

Children need "hands-on" practice to develop conceptual understanding.

To foster both social and academic development, children need repeated encounters with real-world situations and/or concrete materials to test and assess their ideas. In mathematics and science, for example, the importance of hands-on learning is widely recognized. Similarly, collaborating with classmates helps students understand abstract concepts such as fairness and responsibility. For both social learning and academic content, these blueprints focus on developing students' understanding— not merely having them follow formulas.

Children need to feel a measure of control over their learning.

Blueprints encourage students to participate actively, to explore knowledge and ideas, to practice making good choices, and to take responsibility for their learning. For example, teachers set learning goals but give students leeway to determine how to reach those goals; students are also given responsibility for working within their groups to find their own ways to resolve difficulties, both academic and interpersonal; and teachers are encouraged to intervene only when a conflict within a group becomes unproductive.

Children learn best when presented with challenges that are neither too easy nor too difficult.

Blueprints present challenges that can be addressed in more than one way, leaving children choices about the form and content of their work. So, for example, one group's product may be more artistically illustrated, another's may contain more text, and a third's may be better organized— but so long as each meets the goals of the activity, each group can feel successful and be recognized as successful by others.

Children are more willing to take on challenging tasks in a supportive environment.

In classrooms where children are free to learn from their mistakes, do not suffer threats and punishments for misunderstandings, and feel they belong to the group, they are also free to take the risks of learning new material, trying new ideas, and extending their feelings of mastery over their surroundings. Blueprints help students anticipate and analyze their successes and problems in ways that create supportive groups and a supportive classroom.

Children are naturally motivated to learn about topics they consider important, relevant, or fun.

Blueprints engage children's intrinsic motivation to learn by structuring activities that are challenging, meaningful, and fun. Each blueprint offers suggestions for ways you might introduce the activity to help students make connections to what they already know or have experienced in other settings; other ideas can help you show students how the short-term goals of an activity contribute to the broader academic goals and social norms of the class; still other ideas help you showcase what will be especially interesting or enjoyable about the activity.

Children are more likely to internalize learning when they reflect on what and how they learned.

The act of expressing what they have learned, or of hearing it in a new way from a classmate, often deepens students' understanding and helps them make the new learning their own. To help students internalize their learning, every blueprint includes the reflection activity "What Did We Learn?" so that students can extend their learning with the simple but powerful expedient of reflecting on it.

WHAT ARE THE PARTS OF A BLUEPRINT?

The principles above are incorporated in various ways in each blueprint. As you read through different blueprints, the purpose and value of the different parts of their structure will become clear—and as you and your students become familiar with a few blueprints, each succeeding one will be easier to learn because they share this organizing structure as well as many strategies.

The schematic drawing below is a preview of the parts and purposes of a blueprint.

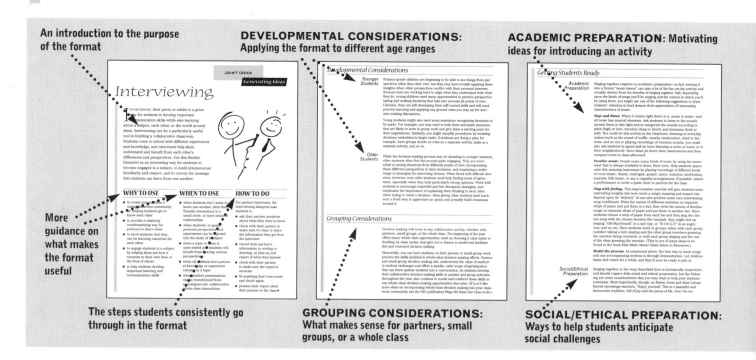

WHAT IS THE TEACHER'S ROLE?

It is your role to choose and facilitate the blueprint activities. You will also make decisions about grouping and the duration of groups. In addition, your students will benefit if you introduce them to a number of simple, informal ways to collaborate, regardless of whether they are engaged in a blueprint activity. Each of these roles is described briefly below. (Also, another DSC publication, *Among Friends,* illustrates through teacher interviews and classroom vignettes the principles and techniques of collaborative learning in a collaborative classroom.)

Choosing Activities to Begin With

Working in groups entails respect, trust, and cooperation—characteristics far easier to attain among friends than strangers. Begin building a sense of classroom community with plenty of getting-to-know-you activities, such as partner interviews in which students get to learn about, understand, and appreciate each other. When students find out what they have in common, and when they learn the interesting things they *don't* have in common, they become "real people" to each other and aren't as susceptible to cliquish or ostracizing behaviors. Likewise, remember that you are a member of the classroom community, too, and let students get to know you.

Whole-class activities are another way to build a sense of classroom community—in the beginning of the year and regularly throughout the year, as well. Activities such as a class collage or mural make it possible for everyone to contribute without having to negotiate the interdependence required in many collaborative activities. Other ideas listed in the Team-Building Index on page iv are simple ways to get students used to each other and to collaboration.

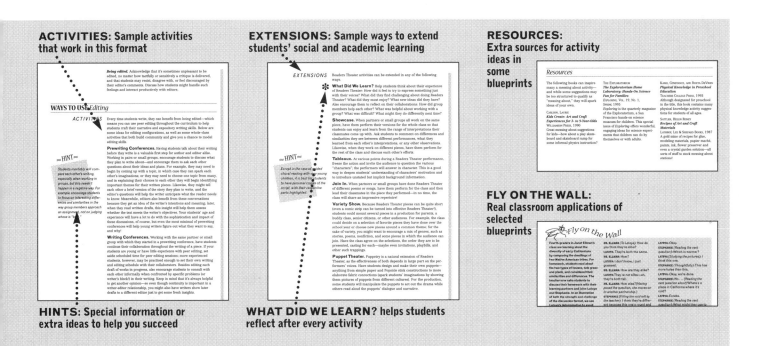

ACTIVITIES: Sample activities that work in this format

HINTS: Special information or extra ideas to help you succeed

EXTENSIONS: Sample ways to extend students' social and academic learning

WHAT DID WE LEARN? helps students reflect after every activity

RESOURCES: Extra sources for activity ideas in some blueprints

FLY ON THE WALL: Real classroom applications of selected blueprints

Acting as the Blueprint Facilitator

As the blueprint facilitator, you have three distinct jobs related to the three stages of any blueprint activity: to introduce the specific activity in a way that gets students motivated and ready to work collaboratively, to observe and intervene as necessary during group work, and to facilitate students' reflection about their academic and social learning at the conclusion of every activity.

Stage 1: Getting Students Ready

You will want to introduce any blueprint activity in a way that is motivating and that provides students with the academic and social preparation needed for successful group work. Each blueprint gives you plenty of helpful ideas about how to do this, and you will come up with many more on your own. In addition, post and review the How To Do directions so that students can ask questions about them and refer to them later during group work.

Stage 2: Group Work

Students are not automatically proficient at collaborating—learning how to learn together takes practice and your occasional intervention. The guiding consideration for how you intervene in group work should be to help *students* take responsibility for figuring out what's going wrong and how *they* can remedy it. When you observe students encountering difficulty, then, the first question to ask yourself is whether you even need to intervene. If students are working on a solution and trying to be fair and respectful in their efforts, you might wait and see how far they get on their own. If they are at an impasse, however, or displaying unproductive or hurtful behaviors, you will want to intervene. In this case, ask a question such as What seems to be the problem? or Who can tell me what your responsibilities are in this group? to help students focus on *their* work rather than *your* evaluation of it.

Whether or not you need to intervene during group work, you will constantly be observing how children work together, any "rough spots" presented by the collaboration or academic content, and any "bright spots" that demonstrate children's developing skills. From these observations, you can learn a lot about students' social and academic progress and challenges, refer to them later as you help children reflect on their group work, and subsequently structure lessons and activities that address or capitalize on what you have learned. (Many teachers find it helpful to take notes during their observations of group work.)

Stage 3: What Did We Learn?

At the conclusion of any collaborative activity, take some time to help students reflect on what they have learned academically and socially. Each blueprint's What Did We Learn? activity suggests some questions and activities that help students think about and consolidate their learning. In addition to these suggestions, draw on any of the alternatives on the next page as ways to help students articulate and internalize their learning.

GUIDED REFLECTION: ALTERNATIVES TO WHOLE-CLASS DISCUSSION

PRIVATE THOUGHTS

Students think privately about how they would answer an evocative question about their own behavior during group work or about ways to work together more successfully in the future.

WHEN TO USE: When you don't have sufficient time for an extended whole-class discussion.

OR: When you think private reflection preceding a whole-class discussion will help deepen the group discussion.

OR: When you want to focus on individual behavior.

GROUP TALK

Students discuss, within their partnerships or groups, a question about their group's interactions.

WHEN TO USE: When you don't have sufficient time for an extended whole-class discussion.

OR: When you think some preliminary small-group discussion will help deepen the whole-class discussion.

OR: When you want students to focus on the functioning of the group rather than their individual contributions to it.

JOURNAL ENTRY

Students write brief entries in their journals about some aspect of their group work or in response to some question relevant to their group work—for example, What did you like best (or least) about the way your group worked? or What did you like (or feel proud of) about your own behavior during group work? or What are you hoping to improve?

WHEN TO USE: When you want students to have a record of their progress.

GROUP PICTURE

Students draw (individually or with their workmates) a picture of something that happened in their group that they really liked.

WHEN TO USE: With primary children to help them become more aware of behaviors conducive to productive group work.

Making Grouping Decisions

Cooperative learning activities can be done in partnerships, small groups, and as a whole class, and each blueprint suggests the appropriateness, advantages, and disadvantages of different configurations for that blueprint. Each blueprint does not, however, reiterate the more general ideas about grouping below.

Partners or Small Groups?

Because children need to learn how to work with one collaborator before they'll be comfortable negotiating the demands of working in larger groups, partnerships are especially important at the beginning of the year—but not only then. With young students, much of their collaboration throughout the year may be built around partnerships, because that may remain the most suited to their collaborative skills. Partnerships may often prove the best configuration for older students as well, especially if they have little collaborative experience, need focused work on their collaborative skills, or face a learning task that requires complex integration of students' thinking.

Small-group work is challenging—with several relationships to manage, more sophisticated collaborative skills are required. On the other hand, small groups can be an enormous boon to learning—students are exposed to a greater number and variety of ideas and opinions and have a broader scope for negotiations, planning, decision making, and problem solving. We recommend that cooperative learning groups never have more than four members—enough to expose students to various perspectives, but not so many as to make it difficult to include and coordinate everyone.

Random, Teacher-Selected, or Interest Groups?

Besides deciding on what size group will best suit an activity, you're also faced with how to group students—that is, who will work with whom. Your options are to randomly group students, deliberately arrange groupings based on your assessment of students' skills and social development, or allow students to work in interest groups.

Random grouping is efficient, can result in fun and surprisingly productive collaborations, and helps emphasize the importance of every child learning to work with every other child in the class. This is particularly appropriate in the beginning of the year, when you want your students to get to know each other and you have little firsthand knowledge of your students that would affect how you might choose to match up students, anyway. As you become familiar with your students, though, you may decide to assign groups or adjust random groupings (if you have made them in private!) to better suit the needs of certain children. In general, most children will be able to work just fine together in random groups—and snags will simply be opportunities for them to learn more about collaborative skills.

For some activities it can be appropriate to let students work in interest groups—Investigating, Model Building, and Expository are blueprints that can accommodate interest groups, for example. But no matter what the activity, only use interest groups *after* students have had many opportunities to work in random and/or teacher-selected groups, and only after you can be certain particular children won't end up feeling unwanted when they join others in an interest group.

Duration of Groups

How long a group stays together depends upon your students' experience and the nature of the activity. As mentioned above, it's important to change partnerships frequently at first, even daily, to get children acquainted and to establish the importance of being able to work with all their peers. Increasingly sophisticated collaboration and complicated tasks, however, challenge students to accommodate more ideas, negotiate more differences, and simply get more done, and such learning experiences may entail groups staying together for three or four weeks. Primary teachers sometimes strike a balance by assigning long-term "learning partners" while also having children work in other collaborations of short duration.

Preparing Students for Informal, Spontaneous Collaboration

As you guide students' participation in the formal collaborative groups that are structured by blueprints, you will be helping them master the basic skills and attitudes of collaboration—skills and attitudes that they can use informally throughout the day in academic and social interactions. (Indeed, the line between formal and informal collaboration will fade as you and your students become experienced at working together.)

INFORMAL COLLABORATIVE STRUCTURES

TWO HEADS TOGETHER

Have students work in pairs to solve a problem. After a few minutes, have one set of partners report their answer. Ask whether the whole class agrees or disagrees with this answer, find out why or why not, and continue until the whole class agrees on an answer.

WHEN TO USE: When you wish to set short challenges or problems for the whole class to solve.

EXPECTED OUTCOMES: It's more fun, increases use of verbal language, and reduces stress for children who are unsure of themselves.

PARTNER CHOICE

Offer students the choice of working on classroom tasks alone or with a partner.

WHEN TO USE: When students have become used to working in pairs.

EXPECTED OUTCOMES: Increases student autonomy and student responsibility; also relieves you of some of the responsibility for knowing when individual students need support to be maximally productive in completing a task and when they need the independence to do it entirely on their own.

PARTNER SUPPORT

When you want students to report to the class on individual products each has made, invite established partners to sit or stand together as each shows and talks about his or her product.

WHEN TO USE: At the beginning of the year, especially in kindergarten and first grade, before children have grown comfortable with their classmates; or whenever a child feels shy or needs a little extra courage.

EXPECTED OUTCOMES: Children begin to feel at ease talking to a large group.

TELL A FRIEND

Every other student turns to the person to the right (or left, just as long as they are all turning the same way) to express what he or she is thinking and, in turn, listens to the classmate's thoughts.

WHEN TO USE: When whole-class discussion gets lively and many students want to share their ideas.

OR: When discussion gets bogged down and few students will say anything in the larger group.

EXPECTED OUTCOMES: Channels or stimulates individual children's desire to participate; deepens understanding of content.

EVERYONE CAN HELP

Let students know that they can always help each other (except on tests).

WHEN TO USE: When students need answers to routine questions such as What is the assignment? or How do you spell *relief*?

EXPECTED OUTCOMES: Children benefit whether they are giving or receiving help, and you are free to spend more time giving the sophisticated help that only you can provide. In addition, the comments you will overhear give you insights into students' thinking processes and learning needs that aren't apparent when you only see their finished products.

For example, you will often find it useful to break into informal partner activities during whole-class discussions, to give all students a chance to voice their ideas rather than just the few you could call on in the larger group. By having a few minutes to discuss the topic with a partner, students are all able to clarify their thinking, express themselves, and hear someone else's perspective. Children learn more—and have more fun—when they talk with each other. Consider some of the informal collaborations you could build into your classroom, such as those described above.

A spirit of collaboration, whether for spontaneous or scheduled group work, cannot be switched on and off. Attitudes of helpfulness and responsibility grow out of experiencing caring and trust throughout the school day, and strong positive relationships among students and teachers are carefully built and nurtured over time. The result is a classroom where students expect to help each other and to support each other's efforts to learn, and where collaboration is the norm rather than the exception. This is the kind of classroom we hope this book will help you and your students enjoy.

JOINT IDEAS

13

19

26

32

 40

45

50

55

Brainstorming

A BRAINSTORM is defined as a "sudden inspiration"—and students in a collaborative classroom frequently are sources of inspiration for one another. Brainstorming is simply a formal vehicle for students to inspire—and be inspired by—lots of wonderful ideas together.

Brainstorming is rarely an end in itself, however—it is usually an important first step in identifying a set of ideas for further consideration. The point of brainstorming is that students spontaneously suggest *any* idea that comes to mind on the subject at hand, without pausing to evaluate or comment on each other's suggestions. They will later evaluate the merit of the ideas, of course, but for now the spontaneity, pace, and safety of such a nonjudgmental activity allow students to enjoy the freedom of sparking each other's imaginations and ideas.

WHY TO USE

- to find out what students know (or think they know) about a topic of study
- to kindle students' curiosity about a topic of study
- to generate students' ideas for possible class activities or topics of study
- to solicit students' ideas about possible solutions to problems—social or academic—facing the class

WHEN TO USE

- at the beginning of a new unit of study
- at the beginning of any whole-class planning or problem-solving process
- any time students need a vehicle for getting their creative juices flowing
- in any situation in which generating a lot of ideas will be a good first step toward arriving at good ideas

HOW TO DO

The Brainstorming blueprint asks students to

- offer any idea that comes to mind
- not judge or discuss any ideas
- record every idea

Developmental Considerations

Younger Students

The trick to brainstorming with young children is to help them move beyond a favorite idea to consider multiple possibilities. Begin by brainstorming subjects for which multiple ideas can coexist without conflict (for example, "animals we might find on our field trip to the farm" or "ways we want our class to be") so that students can learn that their ideas needn't be in competition with each other. After students are comfortable with the brainstorming process, introduce problems that will require consensus building, such as field trip destinations, the class name, and so on.

Brainstorming is also an ideal activity for emergent writers, who are natural list makers. Have students share the task of recording their ideas in small-group or partner brainstorming activities, giving them the option of recording their ideas in writing or drawing. Or you could extend any brainstorming activity by asking students to write or draw about an idea from the brainstorming list that they find interesting.

Older Students

Brainstorming tasks for older students can be more complex and thought-provoking—for example, brainstorming benefits and burdens of a decision or brainstorming speculations about a character's motivations or the possible meaning of a word found in a text. Given older students' developed communication skills and independent thinking, they may need even more practice than primary students in reserving judgment during brainstorming, especially if they feel strongly about the topic.

Grouping Considerations

Brainstorming can be done in partnerships, in small groups, or as a whole class, depending on the topic and students' experience. Whole-class brainstorming is especially useful in the beginning of the year and with students who have not had much experience with brainstorming, to help acclimate the class to the process. Small-group and partner brainstorming have the advantage of giving everyone a chance to talk, and they are also useful for very broad topics that can be divided into smaller subtopics, each to be brainstormed by one or two groups.

Getting Students Ready

No matter how experienced your students are with brainstorming, you may want to review the process with them. Remind them that the goal of brainstorming is to come up with as many ideas as possible and to reserve judgment until later—all ideas are recorded, whether everyone likes them or not. Also review and invite suggestions about any procedural considerations, such as where ideas will be recorded or how many recorders to have.

Fly on the Wall

In Janet Ellman's fourth-grade social studies class, Chris, Gemma, Heather, and Robert have been surveying books about Native Californians, gathering first impressions about the topic. Now they are moving on to their next level of inquiry—brainstorming what they want to learn about the subject. Janet introduced the brainstorming session with a role-play, modeling how students might help one another by responding and asking questions in a nonjudgmental way. Heather has clearly taken the role-play to heart, even when she is taken aback by some of her groupmates' answers!

HEATHER: *(To Robert, her arm over his shoulder)* Do you have any questions?

ROBERT: Yeah. Why do they eat snails? *(He is probably referring to pictures of shellfish remains found in a garbage mound of an ancient Ohlone village.)*

HEATHER: *(Following Robert's train of thought)* Why do they eat raw fish?

(Gemma records this question.)

HEATHER: *(To Chris and Robert)* Oh, do you guys want to write?

CHRIS: No.

HEATHER: Robert, did you ask why they eat snails?

ROBERT: Yes.

(Heather records Robert's question.)

HEATHER: *(To Chris)* What do you want to know?

ROBERT: Why they're naked.

HEATHER: *(Surprised, but accepting)* Do you really want to know that?

ROBERT: *(Rephrasing his question)* Why they're not wearing clothes.

CHRIS: Where do they go to the bathroom?

HEATHER: You don't want to know that!

ROBERT: No—you know that book? There was something else in the book I want to know. *(He escorts the group to the table with the social studies books, and the four look at a book together, then return to their table.)*

MS. ELLMAN: *(Glancing at their chart as she passes)* Good questions. Any others?

ROBERT: Why do they put kids on their backs?

HEATHER: You mean, why do they put them on the ground like the teacher showed us?

ROBERT: No, like the picture in the book—why do they put them on their backs?

(Gemma records Robert's question.)

ROBERT: Heather, I have another question. Why do they kill dinosaurs?

HEATHER: They don't kill dinosaurs. Why do they kill animals? *(She records her question.)* Chris, you haven't gave us a question.

CHRIS: Why are their skins so dark? Why do they eat burnt corn? Where did they come from?

(Gemma and Heather record the questions.)

HEATHER: *(Writing)* And where do the babies come from?

Academic Preparation

Depending on the subject to be discussed, sometimes you may only need to introduce a brainstorming session by suggesting goals and reviewing procedures, while at other times you might want to offer more context. From the suggestions below, choose those that are best suited to the topic and your class.

Help students see the big picture. Brainstorming is almost always part of a larger goal, but students may need some help seeing how the activity relates to previous and future learning. It may be obvious to you, but not to them!

Present background information. For some topics, students might need to have some facts or understand a certain premise before starting their brainstorming. Be creative in finding ways to present this information that will also capture students' interest—for example, read a story, show a video, invite a guest speaker, or lead a discussion to get students primed for the topic.

Give clear, simple instructions. Explain the goals of the activity—if students are working in pairs or small groups, you especially want to be sure the groups all have the same understanding of what topic they are to brainstorm.

Model the process. Early in the year, as students are becoming accustomed to doing partner and small-group brainstorms on their own, role-play brainstorms with student volunteers before the groups start their work. Share your thinking with the class about what you are doing—how you asked a follow-up question to get information you needed, how you rephrased a statement to be sure you understood it, how you refrained from commenting on an idea you really liked, what helped your group organize the process, and so on. Students who have little experience with brainstorming will find this modeling particularly helpful in understanding not only how to brainstorm, but also the social and ethical dimensions of the activity.

Social/Ethical Preparation

The following are some social and ethical aspects of brainstorming that you may want to help your students anticipate.

Dividing the work fairly. When students will be doing their brainstorming in pairs or small groups, have them consider such logistics as how the group might share recording responsibilities.

Listening and responding thoughtfully and respectfully. Ask students to think about different ways they can respond to their classmates' suggestions without being hurtful or judgmental. For example, what are some ways they could ask for clarification of an idea that has been offered without sounding as though they think the idea is "stupid" or doesn't make sense? What responses (e.g., making faces or sarcastic comments) might hurt someone's feelings or make that person reluctant to offer any more ideas?

WAYS TO USE *Brainstorming*

ACTIVITIES

Prior Knowledge List. Knowledge is built on prior understandings, and brainstorming is a great way to help students realize how much they have to go on! As a first step in studying a new topic, have students (as a class or in groups) brainstorm and record what they think they already know about the subject. As they learn more about the topic, have them periodically revisit their lists to note what prior knowledge was validated, modified, or refuted—and what further information they need.

Things We Want to Know. At the beginning of a new unit of study, have students brainstorm what they want to know about the new topic. They will come up with more substantive ideas if they have had some exposure to the topic, so you might want to introduce the brainstorm by having students look through books, examine artifacts or objects, or engage in other activities that pique their interest in the subject. Students' brainstorming lists can give you information about their prior knowledge, help you incorporate their needs and interests into your teaching, and, when revisited, help students recognize what they have learned.

Ways We Want Our Class to Be. Students understand the reasoning behind, and feel committed to the fulfillment of, class norms that they have helped define. At the beginning of the school year, have students brainstorm ideas about what makes for a class where everyone has the best chance to learn and where everyone feels respected and cared for. You might get their thinking started by asking for examples of behaviors that they like or dislike. Younger students will benefit from a whole-class brainstorm, but you could have older students work in pairs after listing a few of their examples on the board. Follow the brainstorm with a class meeting to reach consensus on a list of class norms (see the Discussions and Deciding blueprints on pages 26 and 55 for ideas on collaborative decision making).

Problem Solving and Conflict Resolution. Working together to find solutions to problems facing their class helps students grow socially, ethically, and intellectually. With your class, define and discuss the nature of the problem and then have students brainstorm possible solutions in pairs or as a class. Follow the brainstorm with a discussion of the ideas, using such criteria as fairness and kindness to evaluate each suggestion (see the Discussions blueprint on page 26).

Decision Making. Of course, the strategies described above needn't be limited to problems or conflicts. Use brainstorming as a first step whenever students are making decisions about classroom life—about topics of study, field trips, celebrations, the class name, and so on—followed by collaborative discussions and decision making.

EXTENSIONS

Brainstorming activities can be extended in any of the following ways.

❋ **What Did We Learn?** Have students reflect individually on their academic and social learning in their journals. For example, they could

- write about some way they helped or were helped by another group member during the brainstorming;
- write a letter to another group member, responding to something that person said or did during the brainstorming;
- write about or illustrate a brainstorm idea that struck them as particularly interesting, unexpected, or kind; or
- write about a personal experience that demonstrates an idea generated by the brainstorming.

Alike and Different. If students have brainstormed in groups, another way to help them reflect on their learning is to ask them to talk about how their groups generated ideas and worked together. What similarities and differences were there in how groups worked? What different ways worked equally well? What have they learned doesn't work well?

Sort Things Out. Sometimes a brainstorming session will generate so many ideas that students have a hard time knowing where to begin when it comes time to discuss and evaluate them. In such cases it might be useful for the class to first organize the ideas according to themes, goals, or other categories that help shape the ensuing discussion (see the ORGANIZING IDEAS blueprints on pages 32–54 for suggestions).

Growing Knowledge List. When students have created lists of prior knowledge or of what they want to know about a new study topic, post the lists around the room. As students pursue the topic, encourage them to revisit their lists and add new knowledge, correct misperceptions, and record questions that arise as they learn more on the subject. For example, a first-grade class drew pictures of animals they thought lived in Africa and pinned these to a contour map of the continent; as they learned more about the topic, they pinned new pictures, clippings, and other evidence to the map. (And they unpinned or moved their earlier drawings if new information so dictated.)

≈ HINT ≈

When groups bring their ideas back to the whole class to be listed, they often come up with similar ideas—and it can get a little boring to hear (or list!) the same ideas again and again. After an idea has been shared, simply ask if other groups had the same or a similar idea. This will reduce list-making tedium, encourage students to listen carefully to other groups, help students see that the same idea can be expressed in different words, and acknowledge everyone's ideas in a timely fashion.

Generating Ideas

Interviewing

INTERVIEWING their peers or adults is a great way for students to develop important communication skills while also learning about a subject, each other, or the world around them. Interviewing can be a particularly useful tool in building a collaborative classroom: Students come to school with different experiences and knowledge, and interviews help them understand and benefit from each other's differences and perspectives. Use this flexible blueprint as an interesting way for students to become engaged in a subject, to build interpersonal familiarity and respect, and to convey the message that students can learn from one another.

WHY TO USE

- to create and maintain a caring classroom community by helping students get to know each other
- to provide a relatively nonthreatening way for partners to share ideas
- to show students that they can be learning resources for each other
- to engage students in a subject by helping them see how it connects to their own lives or the lives of others
- to help students develop important listening and communication skills

WHEN TO USE

- when students don't seem to know one another, limit their friendly interactions to a small circle, or have strained relationships
- when students' or guests' personal perspectives and experiences can be injected into the study of a subject
- when a topic or issue is open-ended and students will benefit from hearing various perspectives
- when all students have personal knowledge or experience relevant to a topic
- when student presentations can be transformed from monologues into collaborative whole-class interactions

HOW TO DO

For partner interviews, the Interviewing blueprint asks students to

- ask their partner questions about what they want to know
- check with their partner to make sure it's okay to share the information they got from the interview
- record their partner's information in writing or drawing, or plan an oral report of what they learned
- check with their partner to make sure the report is accurate
- fix anything that's inaccurate and check again
- present their report about their partner to the class ▶

For whole-class interviews, the Interviewing blueprint asks students to

- ask the interviewee questions about what they want to know
- give classmates a chance to ask their questions, too!

Developmental Considerations

Younger Students

Young children have their own ideas about what is significant and interesting—a characteristic that can be both charming and exasperating. In interviews, young children tend to zero in on specifics rather than abstractions—for example, the boys in the Fly on the Wall vignette are far less concerned with discussing the topic of "helping" than they are with accurately representing the physical details of the situation! Accept and enjoy this window into students' thinking, and use whole-class wrap-ups to help students move beyond specifics and draw out larger concepts.

Fly on the Wall

In this first-grade class, Marlene Storey has asked partners to interview each other and draw a picture about a time they helped someone. As Joey interviews Alfonso, he is careful to ask about details for his drawing and to check for accuracy with his partner.

JOEY: Who'd you help?

ALFONSO: I helped Scott, yesterday. Yesterday morning.

JOEY: And, um, how come?

ALFONSO: Because he fell down.

JOEY: And, um, where'd you take him?

ALFONSO: To the Yard Duty.

JOEY: Was it on cement or grass?

ALFONSO: Cement.

JOEY: Okeydokey. *(As he draws)* There's the cement. Now, how far was it to the Yard Duty?

ALFONSO: Um, I don't quite remember . . .

JOEY: About this far? *(He shows Alfonso where he might draw it on the paper.)*

ALFONSO: Yeah, that far—yeah, yeah.

JOEY: *(As he begins drawing Alfonso and Scott)* I think I'll just fill in their heads—kind of get a head start?

ALFONSO: Yeah, looks nice.

JOEY: *(Indicating the figure he's drawing)* That's you, and you're helping Scott—

ALFONSO: —and Scott's fell down.

JOEY: *(Drawing another figure)* Okay, this is Scott . . . he has a smaller head than you. Now, what else do you want me to put in?

ALFONSO: *(Looking over the drawing)* Hmmm.

JOEY: Should I put the blue sky up?

ALFONSO: Yeah, blue sky. And that's it. *(Joey adds the sky.)* Hey, why don't you put the office there?

JOEY: Hmmm, and maybe I should put the gate over here—

ALFONSO: Yeah, the gate!

JOEY: That's the gate. . . . Are you finished?

ALFONSO: Uh, not quite yet—you know why? You need the soft ground next to the gate.

JOEY: Oh, I need the dirt—

ALFONSO: Yeah, the dirt!

JOEY: *(As he draws dots to indicate the dirt)* Speck, speck, speck, speck, speck, speck, speck—

ALFONSO: That's it. That's all you need to do. That's better!

JOEY: Finished?

ALFONSO: Yes, you're finished.

Many students are accustomed to answering questions and may have trouble asking and following up questions in ways that keep an interview going. Model these skills for students, explaining what you do, and give them lots of practice generating their own questions throughout the curriculum.

Also keep in mind that young children find it particularly difficult to report on their partners instead of themselves—they are far more inclined to tell their own story when it comes time to share with the whole class, because these are the details that are most memorable and immediate to them. (That's why activities involving tangible objects, such as Talking Artifacts on page 23, are exceptionally useful with young children—they have something concrete to keep their interview and their report on track.) Before their interviews, remind students to take care in recording their partner's story and when necessary gently steer them back on course during their reports to the class. Of course, role-playing and modeling these skills will prove even more effective than verbal reminders in the long run.

Finally, take the "communication" pressure off emergent writers by having them draw what they learn about their partners, as in the Fly on the Wall vignette. Have children augment their drawings with dialogue or thought bubbles, or short captions, as unintimidating ways to engage their blossoming writing skills in interview activities.

Older Students

Being more verbally skilled than young children, older students may find it difficult to trust someone else to report their ideas accurately. Encourage partners to collaborate closely so that they can adequately portray one another's thoughts and feelings; when necessary, review how to have accurate and respectful reports, as suggested in "Being reported" and the nearby Hint on page 23.

Students of all ages (any of us, for that matter) will find their own ideas especially interesting and will have to work at listening as eagerly to the ideas of others. Older students, however, can more easily be made aware of this tendency and work toward becoming as involved and engaged in the interviewer role as in telling their own story. Challenge student interviewers to take responsibility for asking questions and making comments that help their partner think more deeply about the interview topic.

Grouping Considerations

Interviewing can be done in partnerships or as a whole class, depending upon whether one person has specialized information from which the whole class can learn or everyone has relevant information that can be profitably shared.

Each configuration serves other valuable objectives, as well. In partner interviews, students take turns interviewing each other and then present what they have learned about their partner to the class (via drawings, writing, collages, oral reports, etc.). In doing so they learn to listen attentively and present information clearly to others. Also, partner interviews offer shy students a reassuringly limited audience and a structured way to voice their ideas.

Whole-class interviews, in contrast, can transform traditionally passive class activities—such as show-and-tell, Special Person of the Week, or student oral presentations—into interactive whole-class experiences in which the audience asks questions and responds to the speaker. This makes for a lively learning experience that reinforces the message that students can learn from each other. Likewise, whole-class interviews of guest speakers encourage students' sense of ownership of and responsibility for their own learning.

Getting Students Ready

Academic Preparation

Depending upon the interview purpose and your students' experience, use one or more of the preparation activities below to engage students' interest and hone their interviewing skills.

Introduce the topic. Tell a relevant personal story, read aloud a book, show and discuss an object, or in some other way connect students with the interview topic. If students will be asked specific information in their interviews—for example, to tell a family story or describe a favorite work of art—give students time to gather their data (or collect their thoughts) before the interview.

Invite an interviewer. Ask someone whose job involves interviewing—such as a journalist, social worker, or doctor—to speak to your students about the skills, process, and rewards of doing interviews in his or her profession. An alternative would be to play a videotape of a familiar interviewer, such as Mr. Rogers or Oprah Winfrey, and discuss with students what they observe about a professional's approaches and results.

Discuss questioning strategies. Teach effective questioning strategies by sharing the reasons behind how you ask questions. For example, discuss the difference between closed questions, which only elicit "yes" or "no" answers, and open questions, which evoke more informative responses.

Model the process. Interview and be interviewed by a student, the whole class, or an adult partner. (This gives students a chance not only to learn about the roles of interviewer and interviewee, but also to enjoy learning more about you when you are interviewed!) Afterward, ask students to share their observations about the interviews—what worked, what didn't, what questions seemed most interesting or evocative, what questions they might have asked, and so on.

Social/Ethical Preparation

The following are some social and ethical aspects of interviewing that you may want to help your students anticipate.

Listening carefully. Listening well takes effort and practice. Encourage students to take their role as listeners as thoughtfully as they do other learning tasks—by clearing their desks and giving their full attention to the speaker. Ask students for their ideas on what behaviors might make a speaker feel listened to and what might give

≈HINT≈

Different recording and reporting strategies can accommodate students' varying skill levels—for example, options include drawing a picture with a caption to show to the class, taking brief notes to report to the class, writing an expository paragraph or a story to read aloud, and so on.

the appearance of inattentiveness. For that matter, what can a speaker do to make it easier for a partner or other audience to listen?

Responding respectfully. Help students think about what kinds of responses help people feel "safe" expressing their thoughts and feelings. For example, how might they respond if their interviewee says something that doesn't make sense to them? That surprises them? With which they disagree? Students may enjoy role-playing the difference between respectful and disrespectful responses.

Being reported. When students report their partner's story or information, it can be very difficult for the partner to refrain from chiming in to add overlooked details or to correct the interviewer's rendition of their conversation. Ask students to think about how they feel when they are interrupted and why it is important to respect a partner's efforts to report an interview. Invite their suggestions for making the reporting process easier for everyone—for example, interviewers should check details with their partners before reporting, and after a report you could check in with the interviewee to see if she or he has anything to add.

Sharing the floor. For whole-class interviews, discuss with your students how they can share the interviewer role. For partner interviews, at first you will probably need to signal when it is time for partners to switch interviewer/interviewee roles. As your students get the feel for doing interviews, ask for their ideas on how they can assume responsibility for dividing their interview time with their partner.

≈ HINT ≈

Get students in the habit of checking with their partner about what information is okay to share with the rest of the class—sometimes the partner might feel comfortable telling something to one person but uncomfortable having it broadcast to the whole class.

WAYS TO USE *Interviewing*

ACTIVITIES

PARTNER INTERVIEWS

We Are Alike, We Are Different. Interviews about how partners are alike and different can help students appreciate their shared and unique traits—that it's fun to have things in common and interesting to be different. The activity can focus on specific subjects, such as what we like to learn, things we like to do with friends, areas of interest in a study topic, ways we like to get to know people, and so on. Introduce the activity with a whole-class brainstorm about what questions would be interesting and appropriate to ask in the interview. Have younger partners record their information in a three-column collage of magazine pictures or their own drawings—one column each for their unique traits or preferences, and the middle column for how they are alike. Older students can demonstrate more sophisticated comparisons with a Venn diagram.

Talking Artifacts. This activity—in which partners bring in special objects from home, interview each other about them, and share what they have learned with the rest of the class—is another excellent vehicle for helping students get to know each other and build community in the classroom. (It works especially well with young children, as the use of tangible objects helps elicit and focus both their questions and responses.) Encourage students to bring in objects of personal rather than monetary value—for example, a letter from a grandparent, a favorite drawing, a photo of a friend or relative, and so on. Also, have them bring their object in a paper bag and keep it hidden until they are interviewed; this deters children from distracting each other with their artifacts and adds to the fun by heightening "suspense." Introduce the activity by bringing in an object of your own and having the class interview you about it. A useful variation on this interview would be to have students bring in (or bring in a picture of) a particular category of object, such as a favorite book, recording, work of art, or animal.

Someone Like . . . To extend students' thinking about a story the class is reading, have partners interview each other about someone who reminds them of a character in the story—for example, an elderly person with whom they had a special relationship, or a special pet. You could also use this interview before students have read the story, to introduce it and help them make personal connections with the ideas they will encounter in it.

Personal History. Partner interviews about family histories and traditions can enrich and humanize social studies and history lessons—for example, beginning a unit on state history by having partners interview each other about how their families came to the state. Introduce the activity several days before the interviews (perhaps by telling about your own history), so that students have time to gather information from parents or other family members.

Home Interviews. Have students use their interviewing skills outside of school, to interview a parent or other adult about something the class is studying. Before the interviews, have the class agree on three or four questions to use in the home interviews (these should be questions about opinions or universal experiences, not questions that require special knowledge or expertise). Afterward, follow up with a class discussion or activity that allows students to share and benefit from what their classmates learned; similarly, students could share in partner interviews what they learned in their home interviews.

WHOLE-CLASS INTERVIEWS

Student Presentations. Have the class play the role of interviewer during current event reports, book reports, or other such presentations. Encourage the interviewers to probe beyond data and ask for the presenter's interpretation and speculations about his or her topic. An interesting variation would be for presenters to assume the identity of a character from the story or event being reported on and answer classmates' questions from the character's perspective.

Special Person of the Week. Students can take an enjoyable, active role in learning about the Special Person of the Week by conducting whole-class interviews. Ask the Special Person to share some special objects or photos with the class as a springboard for the interview, and model questioning strategies by participating in the interview yourself.

Guest Speakers. Guest speakers can help students learn about their school, their community, and the world, and students can take charge of their learning by interviewing guests. Prior to a guest's visit, have students discuss what they would like to learn from the visitor and prepare interview questions accordingly. Guest speakers might include the following:

- members of students' families
- a substitute teacher (to give students insight into a substitute's experience!)
- school staff, such as a custodian, secretary, nurse, principal, or cafeteria worker
- representatives of different occupations, both familiar and unusual
- world travelers
- experts about something the class is studying

EXTENSIONS

Interviewing activities can be extended in any of the following ways.

✳ **What Did We Learn?** Invite students' comments about their experience of interviewing. What worked well? What might they do differently next time? What do they enjoy about doing interviews? How could they enjoy them more?

Class Book. Have students each create a page (about their partner or about a whole-class interview, whichever is appropriate) for a class book on the interview theme. The pages could also be displayed on a bulletin board.

Graphically Organize. After a partner interview, have students contribute what they learned to a class chart, Venn diagram, mural, or other graphic organization of information. For example, have students graph the number of siblings their partner has, fill in their partner's name on a Venn diagram (who has a pet mammal, reptile, bird, or fish, for example), mark a map showing the places their partner has visited or would like to visit, paint a picture of their partner's home on a map of the community, and so on. (See the ORGANIZING IDEAS blueprints on pages 32–54 for suggestions.)

Dramatize the Interview. Invite volunteers to dramatize their partner's experience or ideas, either solo or with the partner.

Discussions

PROVIDING opportunities for meaningful interactions among students is an important part of building a collaborative learning community. Chief among such opportunities are instructionally focused discussions— conversations in which students talk to *each other,* responding to and building on each other's ideas. Students who have been trained to answer data-recall questions, or who are accustomed to classroom discussions in which they respond only to the teacher's questions and prompts, may initially be baffled by discussions that require exploratory thinking among peers rather than the teacher's approval for giving "right" answers. Experiencing such discussions, however, will help students learn that plumbing ideas, asking questions, and comparing points of view are intrinsically valuable activities—and these students will become learners who can process ideas, not just details.

WHY TO USE

- to help students expand, clarify, and sharpen their thinking
- to help students learn to articulate the thinking behind their opinions and conclusions
- to develop students' confidence in expressing their own ideas and exploring the ideas of others
- to help students learn, grow, and build community through peer interaction
- to develop students' lifelong appreciation for ideas in their own right, not just for the sake of a right answer

WHEN TO USE

- when hearing different interpretations and points of view will enrich students' understanding and appreciation of a study topic
- when students need insight into each other's perspectives on an issue facing their classroom community
- after brainstorming, to begin evaluating the merits of the ideas that have been offered

HOW TO DO

The Discussions blueprint asks students to

- share thoughts and opinions with each other
- listen and respond respectfully to each other
- give evidence
- get clarification
- agree to disagree

Developmental Considerations

Younger Students

It can be more than a little dismaying to launch a classroom discussion and find that otherwise very chatty students now have nothing to say. To increase the likelihood that young children's instructionally focused discussions will generate the same enthusiasm as their spontaneous playground conversations, you will want to choose topics that are naturally interesting and immediate to them: a problem facing the class, a favorite story character in a predicament, an exhibit they have seen in the science center, or other topics that align with significant aspects of students' lives.

It also helps to use concrete examples to get at abstract ideas. For example, a discussion about Frances and Albert in Russell Hoban's *Best Friends for Frances* is more likely to elicit children's ideas about boy-girl friendships than having partners discuss a general question on the topic. Or starting a science discussion with the question What do living things need? will prove harder going than starting with a partner discussion about the needs of the classroom hamster or iguana, or even the students.

Also, younger children may need more guidance than older students in learning how to respond diplomatically to different ideas—for example, learning to say "I have a different idea" rather than "That's stupid." Modeling the process and holding many whole-class discussions before having students try more independent partner or small-group discussions will help children learn these skills.

Finally, don't be discouraged if your students' discussions don't become quite as engaging and fluid as you'd hoped. Taking turns telling their ideas is as close to discussion as some young children will get, but this is nonetheless valuable—such sharing is a chance for children to think and talk about their own ideas and hear the ideas of others, which is the foundation for future discussions that will have more give-and-take.

Older Students

≈HINT≈

You may need to remind students that discussions are "real work"—even when they don't result in a "right" answer, tangible product, or grade. Help students recognize that the abilities to exchange and evaluate ideas are valuable skills that they will continue to get better at as they practice.

All students need to feel safe before participating frankly and willingly in classroom discussions, but older students particularly need their teachers' and peers' encouragement and support to express unpopular or unusual ideas. In addition to your overall efforts to build a caring classroom community, which in itself engenders the safe environment students need for risking self-expression, also model and discuss with students how to be open to different perspectives. Older students often feel passionate about their views, and you will want to encourage that passion about ideas while also helping students express themselves and challenge each other in respectful ways.

In such a supportive classroom community, older students will relish opportunities to discuss interesting issues—especially those that affect them directly. You may need to help them address more abstract topics and engage in more sophisticated conversations, however, by helping them see the connection between a topic and their own lives—for example, how a seemingly distant event touches their lives and their community, how decisions made by lawmakers in faraway cities directly affect some aspect of their lives, the present-day repercussions of a historic event, and so on.

Grouping Considerations

Lively and worthwhile exchanges can occur in whole-class, small-group, or partner discussions, of course, so your choice of configurations will rest on the scope of the topic, your students' experience, and how the discussion proceeds.

If students have had little experience in independent, instructionally focused talk with peers, first attempts at partner or small-group discussion may feel awkward or stilted. To prepare students for such independent discussions, first hold many whole-class discussions in which you model thoughtful listening and responding. Moving into partner and small-group discussions will, in turn, help students become more accustomed to talking to each other—not just to the teacher—during classroom discussions.

An advantage of partner and small-group discussions is that unlike whole-class discussions, in which a few students can carry the conversation, every voice is needed in small-group discussions. And because small-group or partner discussions resemble everyday conversation far more than whole-class discussions do, they are a relatively nonthreatening way for shy or reluctant students to participate.

Getting Students Ready

Academic Preparation

Discussions will often naturally follow from some other activity—reading a story, finding a math or science solution, trying to understand a conflict that happened at recess, and so on. If not, be sure to prime students for the discussion by creating interest and providing necessary background, so that they know what they are discussing and feel inclined to do so. Below are some suggestions for engaging student interest and fostering discussion skills.

Pose a compelling question. Be sure the question or problem you are asking students to discuss is a worthwhile one, and if necessary explain its worthiness and potential interest to the class.

Create a common context. If students have little familiarity with the topic to be discussed—for example, if you spontaneously ask for their opinion on a recent current event—provide information so that students have some shared understanding from which to start in their discussion.

Make things clear. Talk with students about how they can help each other have clear, productive discussions. Encourage them to support

their ideas with evidence from text or their own experience, since this can add interest to a discussion, but don't give students the idea that they shouldn't speak up unless they can prove they are "right." On the other side of the conversation, as listeners, students should feel comfortable asking for clarification when they aren't sure they understand a classmate's idea. You might introduce paraphrasing as a technique for checking understanding.

Begin together. If students are still getting used to having open-ended discussions, you may want to precede their partner or small-group discussions with a brief whole-class discussion on the topic just to get things going and to review the skills involved.

Model the process. Again, if your students don't have much experience with open-ended classroom discussions, you might model one for them. Hold a brief discussion with a student volunteer and then review it with the class: How do students think it went? What did they notice about how you and your partner responded to each other, built on each other's ideas, kept the conversation on track, and so on? What might they have done differently?

Social/Ethical Preparation

The following are some social and ethical aspects of holding discussions that you may want to help your students anticipate.

Listening and responding. Remind students that discussions are not competitions—the point of a discussion is not necessarily to find a "right" answer or to persuade others to their way of thinking. The overriding goal is to express their thoughts and to *listen* and *respond* to each other, in the interest of exploring ideas, seeing issues from all angles, and perhaps learning a thing or two from each other. Even when discussing something that requires a solution, students' first priority should be to hear each other out and understand each other's perspectives—otherwise they might never explore far enough to arrive at a conclusion.

Agreeing to disagree. Even when a discussion is not focused on arriving at a specific conclusion, students may still have difficulty when they encounter disagreement. Remind them that there is a simple strategy for such inevitabilities: At any point in a discussion they can simply agree to disagree with each other. This allows for a respectful airing of differences and reduces the chances that discussions will bog down by students trying to "win" the discussion.

ACTIVITIES

Informal discussion activities, such as those described below, can be adapted to any of the academic or problem-solving topics that are part of everyday classroom life. Some of the following are useful when students need to make decisions concerning the classroom community, others contribute to students' understanding of academic content, and all of them help students learn with and from each other.

Tell a Friend. This activity, in which you ask students to turn to a classmate (not necessarily a "formal" partner) and exchange ideas, is a simple way to manage or encourage discussion of a topic. For example, if a whole-class discussion is particularly lively and many students are clamoring to share their ideas, you might spontaneously suggest everyone "tell a friend" what they are thinking, so that everyone gets a chance to voice their ideas. Conversely, if a whole-class discussion has bogged down, you might use this to get one-on-one conversations going.

Partners Decide. This is a useful way to generate ideas and manage discussion when students are trying to make whole-class decisions: Have partners discuss the issue, agree on a decision, and then share it with the class. For example, after a brainstorming session (such as Ways We Want Our Class to Be or Problem Solving and Conflict Resolution, described on page 17), partners could identify what they consider to be the best idea from the brainstormed list and then explain their reasoning to the class. The whole class can then discuss the pool of partners' decisions and build consensus from there (see the Deciding blueprint on page 55).

Two Heads Together. Partner decisions can also add interest to academic problem solving, such as finding math or science solutions. After partners put their heads together and agree on a solution, have them present their solutions and explain their reasoning to the class. Not only will students develop their ability to articulate their thought processes, but also the whole class will learn from each other as they discuss different approaches to the same problem.

Common Thread. It is relatively easy to have a discussion when everybody has read the same text or engaged in the same inquiry, but not quite as easy when students have read different books or studied different topics. One approach is to have students discuss their work in groups organized around themes. For example, they could share their independent-reading books in groups organized around such themes as love, hatred, growing up, loss, hope, prejudice, and so on (be sure to capitalize on students' individual insights and interests by allowing them to choose which theme group to join rather than assigning them). Content-area discussion groups can be similarly organized: Current event discussion groups could be organized around themes such as the environment, politics, war, and culture; discussions of famous scientists might be grouped by time period or discipline; and so on.

≈ HINT ≈

Allow yourself the flexibility to change and mix the group size midstream in a discussion activity—to either spark, manage, or vary the conversation.

EXTENSIONS A good discussion is often an end in itself or a segue into another activity, but you may also want to extend a discussion activity in one of the following ways.

✳ **What Did We Learn?** Regularly spend time helping students reflect on their growth and development as thoughtful and principled discussants. For example, after whole-group discussions you could ask students what they liked about the experience and what might have worked better, after small-group discussions you could have each group describe something that contributed to the success of their conversation, and after partner discussions you could ask students each to describe something their partner did that they appreciated. Similarly, small groups or partners could describe how they handled difficulties or disagreements in their discussions.

Share Anyway. Even if the ideas generated in a partner or small-group discussion aren't intended for further whole-class discussion (as they would be, for example, in a class decision-making process), students will still enjoy hearing about their classmates' conversations. To wrap up such discussions, have partners or small groups each share a favorite idea or two.

Get Organized! As with brainstorming, some discussions generate such a slew of ideas that students may need to group or otherwise organize them to make further discussion manageable. See the ORGANIZING IDEAS blueprints on pages 32–54 for some suggestions.

Fly on the Wall

Fourth-graders in Janet Ellman's class are learning about the diversity of early Californians by comparing the dwellings of two Native American tribes. For homework, students read about the two types of houses, tule grass and plank, and considered their similarities and differences. Janet now asks students to discuss their homework with their learning partners and joins Latoya and Stephanie. In an illustration of both the strength and challenge of the discussion format, we see Latoya's determination to avoid the assignment she has already successfully ignored once—she did not do the homework—give way under Stephanie's engagement with the topic and her determination to draw Latoya into it.

MS. ELLMAN: *(To Latoya)* How do you think they're alike?

LATOYA: They're both the same.

MS. ELLMAN: How?

LATOYA: I don't know, I just guessed.

MS. ELLMAN: How are they alike?

LATOYA: They're not alike—oh, they're both tall.

MS. ELLMAN: How else? *(Having posed the question, she moves on to another partnership.)*

STEPHANIE: *(Filling the void left by the teacher)* I think they're different because this one's round and this one's straight. How do you think they're different, Latoya?

LATOYA: I don't know.

STEPHANIE: Because one's bigger than the other one?

LATOYA: Okay.

STEPHANIE: *(Reading the next question)* Which is warmer?

LATOYA: *(Studying the pictures)* I think this one.

STEPHANIE: *(Thoughtfully)* This has more holes than this.

LATOYA: Okay, we're done.

STEPHANIE: No . . . *(Reading the next question aloud)* Where's a place in California where it's cold?

LATOYA: Eureka.

STEPHANIE: *(Reading the next question)* What might they use to build the plank houses and keep out the cold? *(Turning to Latoya)* Um, maybe glue or cement?

LATOYA: *(Considering)* Cement . . . yeah, cement, cement.

Sorting and Classifying

PEOPLE "sort and classify" throughout every day, consciously or otherwise—every time they make distinctions between things they like and dislike, for example. Even though that seems such a natural, automatic part of the way we think, children need some practice as they learn how to sort and classify—that is, how to recognize an attribute of an object or idea that both specifically identifies it and links it to others of the same kind. Additionally, sorting and classifying involves a belief or hypothesis about how things are related—which is the starting point of systematic thinking in science, history, and literature. In collaborative activities that involve sorting and classifying, students learn from each other's different ways of characterizing and categorizing things—thereby increasing their own perceptiveness and developing their ability to think critically about meaningful distinctions and commonalities.

WHY TO USE

- to enhance students' ability to observe and describe properties of objects or ideas
- to develop students' ability to see relationships
- to encourage students to see that objects and ideas can be classified in many different ways
- to help students learn to move from the concrete to the abstract in their thinking

WHEN TO USE

- throughout the curriculum, when students have a lot of data that they need to begin to understand
- after brainstorming or discussion, when students would benefit from ordering the array of ideas they have generated

HOW TO DO

The Sorting and Classifying blueprint asks students to

- brainstorm possible categories for the things or ideas being sorted
- examine one of the objects or ideas
- give reasons for what category they think it belongs in
- agree on which category to put it in
- do the same with each object or idea
- change the categories if necessary! ▶

HOW TO DO

The other way to sort and classify would be for students to

- examine the objects or ideas to be sorted
- group together those that are similar
- give reasons for why they think they are similar
- agree on the groupings
- give category names to the groupings

Developmental Considerations

Younger Students

Whereas adults and older children often identify categories and then sort items into those categories, young children are more likely to first group things that they think go together and then identify the category according to their reasoning about why those things go together.

In fact, young children are often stream-of-consciousness sorters, noticing interesting attributes as they stumble upon them and even changing criteria for classifying objects as they go along. They often operate according to their own special logic and may be unperturbed by glaring inconsistencies (such as categories that are not mutually exclusive) while spending much time resolving very specific issues (such as whether dimetrodons are or are not dinosaurs, as in the Fly on the Wall vignette). Gently probe their thinking, but don't insist on imposing your adult logic if they are not yet ready.

Finally, because of their very concrete, specific ways of looking at the world, young children may need some tools to help them with more abstract sorting and classifying tasks. When they are sorting ideas (in a conversation about class norms, for example, sorting ways they like and dislike being treated), have them draw or write visible representations, such as pictures or sentence strips, to make the ideas more concrete.

Older Students

As children get older, they often begin their own "sorting and classifying" with zeal: Many create personal collections of baseball cards, stickers, action figures, jewelry, rocks, stamps, insects, and so on, which they organize according to conventional or personal classification systems. In fact, older students often seem to enjoy the process of sorting and classifying as much as they do the objects themselves. Invite students to share personal collections and describe their method of organization, to help classmates see the range of possibilities and relevance of sorting and classifying.

Because older students have generally grasped the logic of sorting and classifying, they have more energy to spend on content; they can keep the big picture in mind and, especially when they have some familiarity with what they are sorting, can generate *a priori* classification systems. However, thoughtful observation and examination that is the basis for classifying often introduce new insights and issues, as does students' ability to more thoroughly discuss their different ideas about classifi-

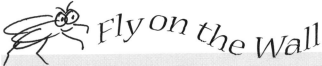
Fly on the Wall

To introduce her combined first- and second-grade class to a story about a boy and his special teddy bear, Maureen Jackson has asked students to bring in one of their "special objects" to show the class. The following day, Maureen further capitalizes on her students' interest by asking them to help her sort and categorize their special objects. Her class responds with a lively mixture of insights, expertise, debate, and negotiation.

MS. JACKSON: Can you give me a category that you notice that's common among many of these things that were brought? Carl?

CARL: We could do a category of all animals.

MS. JACKSON: Okay. *(She writes "animal" on a piece of construction paper and props it on the chalkboard tray; she does the same for all the suggestions.)*

SOPHIA: We could make a category of dolls.

MS. JACKSON: Okay. Arthur, what's your idea?

ARTHUR: *(Supplying his own version of "category")* A caterdero of bears.

JAMIE: Bears are animals.

MS. JACKSON: Okay, some people are saying we may have the same kinds of categories because we have bears and animals. We'll have to solve that problem as we go . . . and maybe it *isn't* a problem.

JUDITH: Put a category of Goofies.

MARK: But there's only one!

MS. JACKSON: There's only one. Hmmm—but could you put a category of Goofy? *(Students indicate general agreement.)* What is your idea, Donna?

DONNA: You could make a category of rabbits.

MS. JACKSON: Of rabbits? Okay, now take a look at some of the other things that have been brought that wouldn't fit under any of these. Josie?

JOSIE: You could make a category of poodles.

MS. JACKSON: Poodles. Ben?

BEN: Dinosaurs.

MONTY: *(Pointing to the object in question)* Dimetrodons aren't dinosaurs.

BEN: Yes, they are.

MS. JACKSON: Oops. *(She stops writing the card.)*

MONTY: No, they're not.

BEN: Yah, they are.

MONTY: No they're not—they lived before the dinosaurs, they weren't dinosaurs!

ALLAN: They weren't *quite* dinosaurs.

MONTY: They aren't true dinosaurs! They just—people *call* them dinosaurs but that's not true, they aren't really dinosaurs!

BETH: They're relatives of the dinosaur.

MS. JACKSON: So what do you think I should write?

BEN: Just write "dinosaurs."

BOBBY: Write "relatives of the dinosaurs."

MONTY: No, what if you just write "dimetrodons"?

MS. JACKSON: Okay. You know, that's an interesting discussion about dinosaurs. You might bring me and the class some information about the dimetrodon.

MONTY: I got some information that I could tell right now about the dimetrodon! It was fierce—had these long teeth for meat eating and short teeth for plant eating!

MS. JACKSON: So, it's a plant and a meat eater?

MONTY: Uh-huh.

MS. JACKSON: Okay. Now, anything else that you've noticed over here to categorize? Wendell?

WENDELL: Maybe we could have a category of stuffed.

SUE: But mostly all of them are stuffed.

RITA: You could make one of all dogs.

DON: Joel's thing is left out. And my thing is left out.

MS. JACKSON: What should I call it, Joel?

JOEL: Comic card?

MS. JACKSON: Okay—does that take care of yours, Don?

DON: No. Rocks.

MS. JACKSON: Yours is a rock, okay.

MARK: You could put "hard stuff."

MS. JACKSON: Okay . . . I'm going to make that as our last category, and then we're going to see if some of these categories can be put together. Do you see some categories that could go together? Beth?

BETH: We can put the bears with the animals.

MS. JACKSON: Okay. Diedre?

DIEDRE: Dogs and poodles.

MS. JACKSON: Dogs and poodles—okay . . . Carl?

CARL: The rabbits, and poodles, and the dogs, and Goofy could go into the animal category.

cations. Help students understand that they may need to revise original categories—evidence that they have learned something new.

Although older students have more developed logic and skills for sorting and classifying tasks, they will not entirely leave behind younger children's stream-of-consciousness approach. When older children are entering new territory—beginning a study of insects or rocks, for example, about which they don't yet have enough knowledge to identify categories—they can use sorting and classifying to help them recognize similarities and differences among the objects and begin building their understanding of the subject. This would necessarily be an exploratory activity of putting things together that go together, much like the approach generally used by younger children.

Grouping Considerations

Sorting and classifying can be done in partnerships, in small groups, or as a whole class.

Getting Students Ready

Academic Preparation

Depending upon the purpose of the activity and your students' experience, use one or more of the following suggestions for introducing sorting and classifying activities and reviewing the skills involved.

Consult the experts. You can introduce sorting and classifying to students throughout the year by drawing attention to classification systems used by experts in various disciplines—geology, astronomy, zoology, botany, art, music, literary genres, and so on. Invite students' thoughts about how categories were defined and the challenges of categorizing some items.

Be open. Make sure students understand that the goal of sorting and classifying is to create a system that *they* think makes sense to *them* for a particular purpose, not to find a single "right" system of classification. Give them an everyday illustration of the different possibilities for classifying the same objects—for example, organizing a kitchen.

MS. JACKSON: Goofy, dogs, and poodles could go in animals—

CARL: And rabbits—

MS. JACKSON: And rabbits.

MARK: Everybody's trying to make animals bigger and bigger.

MS. JACKSON: I know! We have quite a large category there now. Is it a problem?

MARK: There's no problem, but stuffed up and animals are the same thing because all the animals are stuffed up.

MS. JACKSON: That's true, but there may be a problem. *(Holding up a Raggedy Ann doll)* Is that stuffed?

WENDELL: That's not an animal.

SOPHIA: That's a doll.

MS. JACKSON: Well, it's a doll, and it's stuffed, yet it doesn't seem to fit with rabbits, bears, Goofy, dogs, and poodles. Do you see what I mean? Does that make sense? *(Mark nods.)* Okay. Now let's put these things into a graph, and we'll talk some more about using the stuffed category.

We might put cans and jars of food in one cupboard and bowls, pots, and pans in another—until there is a toddler in the house. Then we might reorganize the cupboards so that unbreakable items such as pots and cans are in the bottom cupboard, and breakables such as jars and bowls are in the top. The classification system changed because our purpose changed.

Model the process. Lead a whole-class sorting and classifying activity using items similar to those that students will be classifying in their groups or partnerships. Explain your reasoning as you go along, modeling the decision making students will face in their group work.

Social/Ethical Preparation

Because people classify based on different attributes and different points of view, students will have to discuss each item and reach consensus about their groupings. The following are some social and ethical aspects of the process that you may want to help your students anticipate.

Getting everyone's opinion. Remind students of how important it is to have everyone's input in making decisions—not just to be fair, but also because different insights could lead the group to better conclusions. Ask students to think about the kinds of responses and attitudes that encourage group members to offer divergent or unusual ideas.

Settling differences of opinion. A variety of opinions can broaden a group's thinking and decisions, but that variety can also make decisions hard to come by. Ask for students' suggestions on fair ways to resolve differences of opinion and, depending on how much practice they've had in group decision making, revisit or suggest useful strategies (see the Deciding blueprint on page 55 for ideas).

≈ HINT ≈

To loosen up students' thinking, give groups only two objects and have them name as many categories as they can that apply to both objects.

WAYS TO USE *Sorting and Classifying*

ACTIVITIES

In lower grades, learning how to sort and classify is in itself part of the curriculum. In the upper grades, classifying activities can help students deepen their understanding of many subject areas in the curriculum.

To the Letter. Sorting and classifying activities can help young children learn and practice letter shapes, letter names, and letter-sound relationships. Have partners or small groups sort magnetic, foam, cardboard, or other cut-out letters into categories they devise themselves (and don't be surprised by the very personalized or stylized classifications they might come up with—letters in their names versus those not in their names, letters with points and letters without, and the like). When used in conjunction with explicit instruction about print concepts, such playful activities increase children's familiarity and skill with letters.

Picture Perfect. Interesting magazine pictures or other picture cards are wonderful subjects for sorting, just for the sake of exploration or to meet specific instructional goals. For example, children might sort pictures by beginning or ending sounds, rhyming words (snake, cake, rake, etc.), or some other concept (things made of wood, metal, plastic, fabric, glass; pictures representing different seasons, feelings, etc.). As a variation, students can match pictures with word cards or sentence strips that describe them.

All Sorts of Words. Beginning readers often find words engaging in themselves and enjoy sorting them in different ways—by subject, length, beginning or ending letter, and so on. As with the letter- and picture-sorting activities above, simply "messing about" in this way can help students grasp the mechanics and possibilities of language. Make letter, word, and picture sorts available at literacy centers so that students can repeat sorting activities over and over in different ways and with different classmates.

Sorting to Know You. Small objects often find their way from home to school via students' pockets. Instead of fighting this infestation, take advantage of it with an activity that helps students get to know each other and challenges their sorting skills to boot. Invite students each to bring to class three or four special small objects that they are willing to share with classmates during a special sorting activity. (You might want to specify a size limit—objects that fit in a pocket or the palm of a hand—and you might also want to point out that students can share objects they have already brought in and have in their desks or lockers.) Working in small groups, have students show and tell about their objects and decide how to sort them using material or nonmaterial attributes—for example, they might group objects received as gifts, favorite objects, and found objects; or they might classify by subject matter (all cars go together, all pieces for building together, all action figures together); or they might group objects simply by color or other physical feature. Follow up by having students share what they learned about their groupmates and about classifying. You might also want to provide a time and place for students to play with each other's appealing special objects—during free-play time, for example.

Classified Classroom. Sorting and classifying are designed to help make things more accessible and manageable. Make this literal by having students work in pairs or small group to re-sort and classify their classroom or some part of the room (the materials closet, art area, math center, writing center, etc.), putting things together that go together. Students can create their plans on paper as a first step or just dive in.

Starting with Sorting. Beginning a unit of study with a sorting and classifying activity can both engage students' interest and give you insights into their prior knowledge. For example, have partners or small groups sort and classify objects they will be studying—plants, bugs, rocks and minerals, works of art, poems, pieces of music, and so on—working with real objects, pictures, text, or sound recordings. By forming their own understanding of the subjects' attributes, students will create a context and curiosity for acquiring further knowledge.

≈ HINT ≈

It's easy for more vocal or peremptory students to dominate a sorting and classifying activity. As you observe group work, watch to see if students are discussing their reasons for their classifications and that everyone is participating. If necessary, step in and encourage discussion.

Fieldwork. Many study topics and projects can benefit from sending students "into the field," like scientists, to gather raw data to be sorted and classified. For example, for environmental studies students might classify what they find in a square meter of schoolyard, backyard, or playground; similarly, they could classify litter in a particular area; for science they might classify plants or insects in the neighborhood; for current events they might classify news stories over a period of time; for media studies they might classify advertisements; and so on. Before students collect their data, have a whole-class discussion about what students expect to find—in fact, it might be interesting to list their expectations and later match their findings to the earlier list. Depending upon the location and nature of the fieldwork, have students in groups collect data or have them individually collect data and bring it back to sort and classify with their groups.

Classified Culture. Art and music can seem abstract to students until they understand the times and ideas—aesthetics, purpose, technology, politics, and so on—that influenced such cultural products. Give partners or small groups a variety of art prints, or play a variety of music, and have them classify the pieces and explain their reasoning to the rest of the class. Revisit these groupings and reasons as they further study the art or music, and discuss the similarities or differences between their observations and what they are learning.

As-sorted Stories. Have students think of categories for classifying stories (or poems) that they have read, both in and out of class. Make a class chart and have students use the categories to help them decide what kinds of stories they would like to read or hear as a class; also encourage students to add stories they read throughout the year to the chart.

Organized Ideas. Follow up a brainstorming session or class discussion by having groups classify the ideas that arise—for example, questions they have about a topic of study, ideas for field trips, solutions to class dilemmas, opinions about a story character's motivation, and so on. Such organization can help bring order to a seemingly overwhelming variety of ideas, help students see important emerging themes in their viewpoints, and give them appreciation for the diversity that contributes to their growing knowledge.

EXTENSIONS

A sorting and classifying activity often leads into further related work, or you may want to use some of the following activities to extend students' thinking about their work.

✳ **What Did We Learn?** Give groups or partnerships a chance to share their work with the class and explain the reasons for their thinking. Ask questions that challenge students to think more deeply; for example, ask what different categories have in common, or why certain items are placed in one group and not another, and so on. Also help them reflect on their social and ethical learning: What kinds of disagreements arose, and how were these resolved? What accounted for things going smoothly? What might they do differently or the same next time?

Do You See What I See? Students can have fun "testing" their own and others' powers of observation, as well as the logic of their classifications. For example, to help students focus on the unique attributes of specific items, have group members each write a description of one item in the same category; then have them read aloud their descriptions to see if the class can identify the object they are describing. Or, have groups describe their classification schemes and see if the class can duplicate the group's classification of each object.

Alternate Realities. Comparing or revamping classification schemes will help students sharpen their thinking about categorization and increase their ability to appreciate different answers to the same problem. For example, after groups have made their classifications, have them reclassify everything in a new way and describe the strengths and weaknesses of the two classification schemes. Or, if different groups have been classifying different objects, have groups exchange their objects, classify the new items, and compare their categorizations and reasoning to the other group's.

Quantified. Add a quantitative dimension to sorting and classifying activities by having students graph their results. For example, after sorting and classifying "special objects" they have brought to class, have the class create a graph that shows student preferences at a glance; or after groups have sorted the questions they have asked and answered in content area research, have them create graphs to show the strengths and gaps in their research; and so on.

≈ HINT ≈

Graphic organizers not only help students present information in a meaningful way, but can also encourage students to develop more sophisticated ways of classifying objects. For example, younger students who classify objects according to a single attribute can be nudged to consider multiple dimensions by using a 2×2 (or 2×3, or 2×4) table. Introduce this organizer after students have had many opportunities to grapple with sorting and classifying on their own, though, and are more likely to see the purpose of such a structure.

Mind Mapping

A MIND MAP displays what a person or group knows about a subject and, like a conventional map, can show them where they are and where they might go next in their explorations. Less formal than standard outlining techniques, mind maps are visual tools that help students gain some control over a lot of discrete pieces of information. These graphic representations of knowledge—students' perceptions of a topic's "big" ideas and related groups and subsets of ideas—are especially useful as a first step in a unit of study to identify students' prior knowledge or as a culminating activity to celebrate all that students have learned. And as a cooperative activity, when students work together on mind maps they learn from each other's insights, appreciate their own and each other's learning, and practice their collaborative skills.

WHY TO USE

- to develop students' ability to think systematically and relationally
- to help students connect details to broader ideas and concepts
- to help students represent what they know or have learned

WHEN TO USE

- when all students are likely to know something about the topic and can contribute to the process
- when the topic is open-ended and students can benefit from hearing different points of view
- when you want insight into how students are identifying and connecting the "big" and "little" ideas in a topic
- at the beginning of a unit of study
- as the culmination of a unit of study
- prior to producing a product representing student knowledge, such as a dramatization, a report, or a mural

HOW TO DO

The Mind Mapping blueprint asks students to

- brainstorm categories of information to include on the map
- write these on the map and show how they connect
- say ideas that they think should be included on the map
- discuss which category of information the idea connects to
- agree on where to put the idea
- record the idea on the map
- change categories or create new ones as necessary

Developmental Considerations

Younger Students

Mind mapping is well suited to the emerging literacy of young children, who can use a combination of pictures and labels to represent what they know about a topic. Their early attempts may look more like murals than maps, but don't worry too much about the structure at first. Instead, emphasize the importance of getting everybody's ideas on paper, and work on organization in subsequent mind-mapping projects.

You may also find that young students need help identifying main ideas that support a topic, leaping instead from the general to the specific (for example, they'll name *fish* and *seaweed* as ideas for a mind map of the ocean, bypassing the larger categories of *animals* and *plants*). Modeling the process frequently and brainstorming with the class will help students learn how to name and "nest" categories and ideas.

Older Students

Mind mapping allows older students to organize and record what they know about a topic with minimal text, which means that struggling writers are not thwarted from participating fully and experiencing the satisfaction of contributing to a group product. And because mind maps are graphic as well as verbal, they accommodate students of various writing, artistic, and thinking abilities—and deepen students' appreciation of each other's different skills.

Fly on the Wall

Laurel Cress has asked her third-graders to create mind maps of what they know about the ocean. During a brief whole-class brainstorm about "big categories" with which to start, students quickly suggest a range of main ideas (such as *animals* and *plants*) and supporting ideas (such as *fish*) and then break into groups of four to construct their maps. Listening in on three different groups, we hear how the activity inspires students to pepper each other with ideas, share prior knowledge, and help each other.

Group 1
MALCOLM: Weeds!
ALL: *(Agreeing in unison)* Weeds!

RICH: W-E-E-D-S. *(As Maria, the recorder, writes)*
AGATHA: *(Nodding with satisfaction as Maria finishes)* There we go!
RICH: Put "sea urchins"!
MARIA: Sea urchins?
RICH: Yeah, sea urchins for the animals! *(Points to the animal category on the map, where Maria writes his suggestion)*

Group 2
ANDY: Write in "bass"—a bass is a fish, and you let it grow. You catch a little one and let it grow until it's bigger, way bigger.
JOANNE: Write "flying fish."
DANIELLE: *(Writing for the group)* Flying fish? Okay.

ANDY: No—a flying fish is a shark!
JOANNE: No, it's not.
JESUS: It has—like a sword—has a big ol' nose.
ANDY: Yeah, it has a saw nose.
DANIELLE: How about a hammerhead?
JESUS: Yeah, a hammerhead shark!

Group 3
CYNTHIA: Oh, and there's flounder!
JEREMY: *(Writing Cynthia's idea)* And crabs?
RIANE: Crabs are crustaceans.
CYNTHIA: What are other plants? Is there moss?
RIANE: Uh-huh.

Grouping Considerations

Mind mapping can be done in partnerships, in small groups, and as a whole class, but is perhaps best suited to small groups: enough participants to generate an ample pool of ideas, but not so many people that the pool or the discussion becomes unmanageable.

Getting Students Ready

Academic Preparation

Depending upon the purpose of the activity and your students' experience, use one or more of the following suggestions for introducing mind-mapping activities and reviewing the skills involved.

Introduce the topic. If students will be mind mapping a new topic, make your introduction one that connects them to the subject and invites their expertise. For example, you might begin by reading a story or essay that makes the topic salient and prompts students' thinking about it.

Begin together. Before students break into small groups to make their mind maps, get their thinking started with a brief whole-class brainstorm about categories they might include. Encourage them to continue the brainstorm in their groups and come up with even more ideas.

Model the process. At the beginning of the year, and especially with young children or students who have little experience with mind mapping, give students a lot of practice in whole-class mind-mapping activities before you start having them do mind maps in small groups. Explain your reasoning as you go along, modeling the decision making students will face in their group work: Brainstorm a few categories that will help organize information about the topic, then ask for more information to include in the map and discuss how each idea is related to the topic, the categories or main ideas, and other ideas already on the map. Let students see that as the map evolves, categories and placements sometimes change to accommodate new ideas; help students see how the organization of a lot of "small" information contributes to the understanding of a broader subject or idea.

≈ HINT ≈

When possible and appropriate, encourage students to add interest to the graphic presentation of their mind maps. For example, instead of circling their idea groups they might enclose them in representational shapes, they might use different-colored lines to connect the groups of ideas, they could decorate their maps with drawings or magazine pictures, and so on.

Social/Ethical Preparation

When students do mind mapping as a cooperative activity, they need to incorporate other people's opinions into their idea of how the mind map should be organized. The following are some social and ethical aspects of the process that you may want to help your students anticipate.

Listening to everyone. Discuss why it is important for all group members' ideas to be heard and considered, whether or not others agree with an idea. Ask students what might happen if someone's ideas weren't treated fairly and respectfully: How might that affect the speaker? How might that affect the group's work?

Dealing with disagreement. Discuss how group members might cope with differences in opinion and how they can disagree respectfully. Help students think of creative resolutions, especially considering the flexibility of the mind-mapping format. For example, groups might connect an idea to more than one category; or in mind maps showing what students know about a new topic, they might create a category for "not sure how it fits yet" or "need more information."

Sharing the work. Discuss with students how they might divide the work fairly in their groups—for example, each group member being responsible for recording the ideas in a particular category, or taking turns recording each item, and so on.

WAYS TO USE *Mind Mapping*

ACTIVITIES

The following are some ideas for integrating cooperative mind-mapping activities into the curriculum.

History Map. Have students construct a mind map of what they know about a historical period or civilization. Introduce the activity by doing a brief whole-class mind map of the past year—the important events, issues, people, and so on. As students come up with categories for their ideas—such as politics, popular culture, major events, and the like—help them see how these apply to any historical era. Their history maps will not only help them appreciate what they have learned, but they will also give you insights into the "big ideas" students have constructed from a unit of study and the relationships they see between events.

Place Map. Creating a mind map of their school, neighborhood, or city can help students make personal connections to key concepts in social studies. Introduce the activity by asking the class what a local expert might know about their school (neighborhood, city), and then help them organize this information around such categories as history, famous people, cultural diversity, geography, politics, animals, economy, and so on. Students can then build on this activity to do mind maps of places they are studying in social studies or settings in literature.

Problem Map. Have students construct a mind map of what they know about a social problem—pollution, racism, poverty, war, and so on—either for general interest or because the issue figures in their curriculum or community service goals. Guide the whole class through a preliminary brainstorm about the problem, asking such questions as What might be some sources of the problem? How do you encounter the problem? How does the problem affect you? Others? Explore the distinctions between opinions and facts, and help students appreciate that both are valuable. Have students extend the activity by creating a plan, real or ideal, to address the problem.

Vocabulary Map. Give students lists of vocabulary words from a book they are reading, historical period they are studying, social studies topic, or other suitable subject and have them organize the words into meaningful groups on a mind map. This activity deepens students' understanding of the words' meanings, helps them connect the meaning of words to larger ideas, and creates a framework for understanding the atmosphere and tone of the book, era, character, etc. Students might enjoy extending the activity by using the vocabulary mind maps as springboards for poems about the subject.

Portrait Map. To help students get to know each other at the beginning of the year, have them create portrait mind maps—a self-portrait to introduce themselves to the class or, after a partner interview, a map of what they learned about their partner to introduce him or her to the class.

EXTENSIONS

Whether a mind map is an end in itself or a catalyst for further inquiry, you may want to use some of the following activities to extend students' thinking about their work.

❋ **What Did We Learn?** Give each group the opportunity to show their map and describe the process of developing it. Ask questions that probe their reasoning and that encourage students to see (and learn from) the similarities and differences among the groups' maps. Also help them reflect on their social and ethical learning: What kinds of disagreements arose, and how were these resolved? What did they learn about sharing their work? What might they do differently or the same next time?

What Do We Want to Learn? When students have begun a unit of study with a mind map, have them brainstorm about where their map might lead them. For example, they might brainstorm a list of questions about the topic to inspire further research. Or, if groups have mind mapped separate topics, have each group present its map and let students individually decide which topic they are most interested in studying further. Then create research groups based on students' self-selection.

Expanding Horizons. Display the mind maps around the room and, as students learn more about a topic, have them add to and revise their maps accordingly (preferably in a different color marker than used on the original). The new topography helps students recognize what they have learned and how the boundaries of knowledge can shift and expand.

Get It in Writing. Mind mapping is valuable in and of itself, but it is also a great prewriting activity to help students generate and organize their ideas. The structure of the map easily translates to written reports or narratives: Categories or main ideas become chapters or paragraphs, and so on. The map structure also lends itself to dividing work among group members, with each member assuming responsibility for a main idea or two. (See the Expository blueprint on 149 for suggestions for organizing group writing.)

Visual Translations. Have students use the ideas on a mind map to inspire a group mural or dramatization. Social studies or historical topics readily lend themselves to this kind of translation.

≈ HINT ≈

Students might hesitate to begin writing their ideas on the "real" map for fear of changing their minds and messing it up. Suggest that they make a draft map on a small sheet of paper first, if there's time.

Venn Diagrams

A VENN diagram is a graphic representation of the similarities and differences between two or more things—ideas, individuals, situations, events, problems, solutions. It is a wonderfully simple method both for helping students compare and organize information and for helping them become deeper thinkers about the complexities and considerations involved in making comparisons. Collaborative Venn diagram activities further enrich this awareness, as students learn from the similarities and differences between each other's comparisons!

WHY TO USE

- to graphically represent the comparison of two or more things
- to develop students' ability to thoughtfully make and learn from such comparisons
- to develop students' ability to make connections between individual ideas and between groups of ideas
- to help students connect details and broader ideas and concepts

WHEN TO USE

- when all students are familiar with the subjects being compared
- when comparing specific topics will deepen students' understanding

HOW TO DO

The Venn Diagrams blueprint asks students to

- name an important or salient similarity or difference *between* the things being compared
- discuss and agree that this is a similarity or difference
- record the idea as an individual or shared attribute on the diagram
- do the same for each suggested similarity or difference
- *or,* begin by describing an important or salient characteristic of *one* of the things being compared ▶

- discuss whether or not the characteristic also describes the other comparison subject(s)
- record the idea as an individual or shared attribute on the diagram
- do the same for each suggested characteristic

Developmental Considerations

Younger Students

Even very young children are adept at making comparisons and do so spontaneously in their everyday life. With Venn diagrams, you'll want to keep the activities simple and straightforward, so that the challenge and fun are in making significant comparisons, not in figuring out the task. Try to keep the emphasis on the having, not the recording, of wonderful ideas—in fact, Venn diagrams needn't depend on students' ability to write. For example, try "wordless" diagrams in which students sort pictures, or provide scribes—a great use of parent volunteers or older student buddies—for more challenging problems.

Similarly, whole-class Venn diagram activities in which you serve as recorder not only help children learn and practice their comparison-making skills, but also are excellent language experience activities. Record students' ideas in their own words and read their words aloud to them; also have them tell you where their idea belongs in the diagram (even if it seems obvious to you), to give them opportunities to elaborate on their thinking and practice how Venn diagramming works.

Fly on the Wall

Students in Becky O'Bryan's combined fourth- and fifth-grade class are reading the book *Freedom Train: The Story of Harriet Tubman,* by Dorothy Sterling. Groups of four are constructing Venn diagrams comparing Harriet Tubman with Tim Meeker, a Revolutionary War–era character from the book *My Brother Sam Is Dead* (by James and Christopher Collier), which they read earlier in the year. The discussion prompts this group to explore the nuances of *responsibility,* illustrating how Venn diagrams can deepen students' understanding of both characters and concepts.

AMY: They both matured in a different way. Tim matured when he had to take the wagon back. And, you know, it was scary. And so did Harriet—

JESSICA: Having to escape for the first time.

AMY: Yeah, she matured that way. So they were both—they both matured scaredly, or something like that. *(She chuckles at the word she creates to convey her meaning.)*

DAVID: Well, I think that Tim—well, he had two people in his family die, and Harriet said none of her slaves have ever died and she'd be more careful, but Tim is—

JESSICA: She's more, like, *responsible.*

DAVID: Yeah, and Tim had somebody in his family die and had that experience.

SUSAN: *(Thoughtfully)* She's not more *responsible.* It's just that she's made more people escape—

AMY: She's *had* more responsibility to do than Tim. Tim hasn't had a lot of responsibility.

DAVID: Yeah, and Tim can't get beat up with a whip or nothing, but Harriet, whenever—

JESSICA: He was kind of safer than Harriet.

Older Students	As older students can make more sophisticated comparisons, they can diagram more than two categories at once and can handle more abstract and challenging subjects. However, don't hesitate to keep the topic of comparison simple, such as comparing the main characters in two books—the sophistication will come in the attributes or ideas the students generate and compare.

Grouping Considerations

Venn diagrams can be done in partnerships, in small groups, or as a whole class.

Getting Students Ready

Academic Preparation	Depending upon the purpose of the activity and your students' experience, use one or more of the following suggestions to prepare for Venn diagram activities and review the skills involved.

Stick to familiar subjects. Before introducing a Venn diagram activity, be sure that students are familiar with what is being compared (often this is a given, of course, as the activity will follow on some unit of study or discussion, but you may need to refresh students' memories if a comparison subject hasn't been studied recently). If students don't know enough about the subjects, they can't meaningfully compare them; the more they know about them, the more likely they are to consider ideas deeply and discover significant relationships.

Model the process. The most effective way to introduce partner or small-group Venn diagrams is by doing whole-class Venn diagrams regularly. Even with experienced students you might want to briefly diagram one or two ideas as a class before they start partner or small-group work, just to get their thinking started and to model the decision-making considerations involved.

≈ HINT ≈

Give students plenty of practice comparing two categories before introducing Venn diagrams that compare three or four—the complexity of the diagram can increase significantly with each additional category.

Social/Ethical Preparation	When students do Venn diagrams as a collaborative activity, they need to incorporate their classmates' perspectives into their notions of the subjects' similarities and differences. The following are some social and ethical aspects of the process that you may want to help your students anticipate.

Listening to everyone. Discuss why it is important for all group members' ideas to be heard and considered, whether or not others agree with an idea. Ask students what might happen if someone's ideas were dismissed or laughed at: How would that person feel? What would happen if they didn't listen to ideas that might have turned out to be really useful?

Dealing with disagreement. Students need to be able to negotiate on two levels with Venn diagrams: First, there has to be some agreement on the characteristics of each subject they are comparing, and then they also have to agree on whether these characteristics are similarities or differences between subjects. These "negotiations" are precisely what lead to rich discussions and new insights, as long as students deal well with differing opinions. Help students appreciate the usefulness of disagreement and think of ways they can disagree respectfully.

Sharing the work. Discuss with students how they might divide the work fairly in their groups—for example, having each group member be responsible for recording ideas in a particular section of the diagram, or taking turns recording each idea, and so on.

WAYS TO USE *Venn Diagrams*

ACTIVITIES

The following are some ideas for integrating cooperative Venn diagram activities into the curriculum.

Partner Comparison. A good way to help students get to know each other and build community at the beginning of the year is to have partners do Venn diagrams about their similarities and differences. Introduce the activity with a whole-class brainstorm about what attributes they could compare—for example, favorite school subjects, hobbies, goals for the year, summer activities, and so on. After partners have finished, have each pair use its diagram to introduce each other to the class.

Classmate Comparison. Whole-class Venn diagrams can also serve as community builders throughout the year as topics arise—and they are also a good way to help students progress to doing diagrams with more than two areas of comparison. For example, students might compare the kinds of books they like to read, what they like to do at recess, what topic they would like to study next, and so on. (Be sure to choose attributes that will help students get to know and appreciate one another, not any that might inadvertently create or emphasize status differences.)

Story Comparison. Venn diagrams can enrich students' experience of literature by deepening their understanding of stories, characters, and themselves. For example, having students compare characters in a story can help them perceive motives and events that drive the narrative, having students compare characters from different stories can give them insight into important themes or authors' writing strategies, comparing ideas and situations in different stories can help them appreciate that fundamental aspects and issues of life face even the most seemingly different people, and comparing their own lives with that of a historical character or a character from a culture different than their own helps them understand their world and their relation to it.

History Comparison. Similarly, Venn diagrams can help students recognize common issues and patterns within or across historical eras, even when comparing historical events or characters that seem quite distant or unrelated. For example, using a diagram to compare slavery

≈HINT≈

Students generally have little trouble thinking of superficial similarities and differences (such as physical appearance or age), but they may need encouragement and practice to think about more subtle and significant comparisons, such as intentions, beliefs, feelings, and so on.

in the United States to apartheid in South Africa would help students recognize important economic, cultural, and racial themes that figured in two systems of oppression in very different times and places; or comparing Columbus's "discovery" of America to the United States first putting a man on the moon would bring up common themes about the motivations and outcomes of competition between nations; and so on.

EXTENSIONS

Venn diagram activities, in serving as starting points for further discussion and deeper exploration of topics, can be extended in any of the following ways.

✳ What Did We Learn? Give groups or partnerships the opportunity to show their Venn diagram to the class and describe the process of developing it. Ask questions that encourage students to articulate their reasoning and any understandings they gained from thinking through the diagram. Also help students reflect on their social and ethical learning: What went well, and what didn't? What might they do differently or the same next time?

Put It in Writing. Have students use their Venn diagrams as the basis for written compositions. Get them started by showing how parts of the diagram can be translated into paragraphs describing the subjects being compared; depending upon your purposes, students could do individual compositions, or they could work with the partner or group with whom they created their Venn diagram.

Diagram Dialogues. Have partners use the understanding gained from their Venn diagram to write a dialogue between the people (or animals, or even things) they compared.

SAMPLE VENN DIAGRAM CONFIGURATIONS

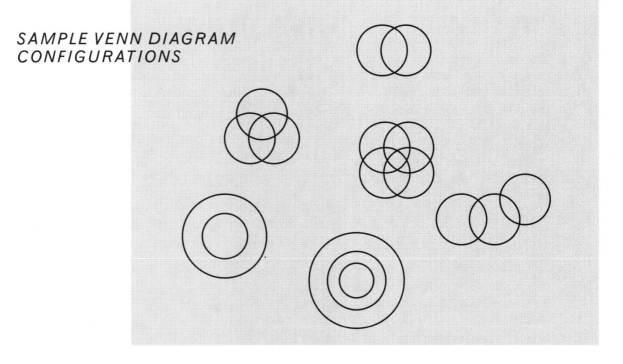

Benefits and Burdens

LISTING the benefits and burdens of a course of action is a simple way for students to organize their own thinking about an issue, realize different perspectives, and learn that most choices in life have advantages *and* disadvantages. Benefits-and-burdens discussions can help students assess and comprehend situations in literature, history, current events, society, and their community as well as decisions to be made in their classroom or personal life. And as they work with their classmates to identify possible benefits and burdens, students will encounter and deal with each other's varying viewpoints—giving them valuable practice articulating their opinions and evaluating the opinions of others. What's more, having identified (and probably debated) the benefits and burdens of a situation, students are prepared to move on to the next step: discussing whether the benefits outweigh the burdens or the other way around!

WHY TO USE

- to help students evaluate choices in literature, history, society, the life of the classroom, and their own lives
- to deepen students' understanding of situations in literature, history, society, the life of the classroom, and their own lives
- to encourage students to see the world from different perspectives
- to develop students' recognition of the complexity underlying most important choices in life
- to help students weigh the contributing factors in making a choice

WHEN TO USE

- when seeing different sides to an issue or situation will deepen students' understanding
- when students need to make choices

HOW TO DO

The Benefits and Burdens blueprint asks students to

- give ideas for what they think are the benefits of a choice or situation
- discuss and agree on whether it's a benefit
- record the idea on the benefits list
- give ideas for what they think are the burdens of a choice or situation
- discuss and agree on whether it's a burden
- record the idea on the burdens list

Developmental Considerations

Younger Students

≈ HINT ≈

A graphic organizer can help students with these activities. Have them create a simple benefits-and-burdens chart by drawing a line down the center of a page and list benefits on one side of the line and burdens on the other.

Benefits	Burdens

When students are comparing multiple options, they could use a 2×2 (or 2×3, 2×4, etc.) chart to record the benefits and burdens of each.

	Benefits	Burdens
#1		
#2		
#3		

The key to doing successful benefits-and-burdens activities with young children is to choose an issue that is interesting and familiar (such as lining up at recess or a dilemma in a story they have just read) and to help them learn and manage the process. Give them a lot of whole-class practice with this format before they move on to partner work, and if necessary break down the discussion into separate sessions. For example, if students are comparing different options (such as choosing between a fish, lizard, or guinea pig as a classroom pet), address one option at a time—discuss the good things and then the bad things about having a fish for a pet in one conversation, discuss the good things and then the bad things about having a lizard for a pet the next day, and so on (and keep a list of the pros and cons they came up with for each option, to use when making a final decision).

Similarly, when students begin doing partner activities, you might have them break the task into a discussion of benefits one day and burdens the next; after a few such practice runs, partners should be able to consider both benefits and burdens in one conversation. Similarly, it is probably best to start out with activities that involve the benefits and burdens of just one subject; once partners have become familiar with the format, they can manage discussions that deal with more than one option in one session (e.g., the fish and the lizard). Also give students the option to either write or draw the items on their lists.

Keep in mind, as well, that young children's speculations about benefits and burdens may at times seem farfetched. For example, one kindergartner declared the disadvantages of having a fish for a classroom pet as "it would spray water in our faces" and the advantages of a lizard as "it would lick us and help us wash our hands," even though she had fish and a lizard at home and they had never done either. Remember that young children's outlandish responses represent the beginning of hypothetical thinking—and their commitment to conscientiously consider every possibility. Encourage these efforts by accepting sincere and thoughtful responses, no matter how unusual.

Older Students

Benefits-and-burdens discussions foster students' capacity to appreciate complexity, subtlety, and ambiguity. Push this to the limits by having older students consider particularly challenging problems or assess the benefits and burdens of a decision from more than one perspective (the benefits for one person or group are not necessarily the benefits for others!).

Grouping Considerations

Benefits-and-burdens lists can be done in partnerships, in small groups, or as a whole class. The format is particularly well suited to partner work, however, in that partner conversations give students significant opportunity and responsibility for participation—encouraging deeper, more thoughtful consideration of the issue and also offering shy or reluctant students a smaller, less intimidating arena for making contributions.

Getting Students Ready

Academic Preparation

Depending upon the purpose of the activity and your students' experience, use one or more of the following suggestions to introduce benefits-and-burdens activities and review the skills involved.

Define terms. Make sure that students understand that *benefits* are advantages of (or good things about) a choice, while *burdens* are the disadvantages of (or bad things about) a choice. With young children, you may simply want to substitute terms like "the good things about/bad things about" or "what you would like about/what you wouldn't like about" for "the benefits/burdens of."

Practice seeing both sides. Students may have trouble seeing that most choices have benefits *and* burdens—especially students who see things in very black-and-white terms, or especially when a choice seems singularly positive or negative. Give them practice seeing both sides by choosing a situation that they are likely to consider positive, such as winning the lottery or being famous, and challenge them to think of burdens that it might incur. Then choose a negative situation, such as being sick or losing a game, and challenge them to think of benefits that might ensue. Ask for their ideas about other such seemingly negative or positive situations that have both bright and dark sides.

Consider the silver lining. Lead students in a discussion about their understanding of the saying "Every cloud has a silver lining." Ask students for examples of benefits that came from something bad that happened to them, giving an example or two of your own to get the storytelling started.

Explore the issue. To get students thinking or to review their understanding of the topic in question, lead the class in a general discussion about the situation or issue before having them move on to a specific exploration of its benefits and burdens.

Look ahead. Make sure students understand that the goal of making a benefits-and-burdens list is to thoroughly explore the ramifications of possible choices—not to immediately jump to *making* a choice—and at this point they are *identifying* benefits and burdens (which in itself can result in some lively discussion and new thinking). Remind them that the follow-up to organizing their ideas in this way will be a discussion of whether the benefits or the burdens outweigh the other, but encourage them not to get sidetracked by such a discussion during their listing process so that they can focus on coming up with as many ideas as possible.

Model the process. Show students a benefits-and-burdens list you made to help you think about a situation, and explain the reasoning involved and any surprising realizations you had. Or, role-play the list-making process with a student partner and model how you might encourage a partner to consider various perspectives.

Social/Ethical Preparation

When students do benefits-and-burdens lists as a cooperative activity, they need to consider their classmates' opinions of the advantages and disadvantages of a choice. The following are some social and ethical aspects of the process that you may want to help your students anticipate.

Taking different perspectives. It helps to imagine another person's point of view when trying to identify the benefits and burdens of a choice, but some students may have difficulty doing so. Suggest some questions students might ask themselves to help think of other perspectives: How might other people be affected by this choice? Who might profit from the choice? Who might suffer? How might this choice make people more (or less) responsible? Kind? Honest? Fair?

Respecting other perspectives. Remind students that their partner or groupmates might have different ways of looking at things. Encourage them to find out *why* their partner thinks that way, not just *what* their partner thinks—and to discuss their notions of benefits or burdens, not just list them. How might they respond to an idea that seems off base or that surprises them? What might be the benefits of hearing different ideas? What might be the burdens?

Reconsidering personal perspectives. Encourage students to think about their own thinking and evaluate their ideas in light of other perspectives. What might be the benefits of deciding that one of your own ideas might not be such a great idea after all?

WAYS TO USE *Benefits and Burdens*

ACTIVITIES

The following are some ideas for integrating collaborative benefits-and-burdens discussion activities into the curriculum.

Fictional Choices. Story characters often face difficult choices involving values such as kindness, fairness, and honesty; they also often face issues that are immediately relevant to students' lives, such as peer pressure, gangs, substance abuse, and family responsibilities. Have students list the benefits and burdens of choices faced by story characters: to deepen their understanding of stories, to further their development as thoughtful and reflective readers, to motivate their learning by helping them see the connection between literature and "real life," and to give them practice in thoughtful decision making.

Social and Historical Choices. Have students discuss and list the benefits and burdens of historical choices (such as starting the Revolutionary War), social conditions (such as our nation's diversity), sociopolitical systems (such as democracy and autocracy), and other such topics that arise in the curriculum. Few social and historical situations carry *only* benefits or burdens—and students can gain great insight into the complexity of the issues they are studying by assessing the benefits *and* burdens.

Classroom Choices. When students are making decisions affecting the life of their classroom—such as field trip destinations, class norms, conflict resolutions, and the like—they could use some even-handed aids for evaluating their options. Help students brain-storm, discuss, and narrow their choices (see GENERATING IDEAS on pages 13–31), and then have them make benefits-and-burdens lists about the remaining possibilities. The resulting pool of ideas will help students realize all sides of an issue before discussing and agreeing on a decision (see Deciding on page 55).

EXTENSIONS

Listing benefits and burdens, of course, is a prerequisite to then weighing those benefits and burdens against each other (and some-times reaching decisions based on that, as in the Classroom Choices activity). In other words, *every* benefits-and-burdens activity is followed by such a discussion.

In addition to that discussion, benefits-and-burdens activities can also be extended in any of the following ways.

✱ **What Did We Learn?** Give groups or partnerships the opportunity to present their benefits-and-burdens lists to the class and explain their decisions. Ask questions that encourage students to articulate their reasoning, and invite students' descriptions of how and why their thinking changed during their conversations. Also help students reflect on their social and ethical learning: What went well, and what didn't? How did they help each other see things from various perspectives? What was difficult or easy about that? What might they do differently or the same next time?

Two by Two. Another way to have students share and learn from each other's ideas (either before or instead of whole-class sharing) is to have pairs of partners get together and present their benefits-and-burdens lists to each other.

Alternate Means. When students identify compelling benefits of otherwise damaging choices (for example, the supportive community of a gang or ending a war by dropping an atom bomb), extend the activity by asking them to discuss other ways they might attain those benefits.

Another Look. In cases where students were asked to define benefits and burdens from the perspective of one character or historical figure, have them make new lists based on another character's or person's point of view.

Two people looking at the same benefits-and-burdens list might still arrive at different decisions—so when students have made their lists and move to the decision-making process, be sure they understand that there may not be one "correct" decision to be made.

Blueprints for a Collaborative Classroom: Joint Ideas

Deciding

EVERY TIME students work together, they have to make decisions together—and if we could, we'd give you a step-by-step formula for students to follow every time! No such formula exists, of course, but we can suggest considerations and strategies that students can apply as they learn to make thoughtful, fair, effective decisions together.

Making decisions together isn't always easy, of course—that is, decisions that truly honor everybody in the group—because it can entail concessions and consensus building. It's worth the effort, though, to help children learn to make collaborative decisions—they not only feel that their participation in group work and the classroom community is meaningful and worthwhile, but also they are invested in decisions they have arrived at themselves and are correspondingly committed to abiding by them. Above all, they acquire lifelong skills in perspective taking, negotiation, and responsibility to themselves and others.

WHY TO USE

- to enable students to assume autonomy and responsibility in guiding their group work and their own learning

- because students are more invested in decisions they have arrived at themselves

- to make group decision making a community-building, rather than community-dividing, activity

- to help students appreciate when compromise is a winning solution

- to teach students the life skills of perspective taking and negotiation

WHEN TO USE

- whenever students are collaborating and need to arrive at a decision together

HOW TO DO

The Deciding blueprint asks students to

- look at the nature of the decision to be made

- look at the different tools they have to help them make decisions, and try the one(s) that suit the decision at hand

- make sure their decision is kind and fair and that everyone can live with it

Developmental Considerations

Younger Students

Primary-grade children are beginning to be able to see things from perspectives other than their own, but they may have trouble applying these insights when other perspectives conflict with their personal interests. Because they are working hard to align what they understand with what they do, young children need many opportunities to practice perspective taking and making decisions that take into account all points of view. Likewise, they are still developing their self-control skills and will need practice learning and applying any ground rules you may set for decision-making discussions.

Young students might also need some assistance recognizing decisions to be made. For example, you may need to help them anticipate decisions that are likely to arise in group work and give them a starting point for their negotiations. Similarly, you might simplify procedures by isolating decisions embedded in larger tasks: If students are doing a play, for example, have groups decide on roles as a separate activity, tasks as a separate activity, and so on.

Older Students

While the decision-making process may be daunting to younger students, older students often find the process quite engaging. They are more adept at seeing situations from different points of view, incorporating these different perspectives in their decisions, and employing a wider range of strategies for narrowing choices. When faced with difficult decisions, however, even older students need help finding areas of agreement, especially when they hold particularly strong opinions. Work with students to encourage respectful and fair discussion strategies, and emphasize the importance of explaining their thinking to each other when trying to reach a decision—thus giving other students (and teachers!) a fresh way to appreciate an option and possibly build consensus around it.

Grouping Considerations

Decision making will occur in any collaborative activity, whether with partners, small groups, or the whole class. The beginning of the year offers many whole-class opportunities, such as choosing a class name or deciding on class norms, that give you a chance to model and facilitate fair and reasoned decision making.

Meanwhile, you can have students, in their partner or small-group work, practice the skills modeled in whole-class decision-making efforts. Partner and small-group decision making also underscores the value of student-to-student exchanges and offers a smaller, safer scope of participation that can draw quieter students into a conversation. As students develop their collaborative decision-making skills in partner and group activities throughout the year, also continue to model and reinforce these skills in any whole-class decision-making opportunities that arise. (If you'd like more ideas on incorporating whole-class decision making into your classroom community, see the DSC publication *Ways We Want Our Class to Be*.)

Fly on the Wall

Maureen Jackson's combined first- and second-grade class has finished a peer editing project. During a follow-up discussion about how group members worked together, Robby protests his group's decision about how to take turns. Maureen guides the class in generating solutions—in which fairness is a central consideration.

ROBBY: That was really unfair, 'cause I had to be last always. We just kept doing it and I always had to be last.

MS. JACKSON: Was that all right?

ROBBY: I didn't like it.

MS. JACKSON: You didn't like it. Did you tell them that?

ROBBY: I told them, "No fair."

MS. JACKSON: What happened?

LINDA: (A fellow group member) Someone *has* to be last.

MS. JACKSON: How do you work that out?

SAMANTHA: Josh said that he wanted to be first, so then he did it and then Linda did it and then I did it and then Robby did it.

ROBBY: And then Josh did it and then Linda and then Samantha. I just kept being last every time we did it.

MS. JACKSON: So if this happens again, do you think you might say something?

ROBBY: I did, but they just didn't do it. They just kept doing it that way.

MS. JACKSON: What could you do next time?

ROBBY: Could we switch it?

MS. JACKSON: I don't know. Josh, what could you do next time?

JOSH: Talk about it?

MS. JACKSON: How could you solve it so he doesn't always end up being last? He's feeling like he's always last.

JOSH: Let him go first.

MS. JACKSON: Somebody has to go last next time. Is there a way to fix that so it doesn't feel like you are the one going last every time?

MELINDA: Take turns being first.

MS. JACKSON: How would that work?

MELINDA: Like they would just like, maybe do "rock, paper, scissors" to see who went first and then they would get in twos and then the two winners would do it against each other and that would be the order. Then after they went around, the person who was first would go to the end and they would keep on doing that.

MS. JACKSON: So one way of sharing the turns would be playing a game. Another idea?

GILLIAN: See, Robby was last, so after they do all their turns, then Josh goes to the end and Robby goes to the front and the two people are in the middle and then the next person that's behind Robby goes there, then the next person goes there, and they've all been first once.

MS. JACKSON: So clearly there's a way of dealing with four people. Usually we deal with two, but there is a way of working with four people, but it's a much more difficult thing to do.

Getting Students Ready

Since decision making is inherent in every collaborative activity, it will rarely be treated as a separate blueprint unto itself and you will rarely be devoting separate academic and social preparation to it. Instead, each blueprint's Getting Students Ready section highlights considerations of respect and fairness that pertain to any decision making that occurs during the activity.

At the beginning of the year, however, you may want to set aside some time to talk with students about helpful decision-making strategies, tools, and behaviors, such as those suggested below. Likewise, when a collaborative activity seems to involve a lot of (or sophisticated) decision making, you may want to help students anticipate challenges by reviewing these ideas, and as you observe group work you can remind students of these suggestions as the need arises.

Review tools. Depending upon the nature of the decision being made—who it affects, and how—students could resolve differences of opinion in many ways. The main thing they should think about is whether their way of reaching a decision is fair and appropriate to the nature of the decision being made. For example, deciding who goes first in a game can be solved in a fairly arbitrary manner, such as drawing straws, because the decision isn't one that will hurt someone's feelings or result in an injustice. In contrast, a decision about who will do different tasks for a group project requires more thoughtful strategies that weigh and respect individual wishes, group needs, and practical considerations. Below are some different tools that can help children make decisions.

- *Narrow the choices.* When students have many ideas to choose from, before even trying to decide on one they might try to eliminate some options with quick, pragmatic strategies such as the following:

  "Unlivable Only": Students name the choices they can't live with and explain why (which helps eliminate unpopular ideas and helps students clarify their thinking).

  "Livable Only": Students name all the choices they can live with (which highlights areas of common agreement and weeds out truly unlivable ideas).

  "One Why": Students each choose the option they consider best and explain why they chose it (which helps students clarify their thinking, eliminates less popular ideas, and highlights deep disagreements).

  "Three Straws": Students cast three straw votes in any way they choose—all their votes for one option, one vote to three different options, etc. (which eliminates all but a few choices while also allowing students to express the strength of their preferences).

- *Vote.* Decisions can be reached by voting, but you will want to help students be aware of the consequences of voting so that they can see when it's an appropriate strategy. The problem with voting is that it divides a group into "winners" and "losers," which does little to contribute to a sense of community or collaboration; also, students might quickly jump to taking a vote when further discussion and negotiation might have resulted in a more fair and widely pleasing decision. Nonetheless, voting can be an efficient decision-making tool when group members are fairly amenable to all ideas but must choose one to go with—since none of the ideas are "unlivable," no one will be unduly disregarded or resentful of the vote result.

- *Leave it to chance.* When decisions don't require reasoned discussion, it's efficient to handle them with luck-of-the-draw devices, such as choosing straws or "eeny-meeny-miney-moe." For example, in the Fly on the Wall vignette Melinda suggests playing "rock, scissors, paper" to designate who will *first* go first—an efficient and appropriate solution because eventually everyone will get a turn at being first, but *someone* has to get things started.

- *Take turns.* Another expedient approach is for group members to take turns making decisions.

- *"Give in."* Who hasn't stuck to their guns well past the point of reason or common sense? Sometimes the point being argued simply isn't worth that kind of stubbornness! Help students recognize that letting others "get their way" is often a measure of maturity, and encourage them to be thoughtful about assessing when their resistance to a suggestion is disproportionate to the significance of the decision being made.

- *Reach consensus.* Building consensus is a sophisticated and often time-consuming process—and an important lifelong skill. Our basic definition of a consensus decision is that everybody concerned can live with it, *even if it's no one's first choice*—and it's a definition that can accommodate significant differences of opinion when reaching a decision! Very often, students will find that they can make concessions or combine their ideas to arrive at satisfying (even rewarding) decisions, but they must be willing to invest some discussion and negotiation to get to that point. Help students think about why it might be important to make that effort for decisions that affect the whole group. What might happen if one group member feels her or his opinions have been completely disregarded? How would they feel if this happened to them? How might it affect their own work and the work of the group?

Review "steps." Students will need practice not only in learning how to weigh the considerations described above, but also in remembering to do so! As necessary, remind students to be thoughtful and deliberate about making decisions by following the "steps" below.

- *Look at the nature of the decision to be made.* In other words, what is the significance of the decision and how might it affect group members and group work? Thinking about this will, in turn, inform children's thinking about the next step.

- *Look at the different tools they have for making decisions, and try the one(s) that suit the decision at hand.* The more students try their hand at collaborative decision making, the more they will have insight into how and when to use the tools reviewed above.

- *Make sure the decision is kind and fair and that everyone can live with it.* Encourage students to appreciate that the goal of a decision-making process is not just to *reach* a decision, but to reach a decision that helps them complete the task at hand *and* treat each other well.

Model the process. Throughout every school day, you can teach students about responsible decision making by explaining your own decisions and reasoning to them; and as mentioned above, of course, you will also want to regularly engage in whole-class decision making, to model and guide the process for students.

Social/Ethical Preparation

When students need to make a decision, it is important that they understand the behaviors that will help them do so. The following are some social and ethical aspects of decision making that you may want to help your students anticipate.

Following ground rules. When students are trying to make decisions and build consensus, strongly held opinions might affect some students' ability to proceed fairly and respectfully. A few basic ground rules, such as the following, can help keep things civilized; you might want to post and review these before activities that involve a lot of collaborative decision making:

- One person speaks at a time.
- Listen to each other.
- Allow each other to disagree.
- No put-downs.
- No finger-pointing or blaming.

Respecting different points of view. Remind students that the whole point of collaborative decision making is to hear and *consider* everyone's point of view—not dismiss any out of hand. Emphasize the importance of finding out reasons behind people's thinking, and suggest questions students might ask themselves to help them understand other people's points of view: How might I feel if I were in their shoes? Why might they be saying "no"? Why might this be so important to them?

Encouraging different points of view. Collaborative decision making means that everybody's ideas are included and honored in the discussion, even if they don't prevail in the decision. Discuss responses—including ways of disagreeing—that might make people feel willing or unwilling to share their thoughts and feelings.

Reaching agreement by principle, not pressure. Explore the difference between persuading others that an idea is agreeable, and badgering them into agreeing.

Learning from the past. If in previous decision-making situations students have identified aspects of the process that they need to work on, remind them of that resolve.

WAYS TO USE *Deciding*

ACTIVITIES

As mentioned earlier, almost any collaborative activity is also a decision-making activity (an exception being the Brainstorming blueprint, which generates the ideas to be decided on), so it would be redundant to propose specific Deciding activities here. We thought it might be useful, though, to point out blueprints in this book that involve many or significant collaborative decisions and that might require extra attention to decision-making strategies and behaviors:

- Sorting and Classifying
- Mind Mapping
- Venn Diagrams
- Benefits and Burdens
- Investigating
- Academic Problem Solving
- Partner Reading

- Poetry
- Narrative
- Expository
- Graphic Arts
- Readers Theater
- Role-Playing
- Model Building

EXTENSIONS

Each blueprint encourages students to reflect on how they worked together and what they accomplished, which necessarily includes decisions they made together. Based on your observations of group work and the kinds of decisions students faced, you might want to use the suggestions below to focus specifically on this aspect of their collaboration.

Fly on the Wall

Students in Janet Ellman's combined second- and third-grade class have invented a dominoes math game during free-play time. Janet invites the class to formalize the game by developing a recording sheet for partners to use when they play the game. The first step is deciding on a name for the game—and treating each other respectfully and fairly while exploring the different possibilities.

MS. ELLMAN: What could we call this game? We could call it anything we want, but we should all call it the same thing. There might be confusion if you're calling it one thing and someone else is calling it something else.

JACKIE: (Shouting spontaneously) Dominoes!

MS. ELLMAN: Raise your hand so we can share our time fairly. Other suggestions?

JEFFREY: Tile Patterns.

NICHOLAS: We could vote.

MS. ELLMAN: Does anyone have another way besides a vote? You know what bothers me about votes? If one person wins, another person—what?

STUDENTS: Loses.

MS. ELLMAN: And I'm afraid that person might feel bad. Is there a way we could combine the two names?

A FEW STUDENTS: Domino Patterns!

MS. ELLMAN: I want to make sure everybody is joining the conversation. (Now that they are struggling with a problem of real importance to them, students have a hard time containing themselves and there is much discussion among them.)

A FEW STUDENTS: Counting Dominoes.

MS. ELLMAN: How about Counting Dominoes? Does that make sense?

LAYLA: Domino Tens.

MS. ELLMAN: Okay, let me get this down—what did we end up with? (She writes on butcher paper.)

Counting Dominoes, Domino Patterns, Domino Tens.

MEGAN: That doesn't sound right.

NICHOLAS: We could *vote*.

MS. ELLMAN: Voting worries me because if someone wins, someone else loses. Why Domino Tens, Layla?

LAYLA: We're counting by tens, not by ones.

MS. ELLMAN: What do you think? I'm going around the circle to hear everybody and what they think. Megan?

MEGAN: Domino Flash.

STUDENTS: Yeah! Yeah!

MS. ELLMAN: Thumbs up if you can live with it. (Everybody raises thumbs except Ashley and Bryan.)

MS. ELLMAN: (Lightly) You held your thumb down—can you tell me why?

ASHLEY: I'm just kidding.

MS. ELLMAN: Okay. (She returns to the butcher paper and writes Domino Flash on the top.)

✳ **What Did We Learn?** Encourage students to reflect on both the content of their decision and on the process of reaching a decision itself. What went well? What interesting ideas or approaches did they learn from a classmate? What might they work on the next time they need to make a decision together?

Share Decisions. When partnerships or small groups have had to make decisions about their own work, the rest of the class can learn from each group's decision-making process. Have each partnership or group report highlights to the whole class—their decision, additional issues that arose in their discussion, how they agreed on a decision, and so on. Help students appreciate similarities and differences in the way groups approached the problem and the decisions they made.

So What Happened? Be sure students have a chance to evaluate their decisions at a later date (the timing of the evaluation will depend on the nature of the decision). And give students a chance to modify their decisions when necessary—students need to learn how to learn from their mistakes, adapt to circumstances, and see that even the best-laid plans have room for improvement!

Messing About

MESSING ABOUT capitalizes on the sheer fun of playing with any idea or thing—exploring how it works, experimenting with its use, enjoying it for its own sake. Such play is an important foundation for learning, for children and adults alike. "Messing about" with concepts and objects has been the starting point for many contributions in science, math, and the humanities, and it can be an important starting point for classroom learning, as well, in two ways: Before a lesson, students benefit from messing about with books or materials to be used in that learning activity, to engage their interest and begin building understanding of the lesson's concepts; students also benefit from having regularly scheduled time set aside for messing about at learning stations devoted to any variety of subjects or materials, as an ongoing means to pursue learning of their own choosing. The beauty of these activities is that, no matter how formally or informally students come together to mess about, collaboration occurs spontaneously as they share their observations and ideas and ask for and offer help. Such open-ended exploration and collaboration spark students' curiosity, tap their intrinsic motivation to learn, offer them hands-on learning experiences, and give them a chance to inspire and learn from each other.

WHY TO USE

- to nurture and capitalize on students' curiosity about the world
- to immerse students in self-directed learning experiences that will form a foundation for further learning
- to promote experimentation, observation, and scientific theory building
- because messing about is the mother of innovation and invention

WHEN TO USE

- when students need to be introduced to novel materials that will be used in directed instruction
- after students have used materials in directed instruction and can further their own exploration
- regularly each week, to foster and satisfy students' spirit of inquiry
- regularly each week, to help students create a database of experience that will lend meaning to subsequent learning

HOW TO DO

The Messing About blueprint asks students to

- decide on a starting activity, if they will be messing about at stations
- read any special instructions at the station
- as they work, talk with others at the station or in their group about what they each are doing and noticing
- if something interesting happens, try it again and see if the same thing happens
- continue trying other ideas that occur to them

Developmental Considerations

Younger Students

Messing about is an ideal format for both younger and older children, but for somewhat different reasons. More than anything, young students need to immerse themselves in the world—to figure out what things do and how things work. Many and varied opportunities to mess about—everything from discovering how water behaves at the water table to testing how people behave in the dramatic play area to poking around in books—help young children develop a database that is the foundation for future learning.

Older Students

In the upper grades, learning becomes serious business, and teachers feel increased pressure to cover a wide range of topics and material. As a result, older students often have few opportunities to engage in leisurely exploration—even of their textbooks! Messing about is a refreshing antidote to the fast-paced, teacher-directed lessons that often dominate the classroom, even despite best efforts to remain child centered. When students have opportunities to ask questions and pursue answers for themselves, they can arrive at important understandings about problems they find significant and relevant—a reminder of what learning is all about and that intrinsic motivation is our ally in the classroom.

Still, it may have been a long time since older students were allowed to "play" in the classroom, and they may need help appreciating that messing about involves "real" learning. Give students examples of how messing about has resulted in discoveries and innovations; an excellent source for such examples is *Smithsonian* magazine, which often profiles people whose inventions spring from their captivation with some unusual idea or pastime. For instance, the August 1995 issue includes an article about Michael Moschen, who has become "in anybody's view, the most significant juggler of the twentieth century, and probably the most innovative in history" by playing with the laws of physics. Or take a look at the January 1996 issue, in which Massachusetts Institute of Technology artist-in-residence Arthur Ganson describes how his "ability to 'play' in spite of himself" enabled him to become a self-taught engineer, the creator of intricate and beautiful moving mechanical sculptures, and the inventor of the captivating Toobers and Zots foam toys.

Keep in mind, too, that older students can mess about with more sophisticated materials than younger students—batteries, wire, bulbs, bells, and other components of electric circuitry, for example—but that there is also considerable value in older students messing about with such basic materials as water, old appliances, potions, and the like.

≈ HINT ≈

If groups will be formed around interest areas, you may need to limit the number of students who can be at an activity at one time—especially if the activity is a messy one or space and resources are limited.

Grouping Considerations

How students are grouped depends somewhat on the context of the messing about activity. For example, if the activity is to precede a specific learning task, such as a math lesson using manipulatives or a science experiment, students may already be grouped for purposes of the lesson and can do their messing about in those same groups.

≈HINT≈

When students are free to come and go between groups as they like, less assertive students may simply move on when a problem arises rather than negotiate what they need. Watch for students who move from task to task, and observe closely to identify whether there is an academic or social problem underlying their migration.

If students will be doing general messing about at learning stations, though, you might set the tone for thoughtful exploration by messing about with different ways of grouping students. For example, you could simply augment the spontaneity of messing about by having students informally group themselves around their shared interest in a station (in which case you also might need to become accustomed to the fact that groups formed this way will be fluid—losing and gaining members as students' interest in an activity ebbs and flows).

After students have had some experience working at stations, you might try out more formal (and perhaps challenging) grouping arrangements—for example, assigning partnerships to work together at the station(s) of their choice. Such an option helps build community by bringing together students who otherwise might not have much interaction, and it also gives students valuable practice in negotiation and compromise as they agree on what activities to pursue.

Yet another alternative is to encourage students to push the limits of a material or problem by having partners or groups spend an entire session at one activity. As you try different grouping arrangements, note the benefits and burdens of each and continue using those that best suit your students and purposes. Try not to jump around too much between systems, however—give students a chance to get used to one system before introducing another, and when possible let students participate in deciding what system to use.

Getting Students Ready

Academic Preparation

Because intrinsic motivation is at the heart of the Messing About blueprint, students need little help connecting with the activities. You might, however, want to use some of the suggestions below to address logistical and content aspects of some activities.

Explore the possibilities. If students will be messing about at stations, review the options before them; tell them about any new materials and activities and reintroduce old, forgotten ones in ways that pique students' interest and expand their possibilities. Explain, for example, "Last month we made animal masks for our play of *Who's in Rabbit's House?* Today I noticed the masks when I was looking in the closet and decided to put them in the dramatic play area. You can use them any way you'd like—to act out *Who's in Rabbit's House?* or to make up a story of your own."

Explain special considerations. Make sure students understand any special instructions or restrictions (including your reasons) for an activity or station. For example, if students need to wear safety goggles when taking apart old radios, make sure to tell them ahead of time. If you do not want students to mix sand with water at the water table, let them know. If only two students can be at the carpenter table at a time, tell them. Post cards at activity areas to remind students of such considerations—but limit these to the essentials.

Connect with prior learning. Help students recall interesting aspects of previous messing about sessions, and get them thinking about where those discoveries might lead them. For example, "Remember when Marta did a subject search on the library computer? What did she do when she got a list of 200 books about animals?"

Focus on process, not product. Remind students that messing about creations, however wonderful, are usually temporary—bubbles pop, block structures must be dismantled and the blocks put away, play dough figures get put in the play dough tub at the end of the session. Help students think of ways they can "keep" their accomplishments, both for posterity and perhaps to build on them in future; for example, they might write a description, draw a sketch or blueprint, take a photograph, and so on. If possible, show the class examples of such records (for instance, Leonardo da Vinci's notebooks).

Model the process. If students are not accustomed to playing with their learning, you may want to model the gist of these activities. For example, mess about with some materials at a station and invite students' observations about what's happening and what they would do next—showing them that messing about *isn't* about finding "right" answers but *is* about asking their own questions and exploring what interests them.

Social/Ethical Preparation

When messing about is organized around interest groups, the fact that students are where they want to be ameliorates problems that can arise in group work. Still, whether in informal or more structured groups, difficulties may arise over choosing what to mess about with, what kind of messing about to do, and how to share materials while messing about. The following are some social and ethical aspects of messing about that you may want to help your students anticipate.

Getting the grouping. If you have used different grouping strategies during messing about activities, be sure students understand which arrangement will be used. Are students expected to stay with a partner? Can partners move freely to different activities, or must they stay with the same activity throughout the session? Are there limits on how many students can be at an activity at one time? Invite students' suggestions for and questions about the grouping arrangement.

Starting out. If you find that certain messing about stations have become quite popular, you may need to establish systems to avoid students' mad rush to beat each other to those activities. For example, have students take turns using the station from session to session, or invite students' suggestions about how to negotiate fair use. (It might be helpful to gauge student "distribution" before each messing about session by asking each student at which station they would like to start; then you'll have some idea of whether any negotiation or system is needed.)

Sharing resources. If students have been having difficulty sharing materials while messing about, discuss possible solutions with the class. Ask for students' ideas on how to handle such situations, and have students role-play their suggestions (younger students especially benefit from rehearsing solutions).

Sharing ideas. When students are messing about together, they may be equally inspired by very different ideas about "how" to mess about—what would be interesting to do with the materials, what to do next, and so on. Discuss with students how they might accommodate such situations: Is there a way to try both ideas? Combine the ideas? Remind students of the importance of listening carefully to each other—they may find that their ideas aren't so far apart, or they may even find someone else's ideas more interesting than their own!

Cleaning up. Messing about is often—well—messy. Cleanup is rarely a problem, however, if students agree on a plan ahead of time. Involve students in decisions about how to clean up—for example, having students clean the area where they are working when cleanup time is announced, or having teams in charge of particular areas (whether or not team members used the area that day), and so on.

WAYS TO USE *Messing About*

ACTIVITIES

As mentioned above, messing about in the classroom falls into two categories: regular opportunities for general messing about and lesson-specific opportunities. The latter, of course, depend upon the topic at hand: When introducing new materials in math, science, art, or other subjects, give students a chance to engage in open-ended exploration before presenting specific problems—students will find it easier to attend to the task if they have had sufficient opportunity to mess about on their own first.

But don't stop there! Continue to foster a spirit of collaborative exploration and experimentation in your classroom by scheduling regular messing about sessions, giving students an ongoing opportunity to deepen and extend their knowledge of materials and to use familiar materials in novel ways. The challenges students pose—and solve—themselves often surpass those we set for them. Set up several stations with different kinds of materials that students can mess about with, and be sure to include materials that students are using in more formal learning situations—props from the play they are performing, math manipulatives from their study of patterns, word files and books they have been reading, and so on.

Physical Properties Play. Encourage students to explore gravity, trajectories, and other properties of the physical world by setting up a physical knowledge center with activities such as bowling and pendulum boards. Or simply present the materials—ramps, marbles, cylinders, and the like—and have students create their own games. (*Physical Knowledge in Preschool Education,* listed below in Resources, is a good source of ideas.)

Deconstructive Play. Things are rarely what they seem, and children are often eager to find out what really makes things "tick." Set up a station with old appliances and equipment that students can take apart—motors, computers, clocks, kitchen appliances, typewriters, radios, and the like. Provide tools, such as screwdrivers, wrenches, and pliers—and be sure to supply goggles for safety (and dramatic effect). Have the book *The Way Things Work,* by David Macaulay, available as a resource.

Dramatic Play. Create a dramatic play area with props that promote role taking—characters and situations from social studies, literature, and other areas of the curriculum as well as real-life roles and situations (such as family, school, community helpers, professions, and so on). Change the props periodically.

Literacy Play. Set up a writing station stocked with a variety of paper, small blank books, writing implements, stickers and stamps, staplers, hole punches, envelopes, dictionaries, a computer, and so on. Younger students will enjoy exploring and practicing their emerging literacy skills; for older students, also have available prompts such as addresses—organizations, politicians, the media, authors—so students can write letters about issues the class is studying, books they are reading, and so on.

Potion Play. Young children love to make potions—and having a station set aside for the purpose can help them learn important principles of chemistry (for example, some things dissolve and others don't, mixing two things together can result in a product that resembles neither of the original ingredients, and so on). Provide a variety of ingredients for students to mess about with—salt, sugar, and other common household potion ingredients; or you might just present combinations you know will produce interesting effects—vinegar and baking soda, corn starch and water, water and food coloring, for example. (Just make sure everything you provide is nontoxic.)

Textbook Play. When students are about to start a new book or chapter in a text, give them time to poke around in it. Have partners or groups list questions, ideas, or interests that arise.

Research Play. Collecting resources for a report requires a good deal of messing about. Have groups explore library resources or collections of materials that are available in the classroom. What looks useful? What new ideas are suggested? What's missing?

Learners' Choice. Older students will welcome the opportunity to create messing about activities based on their own interests and experience. Have individuals, partners, or small groups devise activities and scavenge the supplies necessary.

≈ HINT ≈

Children's science museums often have wonderful ideas for simple, hands-on messing about activities. Visit your local museum, take notes, and then replicate your favorite activities in the classroom. Or better yet, take your class on a field trip and invite them to take notes and replicate their favorite activities (or think of new ones).

EXTENSIONS

Messing about activities can be extended in any of the following ways.

✳ **What Did We Learn?** Before cleanup, you may want to set aside a little time for students to demonstrate any interesting creations and discoveries. After cleanup, have a brief whole-class conversation about how everyone worked together, and include your own observations to help students reflect on the experience: What went well? Did any difficulties arise? How were these addressed? What might students do differently next time?

Clean Teamwork. As long as students are on the subject of how well they worked together, you might want to have them evaluate how well they cleaned up together, too. To some extent, the success of cleanup will be obvious—the proof is in the clean room—but you still might want to check in on whether students think the cleanup plan was fair to everyone involved. Invite students' suggestions about more efficient or fair cleanup systems for future messing about sessions.

Keepsakes. As mentioned earlier, the point of messing about is the process, not the product—but recording their products or results helps students remember interesting ideas and perhaps build on them later. Have students record highlights from their messing about in writing or drawing (or photographs, video, audiotape, etc.). For example, the class might keep a running journal or chart at each messing about station, recording anything interesting they discover or wonder when working there ("what we've noticed about sinking and floating," "structures we've built from blocks," and so on).

Prove It! Have partners or groups postulate scientific principles that explain what they observed or discovered while messing about. Discuss competing theories that arise, and have students devise ways to test them. (See the Investigating blueprint on page 70.)

Where Do We Go from Here? Messing about is likely to generate as many questions as it answers! Help students see the value of such questioning by keeping a record of questions that arise from messing about sessions, and from these have students identify an area of interest for more systematic study.

Resources

The following books can inspire many a messing about activity—and while some suggestions may be too structured to qualify as true "messing about," they will spark ideas of your own.

CARLSON, LAURIE
Kids Create: Art and Craft Experiences for 3- to 9-Year-Olds
WILLIAMSON PRESS, 1990
Great messing about suggestions for kids—how about a play skateboard and skateboard ramp for some informal physics instruction?

THE EXPLORATORIUM
The Exploratorium Home Laboratory: Hands-On Science Fun for Families
EXPLORING, VOL. 19, No. 1, SPRING 1995
Exploring is the quarterly magazine of the Exploratorium, a San Francisco hands-on science museum for children. This special issue of *Exploring* offers wonderful, engaging ideas for science experiments that children can do by themselves or with adults.

KAMII, CONSTANCE, AND RHETA DEVRIES
Physical Knowledge in Preschool Education
TEACHERS COLLEGE PRESS, 1993
Although designated for preschool in the title, this book contains many physical knowledge activity suggestions for students of all ages.

MACAULAY, DAVID
The Way Things Work
HOUGHTON MIFFLIN, 1988
This 400-page large-format book is a fascinating collection of annotated illustrations showing—the way things work!

SATTLER, HELEN RONEY
Recipes of Art and Craft Materials
LATHROP, LEE & SHEPARD BOOKS, 1987
A gold mine of recipes for glue, modeling materials, papier-mâché, paints, ink, flower preserver, and even a crystal garden solution—all sorts of stuff to stock messing about stations!

Investigating

CHILDREN ARE naturally interested in learning about the world and constructing theories about how it works, and the Investigating blueprint capitalizes on that curiosity in much the same spirit as did Messing About. The difference, though, is that Investigating suggests a structure to help students systematically reflect on and explain the results of their explorations. Such investigations can stem from observations of the natural world or experiments with inanimate objects and substances, but in either case the students proceed similarly, following the basic scientific method of investigation: Students raise questions about what they see or has happened, develop possible explanations, develop a procedure to test the explanation, analyze the results, and reexamine their hypothesis. But while investigating is systematic, it is also creative—and collaborating on an investigation enhances this creativity by helping students see different points of view, possibilities, and connections.

WHY TO USE

- to increase students' knowledge of the world
- to deepen students' understanding of scientific concepts
- to teach students a systematic approach to discovery and verification
- to answer specific questions
- to encourage a sense of wonder

WHEN TO USE

- when observing will lead to interesting and important learning
- when experimenting will inform students' understanding of a scientific concept
- when students' thinking and learning will be deepened by hearing other possibilities and points of view

HOW TO DO

The Investigating blueprint asks students to

- observe the subject or experiment and record observations
- discuss questions raised by their observations and choose one to investigate further
- speculate on possible answers (hypotheses) to the question and choose one to test
- develop a way to test the hypothesis
- analyze the results of the test
- reexamine the hypothesis, based on what the test results tell them

Developmental Considerations

Younger Students

As mentioned earlier, investigation is a natural extension of messing about, and young children in particular need lots of opportunities to mess about—to explore the world in an open-ended way—before engaging in more structured investigations. (See the Messing About blueprint, page 63, for suggestions.) As children begin acquiring information and ideas from their messing about activities, you might then begin moving them into investigation by helping them develop their observation skills. Even more than the rest of us, young children are inclined to see what they expect rather than what is there, and they may need practice in looking closely at and describing their subjects. Ask questions that help them think specifically about their observations—how things sound, feel, smell, and taste and details of appearance or behavior.

With observation, of course, comes record keeping—another skill that may take some time and practice for young children to master. You might start them off by simply having them record the most interesting or surprising thing that happened while messing about or observing; the format for recording could range from drawings to simple sentences, depending upon your students' skills. (Adding labels and captions to a "scientific illustration" is a good beginning writing activity that encourages literacy development as well as scientific thinking.) As children gain experience recording their observations, encourage a more systematic approach by having them describe what they observed using each of their senses, comparing what happens on several observations, or the like.

Finally, as young children move on to more structured investigations, provide simple prompts that reflect the steps in the process and help students organize their thinking, such as these:

- We noticed . . .
- We wonder . . .
- We think the reason is . . .
- We tried . . .
- What happened was . . .
- Why we think it happened is . . .
- What we're going to try next is . . .
- We think what will happen next is . . .

Older Students

Students of all ages benefit from many of the same investigating activities: observing a class pet, documenting the growth of a plant, watching seasonal changes in a garden, recording phases of the moon, testing various physical properties, and so on. However, older students can tackle more sophisticated concepts and investigations than can younger students—whereas younger children tend to focus on a single dimension or property at a time, for example, older students can take several variables into account and see relationships between them. Challenge their thinking with questions that help them see such relationships and, depending upon time and resources, encourage them to further test their assumptions in light of different variables. Also encourage them to use charts, graphs, or other graphic organizers to help them juxtapose and understand variables and outcomes.

Grouping Considerations

Investigating is well suited to both partner and small-group collaboration, depending upon the scope of the investigation and available resources. If the activity involves few roles or limited access to materials —for example, investigating surface tension by counting the number of water drops that fit on a penny or observing tiny brine shrimp— students would probably do better to work in partnerships than in small groups. (Do have partnerships get together in groups of four to compare notes, however.) If, however, students are tackling a broad topic, such as conducting a schoolwide survey or examining the plant and animal residents of a square yard of playground, four students may be necessary to adequately cover the tasks involved.

You'll find, of course, that different students take to different kinds of investigation—some are passionate about mixing potions, others are thoughtful and compassionate observers of living things, yet others are fascinated by kinetic energy, and so on. You might want to capitalize on these differences by sometimes having students do investigations in interest groups. While it is important for all students to gain a basic understanding of scientific concepts across disciplines, an occasional interest-group investigation will allow them to develop expertise in an area of choice and encourage all students to see themselves as capable scientists.

Getting Students Ready

Academic Preparation

Investigating covers a wide territory, in terms of both content and procedures, and academic preparation may need to address such specifics in addition to the suggestions outlined below.

Explain investigation. Because investigation does follow a scientific process of observation, questioning, hypothesizing, and testing, you will probably want to review those steps each time students embark on an investigation activity. How thoroughly you define and explain each step will depend on your students' experience, of course; the following are some points you might want to consider.

- *Step 1: Observe the subject or experiment and record observations.* Help students understand the importance of making careful observations, as these will be the springboard for whatever questions and hypotheses they decide to pursue. Emphasize that the usefulness and accuracy of their observations depend in large part upon their objectivity as observers—their ability to see what's really there, as opposed to what they *expect* to be there or think *should* be there. Ask students to imagine they know nothing at all about their subject, to observe as though they have never seen or heard of it before.

Also talk with students about how to record what they see—that is, clearly enough so that anyone could understand and use the information. Show them examples from different scientists and disciplines, such as Gregor Mendel's pea-breeding experiments or Leonardo da Vinci's engineering notes, which are reproduced in many encyclopedias and science texts. (Students might enjoy learning that da Vinci wrote his notes backward so they could be read only by reflecting them in a mirror; invite students to speculate on why he might have done this—and see the answer below, under Social/Ethical Preparation.) For younger children, of course, accurate recording might translate into drawing their observations in as much detail as possible or dictating them to an adult or buddy.

- *Step 2: Discuss questions raised by their observations and choose one to investigate further.* Observation naturally leads students to the next step: wondering about what they have seen. Encourage students to note as many and varied questions as occur to them—anything that makes them curious could lead to an interesting discovery! Partners or group members will then need to discuss each other's questions and agree on one to investigate, so it might be helpful at this point to review decision-making strategies, as well, as suggested in Social/Ethical Preparation.

- *Step 3: Speculate on possible answers (hypotheses) to the question and choose one to test.* Introduce the term *hypothesis*—explain that when scientists wonder about why something happens, they try to come up with an explanation that can be tested and proven true or false. Point out that a question (for example, Why are all the earthworms in that corner of the terrarium?) can lead to several possible explanations (for example, earthworms like the dark, earthworms like the tall grass in that corner, earthworms move east, and so on). After partners or group members have chosen a question to investigate, they should brainstorm and discuss possible explanations—and again, choosing one to test may require some reasoned negotiation. (This conversation will probably overlap a bit with the next step, because one way to eliminate a suggested hypothesis is to point out that it can't be tested—which necessarily entails some preliminary thinking about ways to test different suggestions.)

- *Step 4: Develop a way to test the hypothesis.* Inexperienced investigators will need guidance to devise a realistic, conclusive test of their hypothesis. Suggest questions they can ask themselves to think through their test from all angles—for example, What do we plan to do first? What do we expect to happen? How will that prove our hypothesis? What would have to happen to disprove our hypothesis? Also remind them to look out for variables that might skew their results—for example, if we think earthworms move to one corner because they prefer darkness, and not because they like the grass on that side or because they always move east, then how might we test this? How will we know it's *not* the grass? How will we know it's *not* because they like the east? Finally, remind students that their

≈ HINT ≈

Have students write each hypothesis on a sentence strip so that group members can discuss, compare, sort, and classify them: Are some mutually exclusive (i.e., if one is true, the other can't be)? Which explanations are similar? Could more than one of these explanations work? How can they be rewritten to distinguish them?

≈ HINT ≈

Remind students that testing a hypothesis need not be complicated or elaborate. In fact, scientists even have a word to describe simple, effective tests: elegant.

observation and recording skills will again be very important during their test and urge them to pay attention to details!

- *Step 5: Analyze the results of the test.* Students' tests will often be simple enough that the proof (or not) of their hypothesis is patently obvious. As students venture into more sophisticated investigations, however, they may need to spend some time sifting and organizing their data to help them think through whether the test supported or disproved their hypothesis (see ORGANIZING IDEAS blueprints on pages 32–54 for suggestions). They also might need to take another look at what variables affected their test, which is where thorough observation and records come in handy—for example, after a test of static electricity, it might prove useful to have a record of the weather at the time, and so on. As above, this conversation may overlap with the next step—students are bound to begin drawing conclusions about their hypothesis as they think about the test results.

- *Step 6: Reexamine the hypothesis, based on what the test results tell them.* The results of students' tests may not be as simple as whether their hypothesis has been proven true or false—as students think about what the test results mean, they might conclude that the test was more flawed than the hypothesis! If that's the case, they'll need to revisit their hypothesis to think about how they can better test it. However, their results may help them refine (or even discard) the hypothesis—and even should their investigation prove their hypothesis, reexamining it can lead to bigger and better questions to investigate further.

Invite an investigator. Besides explaining investigations, you will want to engage students' interest in the process and show how it works in the "real world." One way to do this is to invite a professional "investigator" to tell the class about his or her work (you might even have students visit the speaker's place of work rather than have the speaker come to the classroom). If possible, expose students throughout the year to a range of disciplines that use the scientific method of investigation—"hard" sciences such as chemistry, botany, and physics as well as behavioral sciences such as psychology and sociology.

Share examples. Help students see how scientific investigations can help us understand important things about ourselves and our world—for example, by having them view and discuss television programs such as public television's *NOVA* series. Likewise, be alert for scientific investigations that relate to topics your students are studying—or that are simply interesting and significant in their own right—and share these with the class. Encourage students to do the same.

Emphasize observation. When students are new to investigation, their observation and recording skills may need particular attention. Have them do activities that help them practice these skills (and that demonstrate the importance of accuracy). For example, have partners each write a description of an object while keeping that object from their partner's sight; then have partners exchange papers and try to draw each other's objects from the written description. Similarly, you could have partners write a description of the same object and then compare their observations—it's always a revelation to be shown a detail that escaped you completely! (The latter activity is useful because it encourages students to focus on observations made with different senses, not just sight, whereas the drawing activity emphasizes the visible.)

Model the process. When first introducing students to investigation, you may want to begin with a whole-class investigation in which you execute the steps based on student input—you might even devote an entire session to each step. Likewise, as students move on to partner or group investigations, you might start them off with a prescribed experiment—that is, a previously designed experiment that will serve as a model for their later, independent efforts—which will reduce their anxiety about content while they become familiar with the structure of investigating.

Social/Ethical Preparation

The following are some social and ethical aspects of investigating that you may want to help students anticipate; depending upon the nature of the activity and students' experience, you may also want to review relevant cooperative skills found in the blueprints for generating, organizing, and choosing ideas (pages 13–61).

Encouraging participation. Leonardo da Vinci wrote his notes backward, so that they could only be read reflected in a mirror, because he was worried that someone might steal his ideas—but he was working alone and missed out on the fun of collaboration! Ask students what they think might be the advantages of sharing ideas and working with others to figure something out. Remind them that investigation activities are all about ideas—one opportunity after another to think up, discuss, test, and rethink ideas—so it's important to make sure everyone feels that they can participate by contributing their ideas. What can group members do to encourage each other to share ideas? What kinds of behaviors would discourage this?

Sharing participation fairly. Besides the give-and-take of ideas, the steps of an investigation also can raise issues about how to share work fairly. Depending upon the nature and complexity of the investigation, help students anticipate issues that might arise—for example, how to keep everyone involved throughout the investigation when there are a limited number of roles, how to fairly allot such tasks as recording observations or executing the steps of an investigation, and so on.

Making decisions fairly. Of course, making decisions is a part of encouraging participation and of sharing work fairly—but decision making is such a central aspect of investigation that it's worth singling out one more time here. Partners or small groups will have to agree on major decisions that affect the direction of their investigation: on which question to focus, which hypothesis to test, and how to test it. Remind students of their responsibility to each other to discuss their ideas respectfully and, as necessary, review decision-making strategies (see Deciding on page 55 for ideas).

Making lemonade. Investigating can be frustrating. Even with the best of planning, things go awry—equipment breaks or malfunctions, subjects wither and die, results take longer than expected—things just don't go as planned. Help students anticipate setbacks, pointing out

≈ HINT ≈

As you watch groups work, keep an eye for the partners or groups for whom "things just don't go as planned." Help these students think of constructive solutions—and help them recognize what they learned from the detour.

that investigators often learn as much from what doesn't work as they do from what does work. Encourage students to make the most of setbacks and use them to their advantage.

WAYS TO USE *Investigating*

ACTIVITIES

The following are a few ideas for using investigation activities in the classroom as well as some suggested resources that are chock-full of inspiration.

Life Cycle. This is a good activity to help students develop their observation and hypothesizing skills. Establish a classroom colony of monarch butterflies, silkworms, tadpoles, or other small creatures that have a short, interesting life cycle. Have partners or small groups daily observe and record data about the changes they see, as well as their speculations about what is happening and what they think might happen next. Also have them record and discuss possible reasons for any discrepancies between their predictions and actual outcomes. Afterward, round out their understanding with related books, magazine articles, videos, and visits from experts.

Still Hunt. Another good activity for helping students focus their observation skills is to have them join a partner on a "still hunt"— which is simply to sit absolutely motionless and experience nature going about its business. Have each partnership choose a place that has both plant and animal life and sit for at least twenty minutes, paying attention to what they see, hear, smell, and feel. (Although this is most effective when done in the wild, it is surprising what a sense of wonder can be achieved in a public park, a garden, or another small slice of nature.) Have partners list in words or pictures everything they observed, discuss their observations, and identify one or two topics they would be interested in investigating further.

Investigative Science. Science curriculum offers all sorts of opportunities for investigation, of course—including opportunities for prescribed activities that help you familiarize students with the investigative process. Before teaching a scientific concept, have students do an experiment that will demonstrate the concept—direct experience of it will make your subsequent explanations much more accessible. (*Great Explorations in Math and Science*, listed below in Resources, is a good source of guided scientific discovery activities.) After explaining and discussing the concept with the class, have groups devise their own experiments that further explore or verify it.

Investigative Math. A cyclical interplay between observation and explanation can be used to investigate concepts in math, too. Again, guided math experiments can provide opportunities to get students comfortable with the investigative process—for example, *A Collection of Math Lessons* (listed below in Resources) includes a chapter that has students use spinners to observe and explain why some outcomes are likelier than others.

≈ HINT ≈

Many worthwhile observation activities can be created by simply exploring the world right outside (and inside) your door. Younger students are especially attuned to the natural world and will flood the class with insect specimens, autumn leaves, and the like with any encouragement at all. Older students may need more encouragement to notice things they have long taken for granted—and to see them with new eyes.

Investigative Reading. Many things that are worth investigating cannot be explored directly. But even when circumstances do not permit hands-on learning—for example, when learning about ancient worlds or distant cultures—students can use the investigative process to examine texts and other information resources. Help students see that the same steps that operate during hands-on investigations are also at work during "minds-on" investigations: After groups read about their subject (the equivalent of the observation step), have them identify a question of interest about the subject, develop a hypothesis, test their hypothesis by seeking out information about the topic, analyze their findings, and reexamine their hypothesis.

Investigative Gardening. Children benefit academically and socially by simply planting a garden—planning the garden, digging the soil, planting the seeds, tending the plants, and watching them grow—but they have the potential to gain even more when their gardening efforts are combined with scientific study. Once students have planted their garden, have them work in pairs or small groups to observe the plant and animal life there and identify a question they would like to study in depth (this would also be a good interest-group investigation).

Investigative Cooking. When cooking is approached with a spirit of investigation—what is happening, and why?—students can learn a great deal about chemistry, physics, and even life sciences. For example, you might have students start out by following a standard recipe and then have them design experiments to probe the effects of different variables in the recipe (for instance, what is the relationship between the amount of yeast used and how long it takes for dough to rise?). For other ideas, see *Incredible Edible Science* (listed below in Resources), which suggests investigations that help students discover what happens "behind the scenes" when they cook.

EXTENSIONS

Investigating activities can be extended in any of the following ways.

✳ **What Did We Learn?** Because investigation involves such extensive collaboration, it's important to help students reflect on the experience and appreciate their successes and challenges. Ask for children's comments on what went well and what didn't (socially and academically), the advantages and disadvantages of collaborating on an investigation, and anything they learned about cooperative investigations that might help them the next time. Also have students share their test results and conclusions, perhaps by

- creating an exhibit to highlight what they learned;
- "publishing" a scientific paper for classmates or parents;
- making an oral presentation at a (mock) professional meeting or conference;
- holding a mock press conference to announce findings and field questions from "the press";
- creating a game that incorporates the content and the methods used in the investigation—and allows players to experience the joys and pitfalls of scientific inquiry; or
- drawing a scientific illustration

Label and Explain. Even when groups are engrossed in their investigation and make important observations and discoveries, they may not have the vocabulary to name the concept or principle suggested by their exploration. Build on students' observations by providing a label and explanation for what groups have learned (for example, "You have discovered that some things *dissolve* and others don't . . .") and challenge them to devise additional tests of the phenomenon. Younger children may find it difficult to fully understand some scientific explanations, but it is important for them to hear the labels and explanations and wrestle with how these fit with what they see.

Recycle. Investigation involves a cyclical interplay between observation and explanation—the end of one investigation is simply the starting point for another. Encourage students to deepen their discovery by designing a follow-up investigation to explore questions raised by the first.

Resources

These resources are just a few of the many books that ask students to investigate important concepts in an interesting, constructivist manner. These come in especially handy when starting students off with prescribed investigations; just keep in mind that while many such resources assume students will collaborate, few provide teachers or students with guidance for how to do so—but they are easily combined with the suggestions included here to arrive at some wonderful collaborative learning.

BURNS, MARILYN, AND BONNIE TANK
A Collection of Math Lessons: From Grades 1 through 3
MATH SOLUTIONS PUBLICATIONS, 1988
This book includes a chapter entitled "Experiments with Spinners," which gives step-by-step instructions for experiments that investigate mathematical concepts.

HIRSCHFIELD, ROBERT, AND NANCY WHITE
The Kid's Science Book: Creative Experiences for Hands-on Fun
WILLIAMSON PUBLICATIONS, 1995
This wonderful book is built on the idea that "science is all around you every day in everything you do." It contains suggestions for activities based on observation and explanation, designed for children to do themselves, as well as activities that help them develop skill and understanding in many aspects of scientific method.

KNEIDEL, SALLY STENHOUSE
Creepy Crawlies and the Scientific Method: Over 100 Hands-On Science Experiments for Children
FULCRUM PUBLISHING COMPANY, 1993
Insects and bugs are perfect subjects for scientific investigation—they are endlessly fascinating, relatively easy to obtain, and require little in the way of maintenance. This book uses the investigative process to teach both information and methods of biological science—and once students have tried some of the ideas in this book, they'll probably have ideas for experiments of their own.

Great Explorations in Math and Science (GEMS)
LAWRENCE HALL OF SCIENCE
Housed at the University of California at Berkeley, the Lawrence Hall of Science is a public science museum as well as a center for teacher education and curriculum research and development. Its *Great Explorations in Math and Science (GEMS)* publications suggest dozens of science investigation activities, including teacher guides that accommodate those who do not have a special background in math or science. (You can contact the GEMS project at 510/642-7771.)

SEELIG, TINA L.
Incredible Edible Science
SCIENTIFIC AMERICAN BOOKS FOR YOUNG CHILDREN/W.H. FREEMAN, 1994
Food is the subject of these edible scientific investigations.

WALPOLE, BRENDA
175 Science Experiments to Amuse and Amaze your Friends
RANDOM HOUSE, 1988
The experiments, designed for children to do themselves, are great springboards for open-ended investigating.

Academic Problem Solving

Throughout the curriculum (and throughout life), students are faced with open-ended problems to solve—that is, problems that could be approached a variety of ways or even have a variety of answers. These kinds of problems are an ideal venue for collaborative work—in pairs or small groups, students can generate more ideas, be challenged by each other's ideas, and stretch their thinking and collaborative skills to arrive at solutions together.

Offering a blueprint for problem solving is not to suggest that there is a simple, universal way to arrive at each and every solution, however—but it does show students that they are each entrusted with and capable of the thoughtful reasoning that all problem solving has in common. And because that kind of reasoning is necessary well beyond the classroom, the activities suggested here concern academic content areas as well as puzzlers to be solved for their own sake—for the fun, for the challenge, and for the sake of developing students' lifelong problem-solving skills.

WHY TO USE

- to learn and practice an approach to solving a wide range of problems
- to deepen understanding of concepts in specific academic domains
- to stress the importance of thoughtful reasoning, not just getting the right answer
- because people of all ages must deal with problems that need to be solved—thoughtfully
- because people of all ages enjoy a challenge

WHEN TO USE

- when there are different ways to approach a problem
- when a problem has more than one possible solution
- when thinking about and understanding a problem are as important as getting an answer

HOW TO DO

The Academic Problem Solving blueprint asks students to

- make sure they have a shared understanding of what the problem is
- generate and discuss possible solutions to the problem
- agree on a solution
- test or review the solution to make sure it works
- decide whether to adopt the solution or try another

Developmental Considerations

Younger Students

While young children certainly can be characterized as concrete thinkers, it would be a mistake to avoid giving them open-ended problems until they are "old enough" to think abstractly—problem-solving abilities should be developed, not simply waited for. Still, there are limits to young children's problem-solving abilities. Left on their own, many young children focus on a single dimension of a problem; they may stick with one strategy, whether or not it is effective, and fail to recognize inconsistencies or feel little need to resolve them. (Sometimes this is because students have not yet achieved automaticity in some skill—for example, emergent readers may invest all their attention in decoding a word and have none left for noticing that their decoded word doesn't make sense in context.) Collaboration goes far to remedy such single-minded approaches—another group member will often bring different skills to a problem, think of different approaches, or draw attention to factors a child working alone may have overlooked or ignored.

To help develop young students' ability to consider different factors and approaches, make it a habit to consult with them on familiar, everyday problems. You don't have to look far to find engaging and important problems—they arise regularly in the classroom: How many rhythm sticks do we need from the music room? How can we divide the cookies fairly? How many cars do we need for the field trip? Students have an interest in problems that really affect them, are more likely to grasp a variety of factors when they are familiar with the problem's context, and can test their solutions on problems that are real. Do we have two rhythm sticks for each student? Did everybody get the same number of cookies? Are there enough cars to get everyone to the zoo?

≈ HINT ≈

To promote student autonomy and to free you to teach rather than to dispense materials, have any materials needed for an activity organized and in a designated place, with students responsible for getting them as their need dictates—as well as for returning them.

Besides providing familiar contexts, also try to provide children with concrete problems—and materials for *solving* them concretely. Young children might have trouble multiplying 20 by 2, but they are likely to understand the problem and have a shot at solving it if it involves, for example, figuring out the number of shoes in a class of twenty children—and if they are allowed the leeway to try solving it in different ways. Some children may decide to draw two shoes for each student in the room and then count the shoes by ones or twos; others may prefer working with manipulatives, such as counters that represent shoes; still others may want to work with the real thing and simply count their classmates' feet (although they may find it's easier to keep track of manipulatives!). And, of course, an additional benefit of solving such a problem in these concrete ways is that children deepen their understanding of a math concept—in this case, what multiplication is all about—and build a foundation for handling more abstract problems.

Finally, build on children's intrinsic interest in playing with ideas—creating riddles, figuring out puzzles, solving mysteries, and so on. When problem solving is playful, children are more likely to try novel approaches and creative solutions than when the mood is strictly no-nonsense.

Older Students As children get older, they become more capable of abstract thinking and reasoning and can solve problems that entail coordinating more than one perspective—for example, enjoying puns that require them to keep in mind two different meanings of the same word. However, when a problem's context or concept is new, older students also need to begin with concrete situations and materials rather than rules and formulas.

Of course, like any other skill, students' problem-solving abilities mature at different rates—and accommodating a wide range of skills can be a major challenge of teaching older students. That's another reason it is so valuable to have students collaborate on open-ended problems—it allows each student to contribute what she or he can to solving the problem and results in each student forming a more complete picture of the factors involved in finding a solution.

Grouping Considerations

Most open-ended problems are probably best solved in partnerships or small groups, which give students the dual benefits of active participation and hearing different points of view. As suggested above for young children, however, you can make whole-class problem solving a regular feature of classroom life, too—and a recurring opportunity to model and develop problem-solving skills.

Getting Students Ready

Academic Preparation ***Introduce the problem.*** One good reason for solving a problem is that it's interesting, right? Communicate a problem's intrigue, drama, or importance with a story, role-play, or other means of connecting students with the problem to be solved.

Review the problem-solving process. Although the problem-solving process is essentially the same whether it involves math, art, science, or language, the specifics will be different in every case. Remind students of the basic steps in tackling a problem—to ground them in the familiar steps and to help them see how they apply to the problem at hand.

- *Step 1: Define and understand the problem.* Before students can solve a problem, they need to understand what it is—which is often the most neglected step in the problem-solving process. Students working together should first agree on a common definition of the problem, as well as what information they need to solve it. For example, in discussing a problem such as how many cars are needed for a field trip, the challenge will be thinking of variables (how many children are in the class) and dealing with ambiguities (different cars have different numbers of seats for passengers).

With young or inexperienced students, and depending upon the problem to be solved, you may want to arrive at a shared understanding of it as a class before students work on it in pairs or groups. For younger children, especially, understanding the problem may begin with simply restating the problem in their own words; listing important information about it together can also help get students' thinking started.

- *Step 2: Generate and discuss solutions to the problem.* This is the fun part of the process—and the part where you'll want to encourage children's autonomy in choosing how to generate solutions. Some problems might begin with brainstorming—coming up with as many plausible ideas as possible and deferring judgment at first, and then discussing all the proffered ideas. Others might require manipulatives or other physical aids, which could prove quite time consuming and labor intensive—to figure out the number of cars needed for the field trip, for example, some students may need to draw cars with different possible seating configurations and discuss each other's reasoning. And others might involve trial and error—venturing different ideas, trying them out, and trying out different modifications. Remind students that success at problem solving is not always defined by a tidy solution—sometimes the greatest benefits derive from students' creative thinking, no matter what the outcome. Also emphasize the importance of discussion—that students should explain their reasoning and listen to each other's ideas, not just barrel over their groupmates to present the "best" idea.

- *Step 3: Agree on a solution.* Not all problems will require groups to agree on a single solution, of course—some open-ended problems invite many plausible solutions. Some problems do have just one solution, though, or ask that students choose one from their different options; in such cases, you might also want to review consensus-building strategies at this point (see Deciding on page 55 for ideas).

- *Step 4: Test or review the solution.* For problems with tangible products or consequences—dividing cookies fairly, for example, or trying out an invention—the test is immediate. For other problems, the "test" will come in the form of reasoned judgment about whether the solution takes into account all the important variables and makes sense; build in a time when students can review the results of such problems.

- *Step 5: Decide whether to adopt the solution or try another.* After students evaluate a solution, have them consider whether they are satisfied or want to try it again.

Model the process. Introduce open-ended problem solving by working through problems as a class—and do this many times with many different kinds of problems until students are familiar with the procedure. Not only does daily classroom life offer many such opportunities, but also when you make decisions for the class you can model thoughtful problem solving by explaining how you arrived at your conclusion (which produces an added benefit: Children are more likely to respect and comply with a decision when they understand the reasons for it).

The following are some social and ethical aspects of academic problem solving that you may want to help students anticipate.

Being open-minded. It helps to have an open mind when collaborating on open-ended problems! Talk with students about what it means to have an open mind and why this might be important when working on a problem that could be solved in various ways or have various solutions. Invite students to tell about a time when they had an unusual and successful solution to a problem or knew someone else who came up with an unusual solution that worked. (Students might enjoy hearing about some real-life solutions that were rejected when people first heard about them—airplanes and telephones, for example; an engaging source for such anecdotes is *Mistakes That Worked: 40 Familiar Inventions and How They Came to Be,* by Charlotte Foltz Jones.)

Giving reasons. Encourage students to explain their thinking when proposing solutions or discussing others' ideas. Ask them why it might be important for other people to hear what they think about an idea— and why it might be important to listen to others' reasoning. Discuss how they can offer their opinions and reasons in respectful ways that help the group arrive at a solution.

Encouraging contributions. Remind students of their responsibility to make sure everybody has a chance to express their ideas. If a group member is quieter or works more slowly, how can the group make sure that person has a chance to contribute ideas? If you are quieter or work more slowly, how can you make sure the group hears and considers your idea?

Making sure everyone understands. Initiate a discussion of how it feels to be in a group when everyone else seems to understand—and you don't! What can make it hard to say so? Why is it important to let group members help you if you don't understand? What can group members do to make sure everyone understands?

WAYS TO USE *Academic Problem Solving*

ACTIVITIES

Below are some ideas for using open-ended problem solving in the curriculum and simply for its own sake, to help students develop their reasoning and collaborative skills. Of course, you'll find many other opportunities that arise throughout the day and throughout children's studies—just be sure to pose problems that have more than one workable solution or that have multiple ways to get to a single solution.

Artifact Guesswork. This activity is a great way to introduce a culture that students will be experiencing in history, social studies, literature, or current events—students of all ages enjoy it and become engaged in the subject to be studied. Introduce the culture or historical period by giving partners objects (real or pictured) from that time or place; if possible, have each partnership study a different artifact. Have partners study the object carefully and discuss what it might be used for, what it might be made of, what it suggests about the environment in which people lived, and what it suggests about the way of life of the people who used it. Remind students to give reasons for their thinking, and have them list their ideas and supporting reasons or "clues." After partners have agreed on the most likely explanation for their artifact, give them a written description of what it really is. Have partners introduce their object to the rest of the class, sharing their original ideas and reasoning about the object and then revealing its actual use, noting the similarities and differences between their ideas and what they learned about the object.

Other Guesswork. You can also use the guesswork strategy with objects such as fossils, rocks, and plant and animal specimens—either to pique students' interest in a new topic or to help them consolidate and apply what they have learned. For example, after a unit on rocks or insects, have partners or small groups use their new knowledge to figure out the identity of a "mystery" specimen; or at the beginning of a unit on dinosaurs, have them study a paleontological discovery and explain what they think it tells them.

Vocabulary Guesswork. In this problem-solving activity, partners or small groups use contextual clues to determine the meaning of an unfamiliar word. First have partners or group members read aloud the passage that contains the vocabulary word (usually this means the paragraph in which it appears, but sometimes students may also have to read the paragraph before or after to get the context). Then have them discuss and list what they think the word means and what clues in the text make them think so (one way to help them think about the word's meaning is to suggest they think of what *other* word, words, or phrases might make sense if substituted for it). After agreeing on the most plausible meaning or comparing ideas with other groups, students look up the word in the dictionary to check its true meaning.

Word Problems. Children enjoy the challenge of tackling word problems that require them to look at language in a new way, such as riddles and puns—some, such as Hangman, are childhood mainstays. An irresistible assortment of other word problems, ranging from easy to nearly impossible, can be found in Herbert Kohl's *A Book of Puzzlements: Play and Invention with Language* (which, appropriately enough, opens with Lewis Carroll's declaration that "a state of puzzlement is good for the young as it leads to a spirit of enquiry").

Here, There, and Everywhere. Have students practice map-reading skills by solving problems about how to get from one place to another. Use different kinds of maps—road maps, street maps, transit maps, aeronautical charts, nautical charts, old maps, contemporary maps, maps with three-dimensional illustrations, topographical maps, and so on, depending upon students' age and experience—and get double mileage from the activity by using maps and destinations that correspond to settings from literature or social studies. For older students, increase the challenge by putting additional constraints on navigation problems—for example, find the shortest route, the quickest route, the least strenuous route, and so on.

Inventions. Have partners or small groups create inventions that solve a problem—something connected to a curriculum area, such as environmental studies, or something that responds to a class or school need. Introduce the activity by inviting an inventor to speak the class about his or her work (a good resource is the Inventor Clubs of America, a national group that has a speaker's bureau and publications for school children; they can be contacted at 800/336–0169).

Math Problems. Many excellent instructional materials, such as the following, use a problem-solving approach to teaching mathematical concepts:

ANNO, MITSUMASA
Anno's Math Games (Volumes I–III)
PHILOMEL BOOKS, 1987, 1989, 1991
These books of math games, which are especially useful with younger children, include many problems that can be used for group problem solving.

BURNS, MARILYN, AND BONNIE TANK
A Collection of Math Lessons: From Grades 1 through 3
A Collection of Math Lessons: From Grades 3 through 6
A Collection of Math Lessons: From Grades 6 through 8
MATH SOLUTIONS PUBLICATIONS, 1988
Problem solving plays a central role in these three volumes of mathematics lessons, which cover a wide range of topics such as number sense; place value; logical reasoning; algebra; patterns and functions; probability; ratio, proportion, and fractions; and geometry. These books are excellent resources, both for their concrete ideas and their insights into teaching and learning.

ROBERTSON, LAUREL, AND SHAILA REGAN, SUSAN STOCKTON ALLDREDGE, JULIE WELLINGTON CONTESTABLE, MARJI FREEMAN, SUSAN URQUHART-BROWN, AND CAROL TENSING WESTRICH
Number Power: A Cooperative Approach to Mathematics and Social Development (Grades K–6)
ADDISON-WESLEY, 1993–96
These books provide opportunities for students to construct and expand their understanding of number as they work with others to solve problems, make mathematical connections, and communicate about their thinking; the lessons are also explicitly designed to help students learn how to work successfully with others.

STENMARK, JEAN KERR, VIRGINIA THOMPSON, AND RUTH COSSEY
Family Math
LAWRENCE HALL OF SCIENCE, UNIVERSITY OF CALIFORNIA, BERKELEY
Family Math was created by the Lawrence Hall of Science EQUALS program, designed to improve math teaching and learning for all students, especially females and students of color. Family Math activities help develop problem-solving skills and build understanding of math with "hands-on" materials. The activities are designed for parents and kids to do together, but many problems can be adapted for small groups or buddies. (You can contact EQUALS at 510/642-1823.)

Science Problems. Science is an obvious gold mine of possible problem-solving activities, and instructional materials full of great ideas are fairly easy to come by. Here are a couple worth looking into:

Great Explorations in Math and Science (GEMS)
LAWRENCE HALL OF SCIENCE
Housed at the University of California at Berkeley, the Lawrence Hall of Science is a public science museum as well as a center for teacher edu-

cation and curriculum research and development. Its *Great Explorations in Math and Science (GEMS)* publications suggest dozens of science investigation activities (some for math, too), including teacher guides that accommodate those who do not have special background in math or science. (You can contact the GEMS project at 510/642-7771.)

Creating Tomorrow's Innovators (Volumes 1–3)
TECH MUSEUM OF INNOVATION
This hands-on museum, located in the heart of California's Silicon Valley, has produced three volumes of open-ended science and technology activities that challenge intermediate students to think like "real" scientists and engineers. (You can contact the Tech Museum at 408/279–7150.)

EXTENSIONS   Follow-up activities to problem-solving activities should emphasize the thinking behind solutions and help students appreciate different approaches and solutions to the same problem.

✱ **What Did We Learn?** Sometimes students' most important learning is demonstrated not by their solution but by the process of getting there—or even the process of *not* arriving at a solution! The trick is to help students make sense of the experience with a follow-up discussion about what they were trying to do, what they did, what was problematic, and what they learned from the process. If a problem has a single "correct" solution, discuss this solution with the class, but also point out examples of groups' sound reasoning—even when their conclusion proved wrong. Also help students reflect on the experience of working together: What were the advantages and disadvantages of working with others on a problem? What went well, and what might they do differently next time? Invite examples of how being open-minded helped groups come up with better solutions or of how groups combined different people's ideas to come up with a solution.

Share and Compare. Have groups describe their solutions to the rest of the class, and encourage students to compare and contrast different groups' solutions: What do the solutions have in common? How are they different? When groups have come up with the same solution, discuss their different approaches.

Put It on Paper. To deepen students' understanding of the problem they tackled—and their ways of tackling it—have them write up a description of their reasoning and results.

Show Off the Solutions. When a problem-solving process results in a tangible "solution," have students contribute these to a classroom exhibit along with brief written descriptions.

Solve It Again. Solving just one problem is rarely enough for students to learn an important concept, achieve sufficient depth of understanding, or develop desired expertise or automaticity. Have students work on a variation of the problem—one of comparable difficulty or one that extends their thinking, depending upon students' results with the first task.

Playing Games

ALL SCHOOL subjects offer constant opportunity to foster children's cooperative skills—yet physical education programs often don't reflect the thoughtful commitment to building a caring community that characterizes the rest of the curriculum. That's no surprise, really, as almost all of our models of physical education and fitness involve competitive and individual sports. Sometimes, the games children play at recess and in their PE classes seriously undermine the values of cooperation we work so hard to promote during the rest of the day.

This needn't be the case, however—games can be structured to focus on fun, good sportsmanship, and playing well, and even encourage children's cooperative, not competitive, play. And because games are intrinsically interesting to children, they are a natural, fun way to build community among students.

WHY TO USE

- to help create a caring community
- to leaven the competitiveness that typically drives physical education programs
- to help students realize that games can be fun and challenging without being competitive
- to give uncompetitive and unassertive children a way to enjoy games

WHEN TO USE

- at the beginning of the year, as part of establishing a cooperative environment
- throughout the year, to sustain a cooperative environment
- throughout the year, as the foundation for a physical education program

HOW TO DO

The Playing Games blueprint asks students to

- put aside competitiveness and any anxieties about winning or losing
- do their best and cooperate with classmates in playing the game
- have fun

Coordinating: Playing Games

Developmental Considerations

Younger Students

Young children love games and will readily adapt to those with a cooperative bent. When teaching young children a game, though, you may sometimes need to break it down into small, clear steps or scale down the challenge. For example, if you're introducing the parachute game described on page 91, don't assume that children know how to grip and manipulate the parachute—show them how and give them a chance to practice moving the parachute together before attempting a game.

Similarly, before games that require large groups of children to coordinate their actions, you might want to have them practice in pairs or small groups at first. For example, a game that asks children to walk about encircled by a hula hoop could be preceded by having students first work in pairs to get the hang of moving in the same direction at the same time.

Older Students

Usually quite accustomed to competitive sports, older students may be suspicious of noncompetitive games—but they may also quickly become converts when they see that cooperative games entail the same physical challenge as do competitive ones. Meanwhile, noncompetitive students will breathe a sigh of relief to be able to participate in games simply for the fun of it, without the stress or peer pressure of having to live up to a "winning" ideal. Nonetheless, even cooperative games might make some students feel vulnerable—competition aside, they may feel they lack the skills to successfully participate in a game or be able to contribute much to it. So, while cooperative games build community, you also want to *have built* community before introducing potentially difficult games, so that students trust each other enough to risk playing them together.

Grouping Considerations

How students are grouped depends largely on the game being played, of course, but you will probably choose to begin the year with many whole-class cooperative games as part of establishing a caring community.

Getting Students Ready

Academic Preparation

Most of these games require little academic preparation, but you may want to introduce or review some pertinent skills or considerations, as suggested below.

Warm up. Begin the game by teaching and practicing any challenging skills as a warm-up. For example, if the game requires doing a locomotive movement in unison, have students practice individually or with a partner before putting it all together. Likewise, if a game entails a sequence of motions, warm up by first practicing each part separately.

See to safety. Warm-ups can also be used to highlight safety issues. For example, if you are doing a parachute game in which some children will run under the parachute while others hold it aloft, have children practice ducking under the parachute in slow motion—and try to make the challenge of moving safely more enticing than having collisions!

Model the process. Because these games are cooperative and accommodate a wide range of physical abilities, the teacher is no longer relegated to an onlooker role but can join in—in other words, there will be no reason for students to cry "No fair if you help them win!" As a player, you can model how to play the game—the "process" as well as the cooperative, noncompetitive objectives.

Social/Ethical Preparation

The following are some social and ethical aspects of playing cooperative games that you may want to help your students anticipate.

Playing with everyone. Remind students that cooperative games are more fun for everybody when all players work together and treat each other well. Ask for students' ideas on handling situations that might arise: How can they make sure everyone is included? What if someone makes a mistake? What can they do if someone isn't participating?

Remembering the cooperative goal. Inadvertently or not, children sometimes introduce a competitive twist into cooperative games—for example, turning Wheelbarrow into a race between partnerships or Centipede into a race between groups. Try to preempt this by highlighting the cooperative aspect of the game; if students want to compete, have them compete against themselves—for example, by reducing their previous time, trying to set a better group record, and so on.

No cooties. For some cooperative games, students will have to hold hands or touch one another—and some children may not want to touch certain classmates. Likewise, they may find themselves partnered with an unpopular classmate or someone they don't want to play with. Talk with the class about the importance of treating everyone with equal kindness and respect. How would they feel if they were shunned during a game? Why might it be important to have many different people as partners?

WAYS TO USE *Playing Games*

ACTIVITIES

Below are just a few suggestions for cooperative games, which fall into three general categories: traditional children's games that are already cooperative, traditionally competitive children's games that have been turned into cooperative efforts, and nontraditional cooperative games. Some suggestions in the last two categories are borrowed from the work of Terry Orlick, who has devoted two decades to collecting, adapting, and creating games that provide challenge without competition. His books *The Cooperative Sports and Games Book* and *The Second Cooperative Sports and Games Book* suggest hundreds of games for different age groups and tailored to a variety of situations (e.g., rainy days) and purposes (e.g., getting to know you, cleaning up); both books are invaluable resources for teachers who would like to bring physical education into the cooperative learning fold.

TRADITIONAL COOPERATIVE GAMES

Jump Rope. Jump rope is inherently cooperative—its success depends upon both the turners and the skippers doing their part. It also can be modified to challenge students with different abilities, for example, by swaying the rope back and forth instead of around, swinging it lower to the ground or higher, using two ropes, and so on. Some jump rope chants, such as counting rhymes or geography chants, even have an academic bent! (A good source for examples of such chants is Carl Withers's *A Rocket in My Pocket: The Rhymes and Chants of Young Americans*.)

Locomotion Games. A number of traditional games have children pool their efforts (or body parts) to get from one place to another in some novel fashion—such as Leap Frog, for example, or the ideas below:

- *Wheelbarrow.* The "wheelbarrow" students walk on their hands, their partners holding up their legs and "steering" them. Although some might associate this only with wheelbarrow races, playing wheelbarrow doesn't necessarily have a competitive aspect—wheeling about is fun in itself, and you could make things even more entertaining and challenging by constructing an obstacle course for students to wheel through.

- *Partner Hop.* Partners stand facing each other or side by side, extend their left legs toward each other, grasp each other's left ankles, and then hop together from place to place on their free right legs. An even more challenging variation is to have partners stand back to back, bend their left legs behind them from the knee, grasp each other's left ankle, and hop about together.

- *Centipede.* Students walk on their hands, resting their feet on the shoulders of the person behind them; the last student walks on all fours.

TRADITIONAL GAMES WITH A COOPERATIVE TWIST

Long, Long, Long Jump. Instead of having children compete against one another to see who can jump the farthest, this variation has children set a collective long-jump distance and then try to better their group effort—the first player begins at the starting line and makes one jump, the second player starts his or her jump from where the previous person landed, and so on. This game is particularly well suited for younger and older buddies to play together.

Volleyball/oon. In this cooperative variation of volleyball, four or five players start out on one side of the net, with no team on the other side. Using a balloon or a volleyball, each player volleys the ball/oon to another player on the same side of the net, then quickly scoots under the net to the other side. The last player to touch the ball/oon taps it *over* the net and scoots under, and the process is repeated.

Crossover Dodgeball. This is a no-loser version of the old favorite, dodgeball: Players start half and half on two sides of the line, but those that get hit by the ball immediately run over to the other side and continue to play, the goal being to end up with all players on the same side. Moreover, multiple balls are in play at once (i.e., beach balls, soft rubber balls, or pillows), so that players are continually throwing, hitting, being hit, and changing sides all at the same time. The game seems to work better with small teams and with about half as many balls as players—for example, use four balls if you have eight players.

NONTRADITIONAL COOPERATIVE GAMES

Planetpass. Group members lie head to head in a double line and use their hands and feet to pass an earthball or other large rubber ball down the line. As players take their turn passing the ball, they get up and run to the end of the line, and so the game continues indefinitely.

Parachute. Parachute games can take many forms, most of which begin with children standing around the periphery of a parachute spread out on the ground, grasping its edge, and lifting the parachute in unison to inflate it. In one variation a subgroup of students then duck under the chute and allow it to gently fall on them, in another they crawl on top of the parachute while students around the edge shake it vigorously to make waves, and in another they try to keep a ball from falling off the parachute as they shake it up and down.

Guide-a-Partner. Without touching, have students guide a blindfolded partner through an obstacle course, experimenting with communication strategies—clapping, stamping, singing, or talking the partner through, and so on.

≈HINT≈

Many cooperative games are ideal buddy activities, since they can often accommodate different levels of physical skill. They are also fun opportunities for buddies to "teach" each other, when one group has mastered a game and wants to introduce it to their older or younger buddies.

EXTENSIONS

While cooperative games may not lead into structured follow-up activities, they do offer good opportunities for students to reflect on their developing cooperative skills.

✳ **What Did We Learn?** Spend some time talking with students about how things went during their cooperative games. What went well? What didn't? How did they make sure everybody was included? What did they do to try to help everyone have a good time? How did they solve any problems in their group? Also ask students about the game itself—what they liked about it, or didn't, and how they think the game might be improved. (For further ideas on helping students think about their cooperative games, consult the Evaluation Methods section of *The Cooperative Sports and Games Book.*)

Our Cooperative Games. After students have had some experience playing many cooperative games (or games of a certain type, such as locomotion games), invite groups to make up their own games to teach the rest of the class.

Singing

SINGING yields a huge return in community with very little investment of time or effort: Singing together creates a special connection between people, it's intrinsically cooperative, and it uses the instruments that all children can play—their voices, hands, and feet. You don't even have to carve out formal music time for singing, either—you can sing songs between other activities, and you can use all sorts of familiar songs throughout the curriculum to build community, to help students learn how to count and read, and to deepen their appreciation of music for its own sake.

WHY TO USE

- to give students a way to express thoughts and feelings
- to create and maintain esprit de corps
- to foster students' aesthetic development
- to help students learn through music
- to make text accessible to beginning readers

WHEN TO USE

- when a song can help students learn
- as part of daily "hello" and "good-bye" routines
- during spare minutes between other activities
- to celebrate a beginning, an ending, or an event
- after a vacation, to help reestablish a sense of community
- every day

HOW TO DO

The Singing blueprint asks students to

- listen to the music
- join in whenever they're ready (or it's their turn)

Developmental Considerations

Younger Students

Songs with repeated lines and predictable patterns (for example, "The Wheels on the Bus" and "Old MacDonald") are the foundation for singing with young children—they are easy to learn, are easy to remember, and present an irresistible invitation to children to improvise their own material. In fact, you don't actually have to "teach" young children songs; they learn them by hearing them over and over, and all you need do is sing the song to them (or play a recording) a few times and let them join in when they are ready. Songs that combine singing and action (for example, fingerplays, clapping songs, and motion songs) are especially appealing to young children because they can join in right away, doing the motions even before they learn the words.

In addition to all the social benefits of singing, songs are a great way to teach reading, as many favorite songs have characteristics that make them ideal texts for beginning readers—familiarity, repetition, rhyme, match to spoken language, and so on. After students have learned a song, write the lyrics on a chart for shared reading and if possible leave the lyrics posted for a while.

Older Students

Like good literature, good songs speak to young people, and they enjoy songs that cover the whole range of human experience—love, hate, war, peace, injustice, justice, despair, and hope. (Good music needn't be somber, though—older students also enjoy humorous songs!) Because older children will have more firmly formed opinions about the kinds of music they enjoy, you can engage their interest in singing activities by tapping into their preferences about both what to sing and how to go about it—for example, mounting variety shows, writing songs together, putting their poetry to music, and so on. Invite their suggestions and also encourage them to share their favorite songs—those that touch their hearts or funny bones.

Grouping Considerations

For the most part you'll probably sing as a whole class, but even whole-class singing has a cooperative twist when students take turns leading and improvising on songs. In the introduction to *Rise Up Singing* (listed below in Resources), Pete Seeger points out that taking turns leading and improvising promotes not only creativity and self-expression, but also social and ethical values: "Musicians can teach the politicians: it's fun to swap the lead. Musicians can teach the planners—economists, engineers, lawyers: plan for *improvisation.*"

Students can also make music with partners and small groups. Songs, like poetry, can be adapted for Readers Theater, with subgroups singing different parts; some action and clapping songs ask students to divide into small groups or partnerships within the whole group; and many rhythm games work best in small groups or with partners.

Getting Students Ready

Academic Preparation

Singing together requires no academic preparation—in fact, turning it into a formal "music lesson" can take a lot of the fun out the activity and actually detract from the benefits of singing together. Still, depending upon the kinds of songs you'll be singing and the context in which you'll be using them, you might use one of the following suggestions to draw students' attention to (and deepen their appreciation of) interesting characteristics of music.

Stop and listen. When it comes right down to it, music is noise—and all noise has musical elements. Ask students to listen to the sounds around them in this light and to categorize the sounds according to pitch (high or low), duration (long or short), and dynamics (loud or soft). You could do this activity in the classroom, listening to everyday noises (such as the sound of traffic, nearby construction, wind in the trees, and so on) or playing recordings of common sounds; you could also ask students to spend ten minutes listening to noise at home or in their neighborhood—have them jot down their observations and then compare notes in class afterward.

Vocalize music. People make many kinds of music by using the instrument that is always available to them: their voice. Help students appreciate this amazing instrument by playing recordings of different kinds of vocal music: chants, madrigals, gospel, opera, oratorios, barbershop quartets, folk music, or any a cappella arrangements. If possible, attend a performance or invite a guest choir to perform for the class.

Sing with feeling. This improvisation exercise will give students some interesting insights into how much a song's meaning and impact can depend upon its "delivery" (it can also produce some very entertaining song renditions). Write the names of different emotions on separate strips of paper and put them in a hat; then write the names of familiar songs on separate strips of paper and put those in another hat. Have students choose a strip of paper from each hat and then sing the chosen song with the chosen emotion (for example, they might end up singing "Old MacDonald" in a sad way, or "B-I-N-G-O" in an angry way, and so on). Have students work in groups, either with each group member taking a turn singing and the other group members guessing the emotion being conveyed, or with each group singing and the rest of the class guessing the emotion. (This is one of many ideas to be found in the book *Kids Make Music!* listed below in Resources.)

Model the process. As mentioned above, the best way to teach songs and any accompanying motions is through demonstration. Let children listen and watch for a while, and they'll soon be ready to join in.

Social/Ethical Preparation

Singing together in the ways described here is intrinsically cooperative and should require little social and ethical preparation, but the following are some considerations that you may want to help your students anticipate. Most importantly, though, as Bessie Jones and Bess Lomax Hawes encourage teachers, "Enjoy yourself. This is a beautiful and democratic tradition, full of joy and the juices of life. Don't be too solemn, or too organized; these are for *play*" (from their book *Step It Down,* listed below in Resources).

Participating comfortably. Some students may be shy about singing, while others may make up in enthusiasm what they lack in tunefulness. In either case, you'll want to encourage participation and discourage students from making fun of each other. Ask students to think about what kinds of behaviors will invite everyone's participation and what might make people reluctant to join in. Why might it be important to encourage participation? What might people miss out on if they didn't feel comfortable enough to participate? What might everyone else miss out on?

Sharing the "work." Discuss strategies for sharing ideas and sharing the lead—choosing songs, leading songs, improvising new words, adding a rhythm section, and so on.

WAYS TO USE *Singing*

ACTIVITIES

Singing is great for any occasion, but there are situations and circumstances for which singing can be especially valuable. The ideas below include specific song suggestions that fit the activity; in many cases, these are followed by parenthetical references to the books and recordings listed in Resources, below, that include the song (books are cited by the author's last name, and recordings are cited by title). Most of these are familiar songs, though—if you don't know them, you may be able to find someone who can teach them to you.

Getting to Know You. Use the following songs to build a sense of inclusion and community—at the beginning of the year, at the beginning of the day, and to welcome buddies and other guests into the classroom community.

"Come on and Join into the Game" (Glazer, 1973)

"Buddies and Pals," for partners (Glazer, 1980)

"The More We Are (Get) Together" (Glazer, 1973; Larrick)

"Zum Gali Gali," for partners (Glazer, 1980)

Names. Songs such as the following can be used to help children learn others' names, simply by inserting a different name into the verse each time it is sung. Use these at the beginning of the year to introduce classmates to each other and any time you want to introduce the class and newcomers (new students, buddies, or visitors) to each other.

"Bow Belinda" (Glazer, 1980)

"Charlie Over the Water" (Glazer, 1973)

"Jump Shamador" (Mattox)

"Mary Wore Her Red Dress" (Seeger)

"Where Oh Where Is Pretty Little Susie?"; also called "The PawPaw Patch" (Seeger; *American Folk Songs for Children; American Play Parties*)

"Peter Hammers" (Glazer, 1973)

"Who's That Tapping at the Window?" (Seeger)

Counting. Songs are an effective and fun way for students to learn and practice counting—both forward and backward. Once students have learned the pattern of such songs, have them improvise their own verses.

"The Ants Go Marching" (Glazer, 1980)

"Five Little Ducks" (Glazer, 1973)

"Five Little Speckled Frogs" (Corbett)

"Peter Hammers" (Glazer, 1973)

"Ten in a Bed" (Glazer, 1980)

"This Old Man" (Glazer, 1973; Seeger)

Anatomy. Many fingerplays and action songs help children learn the names and locations of different parts of the body.

"Head, Shoulders, Knees, and Toes" (Glazer, 1980)

"Here We Go Looby Loo"; also called "Loop de Loo (Glazer, 1980; Mattox)

"I Point to Myself" (Glazer, 1980)

"One Finger, One Thumb" (Glazer, 1980)

"Put Your Finger in the Air" (Glazer, 1973)

"Where Is Thumbkin?" (Glazer, 1973)

Directionality. Songs can help children learn and practice directional concepts such as left and right, in and out, front and back, and under and over.

"Bow Belinda" (Glazer, 1980)

"Go in and out the Window" (Mattox; Metropolitan Museum of Art Staff)

"Here Comes Sally" (Mattox)

"Here We Go Looby Loo"; also called "Loop de Loo (Glazer, 1980; Mattox)

"The Hokey Pokey" (Glazer, 1980)

Cleaning Up. Adapt songs such as "The Mulberry Bush" for cleanup time by improvising verses—for example, "This is the way we clean up the blocks (or books or paints)," and so on.

PARTICULARLY COOPERATIVE SINGING

While it's been noted that all group singing is inherently a cooperative activity, it's also true that some kinds of songs entail more sophisticated levels of cooperation than others. The suggestions below explicitly require and foster cooperation: Call-and-response songs involve an exchange between a leader and the group; in repetitive songs the group sings lyrics improvised by a group member, rounds require cooperation among and between small groups, and many action songs ask students to coordinate their movements with a partner or group.

Call-and-Response Songs. In call-and-response songs, which are especially prominent in the African American tradition, a leader sings a line or verse that the rest of the singers then answer or repeat. Take the lead while the students are learning the song and then let them take over the leader role. This, of course, is when the singing becomes especially cooperative, so encourage students to pay attention to letting everyone take a turn who wants to.

≈ HINT ≈

Can't carry a tune? If you are shy about singing to your class, introduce songs with recordings. It shouldn't take long for the pleasures of singing with the class to help you overcome your anxiety.

"Did You Feed My Cow?" (Larrick; *You'll Sing a Song and I'll Sing a Song*)

"East Coast Line" (Jones and Hawes)

"Hambone" (Mattox; *Step It Down*)

"I'm Going Away to See Aunt Dinah" (Jones and Hawes)

"Little Johnny Brown" (Jones and Hawes; *Step It Down*)

"Miss Mary Mack" (Larrick; Mattox; *You'll Sing a Song and I'll Sing a Song*)

"My Mama's Calling Me" (Mattox)

"Oh, You Can't Get to Heaven" (Larrick)

"Punchinello" (Jones and Hawes)

"Sippin' Cider Through a Straw" (Larrick)

"Sir Mister Brown" (Jones and Hawes)

"Soup, Soup" (Jones and Hawes; *Step It Down*)

"Way Down Yonder, Sometimes" (Jones and Hawes)

Repetitive Songs. Songs with repetitive and predictable patterns are easily improvised on, and students can have fun substituting their own lyrics in the song's pattern. Some songs, such as "The Wheels on the Bus," are designed for improvisation: "The wheels on the bus go 'round and 'round. . . . The people on the bus go up and down. . . . The wipers on the bus go swish, swish, swish," and so on. Be on the lookout for other songs, too (for example, "He's Got the Whole World in His Hands"), which may not have been designed for improvisation but certainly lend themselves to it. Again, encourage students to pay attention to letting everyone interested take a turn improvising.

"Aiken Drum (There Was a Man Lived in the Moon)" (Larrick)

"The Barnyard Song" (Glazer, 1973)

"Bought Me a Cat" (Larrick; Seeger; *American Folk Songs for Children*)

"Come on and Join into the Game" (Glazer, 1973)

"Down by the Bay"

"Kum ba Ya" (Larrick)

"The Mulberry Bush" (Glazer, 1973)

"Old MacDonald" (Glazer, 1973)

"The Wheels on the Bus" (Larrick)

Rounds. "A round is a song that harmonizes with itself," say Avery Hart and Paul Mantell in *Kids Make Music!* (listed in Resources below), and children love achieving this effect in such familiar rounds as the following. The challenge, of course, is for students to stay on track singing their own part of the round as others join in, so give them a chance to learn and practice the song as a class before adding the challenge of singing it as a round.

"Dona Nobis Pacem"

"Down by the Station"

"Frère Jacques (Are You Sleeping?)"

"Hey, Ho, Nobody Home"

"Kookaburra"

"Make New Friends (but Keep the Old)"

≈ HINT ≈

When you invite young children to improvise, don't have too many expectations about their songs' rhyme or content—it's enough just to let them experience the joy of making music and the pleasure of hearing others sing their lyrics.

"Oh, How Lovely Is the Evening"

"Row, Row, Row Your Boat"

"Three Blind Mice"

"Stop the Train" (Hunter; *Windows*)

"White Coral Bells"

Games, Plays, and Play-Party Songs. These three terms, from different historical and cultural traditions, all refer to songs that have corollary motions. The song lyrics provide the rhythm and, often, directions for the accompanying movements. In the liner notes to his recording *American Play Parties* (listed in Resources below), Pete Seeger describes the appeal of this genre: The songs are easy to learn, "with a minimum of belabored instruction"; any number can participate; no musical accompaniment is needed—all you need is a flat surface and "feet that want to dance"; and the songs are fun to sing, "full of fine folk poetry, delightful imagery, and symbolism which stimulates the imagination."

The African American tradition is rich in songs of this type; besides the familiar songs listed below, many can be found in two books listed in Resources: *Step It Down* by Bessie Jones and Bess Lomax Hawes (as well as the recording of the same name), and *Shake It to the One That You Love the Best* by Cheryl Warren Mattox. Students may also know other such songs they would like to teach the class.

"Little Bird, Little Bird" (Seeger)

"The Farmer in the Dell" (Metropolitan Museum of Art Staff)

"Go in and out the Window" (Mattox; Metropolitan Museum of Art Staff)

"The Hokey Pokey" (Glazer, 1980)

"Jim Along Josie" (Seeger)

"Ring around the Rosie"

"Sally Down the Alley" (*American Play Parties*)

"Skip to My Lou" (Seeger; *American Play Parties*)

EXTENSIONS

Singing activities can be extended in any of the following ways.

✳ **What Did We Learn?** Spend some time talking about how the singing went—what students liked, what might be done differently, what encouraged participation or didn't, how they shared the lead, and so on.

Class Recording. Make a tape recording of the class singing their favorite songs and make a copy for each child to bring home. (For a more professional job, ask your local radio station for assistance.)

Hootenanny. A hootenanny is a gathering at which folksingers entertain, usually with audience participation. Once the class has developed a repertoire of songs, host a hootenanny for buddies, parents, senior citizens, or other guests. Have students make a class songbook with words and illustrations to their favorite songs, so that guests can sing along; working in pairs or groups, students might also research cultural or historical annotations for the book. Ask students to write a class song they can include in the book and debut at the hootenanny.

Class Song. Use the Poetry blueprint (see page 135) to have students write a class song, first writing the refrain as a whole class and then having students work in small groups to contribute the verses. It is usually easiest to choose a tune before writing the words, and melodies to familiar upbeat songs work well, such as "This Land Is Your Land," "Row, Row, Row Your Boat," "Take Me Out to the Ball Game," or the like. Writing the refrain as a whole class will help students understand the concept of matching the number of syllables to the number of notes, but don't worry too much about their doing so in their small-group work. Ruth Seeger (see Resources below) notes that children sometimes create verses that do not fit the rhythm of the song and that "traditional singers often insert extra counts to care for such syllables. Children laugh with the pleasure of hearing so many words elbow their way into the middle of a song pattern they know."

Home Songs. Ask each student to collect one or two favorite songs from parents, grandparents, aunts, uncles, or adult friends. Have them compile the songs in a songbook, including illustrations and text that tells about each song and its meaning to the adult who contributed it. Invite students (or the contributing adults!) to teach their songs to the class, and then host a hootenanny and give each family a copy of the songbook.

Lip Synching. Have students experience the glamour of musical stardom by lip synching to a favorite recording for the class! Students can do this individually or in pairs or small groups, depending on who students are mimicking. (In conjunction with this activity, older students might also enjoy hearing you read aloud Gary Soto's story "La Bamba," in *Baseball in April*.)

Readers Theater. Songs make great material for Readers Theater: Have partners, small groups, or the whole class arrange and perform a song using Readers Theater techniques (see blueprint on page 167), but be sure students are comfortable both with Readers Theater and singing together before they tackle this project.

Vaudeville. Vaudeville shows featured a wide variety of entertainment, including singing, skits, magic, card tricks, juggling, and especially comedy. Have students work individually, in pairs, or in small groups to put together a class vaudeville show that gives each student a chance to showcase a special talent or interest. This activity is particularly suited to older students, who will enjoy the humor and pace of a vaudeville show.

Resources

This is far from a comprehensive list of songbooks and recordings, but it does reflect some of our favorites and perhaps some which are new to you.

Songbooks

BLOOD, PETER, AND ANNIE PATTERSON
Rise Up Singing: The Group Singing Songbook
SING OUT CORPORATION
If you can afford only one songbook, this is the one to get—it contains lyrics, chords for guitar or autoharp, and sources to 1,200 songs. Its range— from folk to "oldies"—also makes it especially appealing to older students. An accompanying set of cassettes to help teach the songs is also available from Sing Out (see Recordings, below).

CORBETT, PIE
The Playtime Treasury: A Collection of Playground Rhymes, Games, and Action Songs
DOUBLEDAY, 1989
A book of rhymes, games, and songs that are the bedrock of children's playground culture.

DELACRE, LULU
Arroz con Leche: Popular Songs and Games from Latin America
SCHOLASTIC, 1989
English and Spanish lyrics to popular songs and games from Mexico, Puerto Rico, and Argentina.

GLAZER, TOM
Eye Winker, Tom Tinker, Chin Chopper: Fifty Musical Fingerplays
DOUBLEDAY, 1973
Do Your Ears Hang Low? Fifty More Musical Fingerplays
DOUBLEDAY, 1980
Two collections of fingerplays and action songs that include words, music, and directions for performing the actions.

HART, AVERY, AND PAUL MANTELL
Kids Make Music! Clapping and Tapping from Bach to Rock
WILLIAMSON PUBLISHING, 1993
This is another invaluable book, suitable for three- to nine-year-olds and chock-full of do-it-yourself musical

activities that can be adapted for partner, small-group, and whole-class use.

HUNTER, TOM
Come into My House: A Collection of Songs by Tom Hunter
WEDNESDAY HILL, 1988
Singer/songwriter Tom Hunter says that most of his song ideas "have come from children themselves, and the songs have been written to reflect the realities of children's lives. Each song started somewhere and grew as someone used it and had another idea. . . . The songs won't just sit quietly on the page. They'll keep growing." Hunter's recordings listed below include all the songs in this book.

JONES, BESSIE, AND BESS LOMAX HAWES
Step It Down: Games, Plays, Songs, and Stories from the Afro-American Heritage
UNIVERSITY OF GEORGIA PRESS, 1987
This wonderful collection is based on interviews with Bessie Jones, a member of the Georgia Sea Islanders, a choral group dedicated to preserving their African and African American heritage. (See below for recording of the same name.)

KRULL, KATHLEEN
Gonna Sing My Head Off! American Folk Songs for Children
ALFRED A. KNOPF, 1992
A collection of "good songs that have stayed good songs" for children seven and up.

LARRICK, NANCY
Let's Do a Poem: Introducing Poetry to Children
DELACORTE, 1991
The author believes that songs are a natural way to introduce poetry to children and has included in this book a chapter of music activities, "Music Has Winning Ways," that engage children in music and poetry alike. She also offers a useful resource list of suggested songbooks for children.

MATTOX, CHERYL WARREN
Shake It to the One That You Love the Best: Play Songs and Lullabies from Black Musical Traditions
WARREN-MATTOX PRODUCTIONS, 1989
The music in this beautifully illustrated collection is accompanied by brief historical notations, commentaries, and directions for performing motions.

METROPOLITAN MUSEUM OF ART STAFF
Go in and out the Window: An Illustrated Songbook for Young People
HENRY HOLT & CO., 1987
A feast for the eye and the ear, this book includes lyrics and music for sixty-one traditional children's songs, each illustrated with art from New York's Metropolitan Museum of Art.

NATIONAL GALLERY OF ART
An Illustrated Treasury of Songs
RIZZOLI INTERNATIONAL PUBLICATIONS, INC., 1991
A collection of traditional American songs, ballads, and nursery rhymes illustrated with art from the National Gallery of Art in Washington, D.C.

OROZCO, JOSÉ LUIS
De Colores and Other Latin-American Folk Songs for Children
DUTTON, 1994
Appealing songs and whimsical illustrations make this a popular collection of Latin American children's songs, which includes English translations printed side by side with original Spanish lyrics.

SCHOENBACH, RUTH (EDITOR)
Canciones de Compañeros: A Book of Spanish Songs for Children
SHUMBA PUBLICATIONS, 1985
This wonderful collection of children's songs from all over Latin America is presented in the original Spanish with English translations and includes an inviting audiocassette. (Note: The book is available in the United States through Iaconi Book Imports, San Francisco.)

SEEGER, RUTH CRAWFORD
American Folk Songs for Children
DOUBLEDAY, 1948, 1980
This is the single most important song-book resource for teachers of young children—in addition to music and lyrics, Seeger provides practical and reassuring tips for teachers. The companion recording (see listing below) points out that "these songs are like the language from which they spring: rich and full of variety. There is something for everyone. Not only are these songs part of history, but they are part of our present—they express things that will always be part of life, American life."

Recordings

FROM THE AFRICAN AMERICAN TRADITION

JONES, BESSIE
Step It Down: Games for Children by Bessie Jones
ROUNDER RECORDS
Bessie Jones and her children's chorus sing and clap their way through eighteen African American games for children; their enthusiasm is infectious, and listeners will not be able to resist joining in.

FROM LATIN AMERICAN CULTURE

Latin American Children's Game Songs
FOLKWAYS RECORDS
Recorded in Puerto Rico and Mexico, this collection is especially appealing because the songs are sung by children; the recording also includes printed lyrics in both English and Spanish.

OROZCO, JOSÉ LUIS
De Colores and Other Latin-American Folk Songs for Children
José Luis Orozco sings the songs featured in his book of the same name.

AMERICAN PLAY-PARTY SONGS

SEEGER, PETE, MIKA SEEGER, AND REV. LARRY EISENBERG
American Play Parties
FOLKWAY RECORDS
A recording of traditional play-party songs, including liner notes that describe the origin of American play parties, lyrics to the songs on the recording, and the movements that accompany each song.

FOLK SONGS

VARIOUS ARTISTS
Rise Up Singing: The Teaching Tapes
SING OUT CORPORATION
These cassettes present simple vocal and guitar renditions of all the songs in *Rise Up Singing* (see Songbook listing, above), grouped according to the book's six chapters: 231 Songs for Children, 164 Songs about Community and Change, Songs of Faith, 216 (Mostly) Traditional Folksongs, 182 Songs about Living and Struggle, and 204 Songs of Love and Imagination.

SEEGER, MIKE, AND PEGGY SEEGER
American Folk Songs for Children
ROUNDER RECORDS
Containing all ninety-four songs in the book *American Folk Songs for Children* by Ruth Crawford Seeger (see Song-books listings, above), these recordings were made by two of Seeger's children, "partly as a tribute to her and partly as a tribute to her love of music and children."

OTHER TRADITIONAL AND CONTEMPORARY RECORDINGS IN THE SING-ALONG TRADITION

GRAMMER, RED
Can You Sound Just Like Me?
BMG MUSIC
A collection of sing-alongs, fingerplays, and imagination games for preschool and primary-age children.

GRAMMER, RED
Red Grammer's Favorite Sing-Along Songs
RED NOTE RECORDS
A collection of old favorites, both humorous and serious, with special appeal to intermediate-grade students.

GRAMMER, RED
Teaching Peace
BMG MUSIC
Red Grammer describes this recording as "a collection of songs created to help children and their parents break down the 'big idea' of World Peace into the individual daily actions that will make it a reality."

HUNTER, TOM (AND FRIENDS)
Comin' Home
Our Record
Windows
You Gave Me This Song
LONG SLEEVE RECORDS
The songs on these four recordings deal with topics that are important to children—everyday matters (for example, "Pockets," "A Song about Feet") as well as the bigger themes ("I Wonder," "Questions"). All the songs in the first three albums are included in *Come into My House,* listed above in Songbooks.

JENKINS, ELLA
And One and Two: And Other Songs for Pre-School and Primary Children
Looking Forward—Looking Back
My Street Begins at My House
You'll Sing a Song and I'll Sing a Song
FOLKWAY RECORDS
These four recordings present call-and-response and other traditional participatory children's songs.

Dance and Movement

FOR PEOPLE all over the world, dancing is a natural form of communication about life's joys and sorrows, ideas and events. Dance and movement activities capitalize on this natural inclination to express ourselves through motion, be it the simplest unconscious gesture or the most structured choreography, and they can be used throughout the curriculum—to build community, develop physical coordination, augment counting and language arts activities, and to give students a creative venue for responding to the ideas they encounter in their learning. And when children do these activities together, they exercise another whole way of communicating and cooperating with each other.

WHY TO USE

- to foster balance and coordination, both physical and social

- to give students a way to express thoughts and feelings

- to encourage students' improvisation and creativity

- to broaden students' opportunities as learners and contributors in classroom life

WHEN TO USE

- as an opening or closing activity for the day

- with younger and older buddies

- as part of a physical education program

- whenever students can use movement to respond to language, music, and ideas

HOW TO DO

The Dance and Movement blueprint asks students to

- use their bodies to explore whatever movement they're asked to try, or to explore *with* movement the ideas or emotions before them

- work with their partner or group to coordinate this exploration—depending upon the activity, this could mean conversations about how they will use movement to address a topic, or paying attention to each other as they move and adapting their movements accordingly

Developmental Considerations

Younger Students

Young children are apt to respond to dance and movement activities quite enthusiastically, but they may need some practice to work up to doing cooperative or complicated activities. Begin by leading them in simple, specific movements: clapping their hands, stomping their feet, wiggling their fingers, swinging their right arm, shaking their head, shaking their tail feathers, and so on. You can segue into cooperative movement activities by having children do these with partners, too: clap their partner's hand, skip with their partner, hop with their partner, jump with their partner, and so on. After leading a few of these movements, let students take turns calling out instructions.

You can also build confidence (and community) with a variety of simple whole-class movement activities—for example, such familiar movement games as Ring around the Rosie or The Itsy Bitsy Spider. After children have had some fun with these simpler activities, introduce easy cooperative movement activities, such as Part-to-Part (see Ways to Use Dance and Movement, below).

Older Students

Some older students may be self-conscious and uncomfortable about dancing in class. (Sometimes the problem is simply the word *dance*, which can bear some daunting expectations—but even those who do not view themselves as dancers may participate willingly in *movement* activities.) As ever, modeling the process can work wonders, so be prepared to shed your own preconceived notions about what's expected of a dancer and show your willingness to play with movement.

Grouping Considerations

Dance and movement activities occur in partner, group, and whole-class configurations and are sometimes adaptable to all three. It is often useful to start out with whole-class activities that use prescribed movements (for example, the Hokey Pokey), both because they are great community builders and so that students who do not see themselves as dancers can participate relatively comfortably. Likewise, it can be helpful to have students do some individual movement activities at first and let them experiment with different ways of moving before introducing partner activities; then introduce small-group activities when students are ready for more challenge.

Getting Students Ready

Academic Preparation

Preview the possibilities. Help students develop a vocabulary of dance movements by having them spend a few minutes experimenting on their own with the different kinds of movements their bodies can make—smooth and jerky movements, pushing and pulling movements, light and heavy movements, and so on. Likewise, if the activity involves a particular kind of movement (or series of movements), have students practice individually before trying it out with their partner or group.

Preview the music. Before students start their dance or movement activity, give them a taste of the music to which they will be dancing. Have them close their eyes and listen, and ask them to describe or demonstrate the kind of movements the music suggests to them.

Take in a show. Invite a local high school dance class or community dance company to visit your class and engage students in dance and conversation.

Know when to stop. If the activity will be interspersed with directions, have the class agree on the signal you will use to get their attention—for example, a whistle, bell, flick of the lights, hand signal, or the like.

Model the process. For many of these activities, you may need to demonstrate the movements or steps involved. More importantly, you will want to "model the process" by participating in the dance or movement activity with your students as much as possible. If you are a devotee of dance yourself, share this with your students—what you enjoy, why, how it makes you feel, how you became interested in dance, and so on.

Social/Ethical Preparation

For some people, children and adults alike, dancing is a risk-taking activity—they feel shy or awkward and are afraid of being laughed at. To get students thinking about the benefits of encouraging everyone to participate freely, the following are some social and ethical aspects of dance and movement activites you may want to help students anticipate.

Learning to join in. Read aloud Petra Mathers's picture book *Sophie and Lou,* the story of how the terribly shy Sophie finds confidence through her passion for ballroom dancing. Talk with students about Sophie's transformation: Why might it take some time for some people to feel comfortable participating? Why might it be important for people to take their time and do something in their own way? Why might it be more fun to dance with another person than alone? How can something like dancing "liberate" someone?

Encouraging participation. The first few times students do partner or group dance and movement activities, you might need to acknowledge that some students may feel awkward or uncomfortable doing these activities. Ask students for their ideas about why this might be so, and invite their suggestions for how they can encourage everyone's participation—and what kinds of behaviors might discourage participation.

No cooties. For some dance and movement activities, students will have to hold hands or touch one another—and some children may not want to touch certain classmates. Likewise, they may find themselves partnered or grouped with an unpopular classmate or someone with whom they don't want to dance. Talk with the class about the importance of treating everyone with equal kindness and respect. How would they feel if they were shunned during these activities? Why might it be important to have many different people as partners or groupmates?

Accommodating a partner. Remind students that dance and movement activities are more fun (and more challenging) if students really try to work and coordinate with their partner or groupmates. Depending upon the activity they'll be doing, have students role-play how they might need to accommodate a partner—for example, helping the partner learn a step, moving safely with a partner, changing their movements to a change in the music tempo, and so on. Point out that they are learning a different way to communicate with each other, and it might take some practice to do so smoothly—encourage them to be entertained by their efforts, rather than frustrated.

Sharing the "work." For some of these activites, students take turns being leader or calling out instructions, in which case you might want to discuss fair ways to give everyone interested a turn.

WAYS TO USE *Dance and Movement*

ACTIVITIES
The suggested activities below are divided into three categories: movement activities, which generally require an improvised coordination of motions; dancing to imagery, in which children use dance and movement to respond to language or music; and play-party songs, whose lyrics and rhythms prescribe corollary movements.

MOVEMENT ACTIVITIES

These activities are especially cooperative because they ask partners or group members either to coordinate their movements for a particular purpose or to follow each other's lead in performing improvised movements. Many of these activities are performed to the simple rhythm of a drum or metronome; for others, use your judgment as to whether you want to use music, which can add both inspiration and challenge.

Part-to-Part. This is a simple, fun game for young children and a good way to introduce them to partner "dancing." Have students face each other and follow the caller's instructions to connect heel to heel, elbow to elbow, and so on. Take the caller role yourself at first, to give students the flavor of the activity, and then have students take turns being the caller.

Metronome. This partner activity introduces students to the concepts of tempo and beat in dance: Partners take turns improvising a specific movement to the beat of a metronome (or rhythm sticks), which the other partner imitates—for example, a nod of the head, roll of a shoulder, blink of the eyes, and so on. This activity can be done standing, sitting on the ground, even at their desks, and changing the speed of the metronome can add variety and challenge. Begin this as a whole-class activity and then turn it over to the partners.

Follow the Leader. Students line up behind a leader, who performs a locomotor movement to a rhythm—slow walk, fast walk, skip, trot, step-together-step, step-kick, and so on—which the rest of the group imitates. Ideally, the leader also taps out the rhythm, using rhythm sticks or the like, but lacking that you could set the rhythm with a metronome. Begin by taking the role of leader yourself and lead students around the room or dance area a couple of times; once students have practiced the game a bit, have them play in small groups and take turns being the leader.

Body Shapes. Have partners make different shapes with their two bodies—upright, on the ground, or both. Call out any variety of configurations for them to create—a box, a circle, the smallest shape they can make, the largest, a smooth shape, a jagged shape, a high shape, a low shape, and so on. Once they've tried one way to make the shape, have them find another way to do it! Ask students to come up with other kinds of shapes, too (an oblong, a crescent, a steep triangle, a wavy circle, a concave box, etc.), and have them write these on strips of paper; put the strips in a hat and draw and call them at random. Give students plenty of room for this activity.

Body ABCs. In this variation of Body Shapes, have partners use their bodies to create letters of the alphabet (or numbers) with their bodies.

Taking Up Space. We usually occupy space in several standard ways: standing, sitting, and lying down. This small-group exercise helps students expand their definition of the space their bodies can occupy, with a particular focus on level. Ask students to think of themselves as elevators, going up and down the floors of a building. How could they show they are on the top floor, or middle floors, or the ground floor—or even on the roof or in the basement? Have students experiment with this notion individually at first and then in groups. Beat a drum slowly and have students pick up the beat, moving to a different level with each beat, and then freezing every time you cease drumming. Encourage group members to observe each other and play off each other's movements and "levels" and see what kind of interesting group compositions they end up with when the drum stops.

Mirror. This classic movement exercise asks partners to face each other and copy each other's movements, as though one is the reflection of the other in a mirror. Have partners decide who will start out as leader: The leader initiates each action, and the partner copies it. (Halfway through the exercise, have partners switch roles, so that each gets a turn at being leader.) Emphasize that success in this activity is measured by how well students move together, not by whether they can "trick" each other by doing movements their partner can't follow, and that leaders should adjust the speed and complexity of their movements to their partners' capabilities. This is a great movement activity for buddies.

Transition. In this exercise, partners are challenged to use their bodies to create aesthetically interesting compositions. Partners begin by standing face to face: One partner remains stationary while the other moves into a position that incorporates the stationary partner into an interesting composition, and freezes; then the other partner takes a turn. Instruct students to take five turns each and see where they end up (younger students may need your guidance as to when to take a turn), and encourage them to use all levels of space—high, medium, and low. This exercise can also be done in small groups.

Clap-and-Snap. Clap-and-snap games do double duty: They can focus students' attention during transitions between activities and reinforce their understanding of patterns at the same time. In these games, students use their hands to clap, tap, slap, and snap out rhythms. For example, a simple pattern would be clap, snap fingers; clap, snap fingers; clap, snap fingers; etc. A more complex pattern would be tap head, tap shoulders, clap, snap; tap head, tap shoulders, clap, snap; etc. Establish the game with the whole class; then hand it over to students—when students take the lead, it becomes a cooperative activity, and you are free to attend to the details that invariably arise during transition time.

Clapping Syllables. Clapping games can also increase children's phonemic awareness—the understanding that words are made up of distinct sounds. Begin by clapping the syllables in students' names: Ja(clap)-mie(clap); Sue(clap), Rod(clap)-ney(clap), Re(clap)-bec(clap)-ca(clap); and so on. Students can clap in unison or take turns clapping each other's names. In a more sophisticated, guessing-game version, students take turns clapping the syllables and rhythmn of familiar songs and having classmates guess what it is. (These activities can also be done using rhythmn sticks instead of clapping.)

DANCING TO IMAGERY

Dance is a wonderful way for students to communicate their thoughts and feelings as they respond to the imagery of words, poems, stories, and music. Working together, students are called upon to discuss and coordinate their personal responses and ideas, which helps them clarify their thinking, inspire each other, and build their collaborative skills—and students who are not verbally adept may be appreciated for their skill in this physical mode of communication.

Music. Of course, one of the best movement activities for young children is to invite them to move to an interesting piece of music however they please. For a cooperative activity, however, children can work together in small groups to create more formal dance responses to music: Have each group member choreograph a phrase of the music and teach it to their groupmates, allowing for changes agreed on by the group. (You might also have groups perform their finished pieces for the class or for another audience.) Use this activity to highlight academic topics—for example, choreographing to folk music from another culture or to music illustrating patterns from math—or as a stand-alone dance activity to pieces of music that are class favorites.

Lyrics. Having students choreograph movements to match song lyrics is a good introduction to all dance response activities that involve language. Using songs with lyrics that are somewhat prescriptive, students can become accustomed to the concept of responding to words with dance and may find it easier to move on to the more abstract activities described below. Have partners or small groups create movements to accompany old favorites such as "Take Me Out to the Ballgame," "This Old Man," "Buffalo Gals," "Day-O," "Oats, Peas, Beans, and Barley-O," and the like. (See the songbook resources on page 100 for more ideas.)

Words. Evocative words make good movement prompts—and almost any noun, verb, adjective, or adverb can be evocative! Have group members brainstorm and discuss their reactions to a word, or the images it provokes, and then experiment with ways to represent these reactions and images in movement. Encourage students to consider space, tempo, and all kinds of motions as they relate to the word and not to limit themselves to literal translations from word to movement. To introduce the activity, demonstrate a word dance of your own creation or do a whole-class brainstorm to help students see how these space, tempo, and motion elements can work. Have groups finalize the piece that best expresses their feelings about the word and perform it for the class. Give students plenty of category and word suggestions to get them started, for example:

- feelings: surprise, disappointment, delight, fury, eagerness, frustration, curiosity, impatience, shyness, zeal, exhaustion . . .
- animals: elephant, tiger, monkey, alligator, turtle, horse, flamingo, eagle, mouse, spider, snail, duck, owl, shark, fish, whale . . .
- plant forms: seed growing, flower opening, potted plant, seaweed in a current, tree in a storm, tree laden with fruit, field of wheat . . .
- machines: cement mixer, computer, crane, dump truck, washing machine, dryer, skateboard, bicycle, CD player, ATM, desk lamp, photocopier . . .
- toys: rag doll, soldier, wind-up toy, building blocks, Lincoln Logs, balloon, ball, airplanes, cars, trains . . .
- weather: rain, thunderstorm, breeze, gale, tornado, fog, sunshine, snowfall, hail, blizzard . . .

Poetry. Because poetry can be interpreted in individual and multi-layered ways, it makes an effective dance prompt. Students will enjoy "dancing out" narrative poems, and you also might challenge them with poetry that conjures images and emotions rather than tells a story. Have groups discuss feelings and images evoked by the poem, create a group dance incorporating these ideas, and perform it for the class or other audience. (Suggest that groups could designate a group member to read the poem aloud while the others dance, or they could play a recording of the poem, or all the group members could recite the poem as they dance.)

Ideas. When the class is engaged in the study of an emotionally evocative idea or topic, have students work with a partner or small group to create a dance about it. Social studies, current events, language arts, and science might present any number of interesting possiblities: war, poverty, or other societal issues; oceans, rain forests, or other ecosystems; courage, hope, or other universal themes; and issues and dilemmas that arise in stories the class is reading. Give students the option of dancing without music or choosing music that conveys the mood of their dance.

PLAY-PARTY DANCING

Play-party songs arose from nineteenth-century American religious traditions that prohibited dancing and dance music—in effect, participants circumvented the prohibition by singing songs without instrumental accompaniment and doing movements that acted out the lyrics of songs. Many of these traditional play-party games are cooperative in that dancers match or coordinate their movements. Some songs, such as "The Hokey Pokey," entail only limited cooperation—children simply have to do the same movement at the same time; others, such as "Shoo Fly, Don't Bother Me" and "Go in and out the Window," divide students into partnerships or small groups and require more complex coordination. In general, though, play-party games are relatively simple, and, because the songs' lyrics tell participants how to move, these may be preferred by children who are not comfortable with creative or improvisational dance. (For play-party song ideas, see suggestions on page 98 in the previous chapter, "Singing.") And if students enjoy play-party dances, you might introduce them to even more formal cooperative dances from different cultures and traditions—square dancing, Greek line dancing, and so on.

EXTENSIONS

Dance and movement activities can be extended in any of the following ways.

✳ **What Did We Learn?** Most dance and movement activities do not have a product—the value is in the doing. Do spend some time talking with students about how the activity went, however. How did they feel about the activity? How did they feel about the music? What went well? What was difficult? What problems did they have, and how did they resolve them? What did they learn about the music to which they danced, the material that inspired their dance, or their own dance and movement abilities and preferences? What did they learn about communicating and coordinating with others?

Share Ideas. Give students a chance to show each other any movements or aspects of their dancing about which they are particularly enthusiastic—an interesting configuration at which they arrived, a perfect gesture, and so on. Remind students that there are many approaches to the same idea or issue by asking questions such as Who did it another way? or Who had a similar idea?

Showtime. Depending upon the project and students' level of engagement, you may want to encourage students to perform their dances for an audience—each other, a buddy class, parents, other classes, or the like. Give groups time to plan costumes, lighting, props, and so on. Before the event, have a conversation with the class about how to be a polite audience when their classmates are peforming.

Music Video. Instead of or in addition to a performance, students could film a video of their work. If so, encourage students to think about how to successfully translate their work to tape: What camera angles will best display the dance? Should they modify any of the choreography to suit the limitations (and possibilities) of taping?

Partner Reading

W HO HAS not had the experience of reading something—a cartoon in the morning paper, a paragraph from an article, a book—and feeling great delight or dismay at what we've read, been compelled to share it with another? Partner reading affords students that same gratification, and more: When students read and discuss text with a partner, they can help each other with the mechanics of reading, they have someone to whom they can express their pleasure or interest in what they have read, and they can acquire new insights from their partner's response to the reading as well.

Typically, the partner reading process simply consists of two students taking turns reading aloud to each other from the same text—storybook, textbook, or anything else— followed by partner discussions or activities that prompt students to think about important ideas or issues in what they have read (and perhaps some whole-class discussions to share their thinking with their other classmates, too). Partner reading is an involving strategy that can replace more traditional round-robin reading—and the opportunity and responsibility for such collaborative reading and conversation help students appreciate not only what they have read, but also each other.

WHY TO USE

- to develop students' reading and comprehension skills

- to enhance students' speaking and listening skills

- to deepen students' understanding of themselves, their classmates, and characters and events in literature

- to increase students' enjoyment of reading

WHEN TO USE

- when students will be reading a story that prompts a lot of ideas and discussion

- when students can use help and support reading challenging text

- when students will be reading nonfiction and can help each other master the information in the text

HOW TO DO

The Partner Reading blueprint asks students to

- decide how to divide the reading

- take turns reading aloud to each other

- help each other with the reading

- discuss what they've read

Developmental Considerations

Younger Students

In the early grades, as children are newly developing their literacy skills, the demands of partner reading have more to do with the mechanics of reading text than with in-depth reflection on issues. To introduce partner reading, select books that students can read fluently (or "pretend-read"), to build their confidence and pleasure in reading before moving on to more challenging texts. For example, start off with wordless books: They invite children to engage in and enjoy reading behaviors without the constraints imposed by print and are a natural transition to beginning reading. Even independent readers enjoy creating text about wordless books and benefit from learning and practicing important concepts and behaviors, such as directionality, book language, and story conventions.

Another important strategy for facilitating young children's partner reading is to read a book aloud to the whole class at least once before students read it with a partner. Their teacher's first read-through is a significant aid for beginning readers: They hear new vocabulary and acquire a context for deciphering it when they encounter it on their own; the content also becomes familiar, which enables beginning readers to "read" from memory by mapping spoken language onto print—an acceptable strategy in early literacy development. (You needn't read aloud wordless books, however, unless students have very little experience with them; even then, just read a page or two to help children see the range of information and detail they can include in their telling of the story.)

Even with thoughtful planning and preparation, though, you may have one or two students who need additional assistance during partner reading. In such cases, you may want to sit in as a third "partner" and facilitate reading and discussion with these students.

≈HINT≈

While you will want to consider your students' reading skills in selecting books, partner reading can work even when the text is difficult. Intense interest, an encouraging environment, and thoughtful preparation can help students rise above their independent reading levels. Your enthusiasm for a particular book can go a long way in inspiring partners to new levels of reading and understanding.

Fly on the Wall

Maureen Jackson's combined first- and second-grade class is about to start a partner read, but before Maureen hands out the books she asks partners to decide how they will divide the reading. Partners Samantha and Robbie each contribute uniquely to a satisfactory solution for their partnership.

SAMANTHA: How about you read two pages and I read two pages? *(Robbie thinks about Samantha's suggestion.)* Or how about, do you want to read a sentence and I read a sentence?

ROBBIE: When I was with Michael it took forever.

SAMANTHA: Do you want to read one page?

ROBBIE: Yeah, that's a lot better. When I did the sentences with

Michael, it was no good. You know why?

SAMANTHA: Why?

ROBBIE: Because it took forever.

SAMANTHA: *(Nods in acknowledgment)* So we'll do the page—you do a page and I'll do a page?

ROBBIE: Yeah.

SAMANTHA: Okay.

≈HINT≈

Older students usually enjoy reading aloud, but you may encounter some resistance—perhaps from students who don't want to be "held back" by those who read more slowly or from students who may per-ceive the activity as a test of their decoding skills. Both cases reflect how important it is to highlight the purpose and benefits of partner reading (or any reading, for that matter): It's not about how much or how well you read, but about what you get out of it. The value of reading is in the issues and ideas the text asks its readers to consider, and as with any cooperative learning activity, partner reading enables students to help each other understand, broaden, and enjoy what they are learning.

Time will also help make your case: As students become more practiced in partner reading—experiencing its benefits and developing trusting working relationships with their classmates—any reluctance or self-consciousness will subside. Begin with stories and textbook passages that are relatively short and within the reading range of most of your students, and let subsequent choices be guided by curriculum topics as well as by students' interests and developing skills. As the year pro-gresses and partners become more proficient, they can also exercise more autonomy in managing the partner reading process; for example, they may decide to decrease how much they read aloud, sometimes instead reading silently and asking one another for help as necessary.

Grouping Considerations

≈HINT≈

Obviously, partner reading means that students work in pairs—but many factors can influence how you pair students and the success of their reading partnerships. In general, teachers find that partnerships are most successful when partners' decoding abilities are not too far apart—so, for example, you might accomplish this by pairing students who have high or low decoding skills with students whose skills are somewhere in the middle.

Because success in partner reading also depends upon a number of other social and academic factors, however, it is not *essential* for students to have similar reading skills. Students may have other abilities and talents to offer, and they can learn to recognize and appreciate their own and their partners' contributions. For example, when one partner can read with relative ease and the other has a higher level of empathy or converses with ease, their collaboration enhances both partners' learning. This, in the end, is what really makes a partnership successful—that each student feels he or she can make a meaningful contribution to partner work.

You may also have reasons for pairing students that are not related to reading ability at all. At the beginning of the year, random pairings give you—and your students—a chance to see how different children work together; sometimes pairing can simply provide an opportunity to bring together students who otherwise might not get to know each other. Also keep in mind that when the class has developed into a supportive and trusting community, an intuitive (or even risky) pairing may, for a particular book, yield surprising and positive results.

Finally, sometimes partnerships needn't be partnerships at all: While reading in pairs generally ensures the greatest student participation and engagement, you may encounter circumstances when a larger reading group is necessary or even preferable. For example, when a student is absent, his or her regular partner might join another partnership temporarily; likewise, a permanent group of three may be the best solution for students who are frequently absent. And of course, a class will not always comprise an even number of students! On occasion, the content of the reading—a play with four main characters, for example—will also suggest a particular group size.

Getting Students Ready

Academic Preparation

Depending upon the material to be read and your students' proficiency, use some of the suggestions below to get students thinking about the text and to review reading strategies.

Make introductions. Before starting a reading, introduce it to the class in ways that engage their interest or connect it to their prior knowledge. Use your favorite strategies for introducing students to people, ideas, or issues they will encounter in a text (but without giving away so much that there's nothing left for students to discover themselves!). With expository text, for example, discuss what students know or hope to learn about the topic; you might also do activities that increase students' personal connection to the material—how about introducing astronomy with a Family Science Night stargazing event, for instance? Or when introducing a work of fiction, start with a conversation about an important theme in the book—not about how it figures in the story, but about what students understand or feel about it in general.

Deal with difficulties. Ask students for what strategies they might use when they encounter difficult words or passages as they read aloud, and offer your own favorite reading strategies as well—for example, break the word into parts, sound it out, ask yourself if the word you think it is makes sense in context, ask your partner, and so on. (Also remind students to return to the beginning of the sentence after they have figured out the word, to reestablish context.) Post everyone's ideas for handy reference.

Face the facts. Reading for information is especially challenging for elementary school children: Nonfiction generally contains greater volume and density of information than fiction, and familiar comprehension clues such as character, plot, and setting prove inapplicable to expository text. Fortunately, reading for information is well suited to collaborative effort—as students tackle such reading tasks together, they can help each other understand the material and gain experience with nonfiction reading strategies. Review these strategies before partners read textbooks or other nonfiction that emphasizes reading as an investigation. (For younger children especially, cover each of the following steps in a separate, short lesson.)

- *Discuss the topic before reading.* Reading comprehension is directly related to students' prior knowledge, and as mentioned above, it is important to introduce both fiction and nonfiction with activities that "connect" students to what they will be reading. With nonfiction it is perhaps particularly important to have a class discussion about the topic beforehand, both to help you assess student knowledge and to provide students with information that helps them relate what they will read to what they already know.

- *Survey the material.* Next, have partnerships survey the material to be read. A survey involves "investigating" all aspects of the material not included in the main body of the text—introductions and conclusions, headings, subheadings, charts, graphs, photographs, and anything else that might provide clues as to what the material is about; partners then discuss what they have concluded about the topic from these clues.

- *Read the text.* Have partners read and discuss one section of the text at a time (with very difficult text, this may mean one paragraph at a time). This allows students to build a momentum of comprehension that makes the reading increasingly accessible, rather than increasingly daunting.

- *Probe students' thinking.* Provide partners with some provocative, open-ended questions designed to enrich their understanding of the reading. Or challenge them to ask each other questions that will help their partner learn.

- *Use the new knowledge.* Follow up with one or more experiences (such as those suggested in Extensions, below) in which students apply the information presented in the reading.

Take time. Give students a realistic timeline for the work expected of them and make sure they understand the schedule and your reasons behind it. You may choose to keep the whole class on the same schedule (especially at first); or you may give students the leeway to work at different paces, once students have become comfortable with partner reading and have developed the necessary skills, habits, and judgment to work productively at their own pace.

Plant a seed. Partners' understanding and enjoyment of their reading will depend heavily on their ability to have a conversation about it, yet you may find that some students have had little or no experience holding independent, instructionally focused conversations with peers. Provide them with some framework for their partner conversations by suggesting a few questions to get them started—very broad questions, such as What was your favorite part? or What are you wondering about? or more specific questions that encourage students to think about significant issues or ideas in the text. Offer just a couple of conversation starters, though, so that students have the freedom (and responsibility) to direct their own conversations, pose their own questions, and come up with their own ideas. (See the Discussions blueprint on page 26 for some ideas about helping students hold instructionally focused conversations.)

Model the process. Successful partner reading builds on behaviors that you model throughout the curriculum when you read aloud, facilitate class discussions, and "think out loud" about ideas you encounter in text. It is also valuable, of course, to specifically model partner reading with a student volunteer—for example, to demonstrate how you might negotiate how to divide the work, some of the reading strategies described above (but not all of them at once), and so on. Give your volunteer an idea of what to expect during the role-play, but don't script it.

Social/Ethical Preparation

The best preparation for partner reading is creating a safe and supportive classroom environment, so that students have the comfort and confidence to read aloud to each other (and risk making mistakes), ask for and offer each other help, and discuss their thoughts and feelings about what they have read. In building such trusting relationships, the following are some social and ethical aspects of partner reading that you may want to help your students anticipate.

Sharing the reading. If your students are new to partner reading, they may need some direction in figuring out how to divide the reading task. Younger students, especially, might need explicit guidance—for example, that partners seated on the left read aloud the pages on the left side of the book, and partners seated on the right read the pages on the right side. (When very young children are still at the stage of "telling" books from pictures, it might work best to alternate reading the whole book.) As they gain experience, students will be able to decide how to fairly and logically divide the task of reading aloud, but it is still probably a good idea to review the possibilities with them—for example, alternating sentences, paragraphs, pages, sets of pages, and so on. Also be sure they understand that if the system they've agreed on doesn't seem to be working, they should feel free to modify it as they go along.

≈ HINT ≈

When a reading presents particularly challenging issues or ideas to discuss, you might encourage conversation by pairing up partnerships and having four students wrestle the topic around.

Offering and asking for help. These are two sides of a coin, linked by common concerns of trust, tact, and timing. Discuss with students how partners might treat each other when one of them has difficulty with some word or sentence while reading, and encourage them to take the partner's perspective: How does it feel to ask for help? What might make it easier (or harder) for a partner to ask for help? Should a partner wait to be asked for help or jump in with a suggestion? What makes the difference between seeming impatient and seeming helpful?

Sharing ideas. Partner reading isn't just partner *reading,* of course—it also includes partner discussion of ideas in the text. You might want to review with students some of the social and ethical aspects of holding respectful and productive conversations (see the Discussions blueprint on page 26).

WAYS TO USE *Partner Reading*

Since partner reading suits almost any circumstance in which students might practice their reading skills, build their reading comprehension, and learn to work collaboratively, its possibilities as a flexible format are endless. Below are just a few ideas for using the format in different ways.

ACTIVITIES

Buddy Reading. Partner reading can be easily adapted for cross-age buddies: Younger buddies enjoy and learn from challenging books read to them by an older buddy, and even tentative readers gain confidence when they read to an admiring younger child.

Family Reading. To highlight the value and enjoyment of parents and children reading together, hold regular Family Reading nights when parents read with their children in a low-key but festive celebration of family literacy. (Be sure to serve refreshments!) Such events allow children to "show off" their skills and parents to share in important aspects of their children's learning—and may also encourage families to do more reading together at home.

Picture Books. Although generally considered the domain of younger children, many picture books convey important ideas that speak to people of all ages—and the pared-down expression of such ideas in text and graphics is often a source of their power. Talk with older students about picture books: What were their favorites when they were younger? Why? What do they think picture books have to offer all readers? Have students do a partner read of a picture book, including a discussion of the ideas in the story—as indicated in both words and pictures.

EXTENSIONS

Partner reading activities can be extended in any of the following ways.

✳ **What Did We Learn?** Depending upon time and topic, you will sometimes want to bring the whole class together so partners can share their responses to what they've read. You needn't do this after every partner reading session, of course, nor is it a good idea for the whole class to discuss every question discussed in partnerships. Instead, pick one or two issues based on your sense of their importance to the class and/or your assessment of students' enthusiasm for a particular topic. While you're at it, inquire about what students are learning as reading partners: What do they like about reading with someone else? What works well, and what poses difficulties? How might those be addressed? What might they do differently the next time they read with a partner?

Get Organized. In partnerships, students can also reflect on what they have learned by thinking about how their ideas connect to, overlap with, compare to, contrast with, or otherwise relate to each other. See the ORGANIZING IDEAS blueprints on pages 32–54 for some suggestions.

Only Connect. Have students connect ideas from their reading to their own lives, to other pieces of literature, and to other disciplines, such as drama, art, music, and dance. For possible activities, see Singing on page 92, Dance and Movement on page 102, Graphic Arts on page 157, Readers Theater on page 167, and Role-Playing on page 174.

Write On. Have partners record and extend their ideas by writing collaboratively about them. For possible activities, see the Poetry, Narrative, and Expository writing blueprints on pages 135–156.

Partner Reading Curriculum. Two programs that incorporate partner reading throughout are published by Developmental Studies Center. See *Reading, Thinking & Caring* and *Reading for Real* in Teacher Support Materials from Developmental Studies Center on page 188.

Rehearsing

WHEN a learning task involves practice or memorization, two heads can definitely be better than one! Working in pairs, students can help each other with two kinds of rehearsal tasks: memorization of information, such as a poem or song, math or science facts, skits or plays; and delivery of information, such as portfolio presentations, speeches, or any other public presentation. Partners take turns rehearsing, one student presenting while the other listens: For memorization tasks, the listener provides cues and encouragement to the reciter; for presentation rehearsals, the listener plays the role of a "practice audience," listening silently and offering moral support. Then they switch roles. The process benefits both presenter and listener, because listening also facilitates learning—the listening partner practices an important communication skill *and* absorbs the presenter's information. Taking turns helping each other rehearse, students experience both sides of a partner relationship—being "the helper" and "the helped"—and gain appreciation for how valuable it can be to work with a colleague.

WHY TO USE

- to help students develop their presentation skills
- to help students memorize
- to make memorizing more fun
- to increase automaticity in areas such as math and spelling

WHEN TO USE

- when students need to practice how they want to present material
- when students need to learn material for a play, speech, or other presentation
- when students need to learn a poem or song
- whenever achieving automaticity is necessary or desirable

HOW TO DO

When students need to memorize material, the Rehearsing blueprint asks them to

- read aloud together the material to be memorized
- decide who will recite and who will listen first
- ask their listening partners for a cue when they get stuck
- give their reciting partners a verbal or visual cue only when asked
- switch roles
- continue until both partners have memorized the material ▶

HOW TO DO

When students need to practice presenting material, the Rehearsing blueprint asks them to

- decide who will present and who will listen first
- present the material as though to an audience, without pausing for questions or comments
- listen to their presenting partners without interjecting comments or questions
- switch roles
- continue until both feel comfortable with their presentations

Developmental Considerations

Younger Students

If your students are not yet reading, do whole-class rehearsals of material to be memorized before moving on to partner work; after the class has memorized the material, partners then can help each other work toward automaticity. Prereaders will also benefit from visual reminders, such as physical movements, that go with material they are memorizing—both to help them remember when they are reciting and to offer as cues when they are listening to their partner recite.

Alternate partner and whole-class rehearsing to make sure students are memorizing accurately, and observe partnerships to see if any are floundering—you may need to do a little extra work with these students, such as coaching them yourself a bit. If a number of partners are having trouble helping each other rehearse, increase the amount of whole-class rehearsal.

Older Students

Throughout the curriculum, older students are presented with many opportunities to help each other learn material—and they also make ideal rehearsing partners for younger buddies. They are able and patient listeners for their young partners and benefit socially from taking the role of helper; they can also benefit academically from listening, even when the material being memorized seems remedial—it's a chance to brush up on the basics!

Grouping Considerations

Rehearsing generally works best in partnerships, but some work that begins in partnerships can be expanded to small groups—for example, when the rehearsal is for a play or other performance.

Academic Preparation

Talk about why. Students may not relish the prospect of doing memorization, and you may need to discuss the value of developing their memory or of the particular activity with them. Why, for example, do they think it might be important to have a good memory or to achieve automaticity in math facts and spelling words? If students have not had much experience working with partners on memorization, also talk about the benefits of tackling such tasks with another person.

Begin together. If all students will be memorizing the same material, review it with the whole class and highlight any difficult spots. If students are prereaders, begin the process by rehearsing the material as a whole class and then have partners work together to perfect their memorization.

Get a cue. Invite students' ideas for different kinds of cues they might offer to help a partner remember the material to be memorized—for example, physical gestures, the sound a word begins with, rhymes, and so on.

Model the process. With a student volunteer, demonstrate the rehearsal process, highlighting any aspects of the task that might cause difficulty—for example, asking for cues, not giving cues until asked, examples of cues, and so on. Offer helpful hints and describe what you and your partner did that helped you both learn. An alternative would be to sing a song or recite a poem (a favorite that your students can see you enjoy sharing) and explain how you learned it through repetition; highlight any special techniques you used to help you memorize, such as memorizing one small section at a time or the like.

≈ HINT ≈

Partner rehearsing is useful whether partners are working with the same or different material. In fact, when partners rehearse different material, they are likely to learn their partner's material as well as their own—and reap twice the benefit!

Social/Ethical Preparation

Rehearsing together can be risky business if students aren't thinking about how to best handle each other's efforts—after all, until they memorize or present something perfectly, they'll be making a series of mistakes! The following are some social and ethical aspects of rehearsing that you may want to help your students anticipate.

Listening well. If rehearsals are to be truly useful, both partners have to hold up their end of the activity—in other words, the presenter needs an active listener. Encourage students to be attentive to their reciting partners and to recognize the part they play in the reciters' success. What if a listening partner didn't pay attention? What if a listening partner wasn't prepared to provide cues when requested? How would the presenting partner feel? How might it affect her or his ability to memorize material? How might it affect her or his comfort and ease in making a presentation?

Listening silently. If partners will be helping each other rehearse a presentation, remind them that an active listener can still be a silent listener—in other words, it is important for listening partners to be attentive, but they shouldn't interrupt their partners' delivery. For this

≈ HINT ≈

When students can't hear each other easily, rehearsals become frustrating rather than helpful. Have students take a moment to rehearse their rehearsal voices.

kind of rehearsal, they are to serve as a silent "practice audience" for their partners. (Keep in mind that the Reviewing blueprint on page 129 is useful for when you *do* want students to critique and help shape their partners' work, as opposed to simply serving as a practice audience.)

Helping respectfully. Remind students that some people memorize more quickly than others, and that it is important to offer help in ways that show kindness and consideration, not impatience or ridicule. What kinds of behaviors and responses are truly helpful? What kinds of behaviors might make a partner reluctant to ask for help (thereby slowing down the learning process even more)?

Offering encouragement. Ask students to think of a time when they tried hard to do something and felt discouraged. How do they think their partner might feel if he or she is having a hard time memorizing material or perfecting a presentation? How might partners encourage one another to keep trying? What behaviors might discourage a partner even further?

Switching roles. Each partner will need a chance to rehearse, and at first students may need some guidance as to taking turns fairly—for example, you might suggest that partners switch roles after the presenter has had three tries all the way through the material. Ask students for other ideas and encourage them to think of ways to divide the work that takes into account differences in learning styles and speed. With experience, partners will be able to negotiate their own ways to divide the task.

≈ HINT ≈

Listening partners may have a hard time resisting the urge to jump in and help when their partner gets stuck—so you may need to stress the importance of giving assistance only when the reciting partner asks for it.

WAYS TO USE *Rehearsing*

ACTIVITIES

Words and Music. The Rehearsing blueprint comes in handy when students need to learn a poem or song for a whole-class performance. If the piece has many stanzas or verses, assign certain partnerships to each section and then have the class come together to put it all together. If a song has a repeating chorus, have all partnerships learn the chorus and sing it as a class. Likewise, partners can use rehearsal to help each other learn individual pieces for a class talent show or other such performance.

All the World's a Stage. Partner rehearsing can help student actors memorize lines for a class play or performance, whether or not students are memorizing the same parts. Suggest that listeners cue their partners by reading a few lines preceding the reciting partner's lines, to provide the necessary context. After partners have achieved some measure of facility with their own lines, bring them together with other cast members to begin practicing all their parts together.

All the World's a Soapbox. Nothing can be more nerve-wracking than having to get up and give a presentation before your peers—but having a partner to rehearse with beforehand can ease the trauma considerably. Have partners rehearse together when they have to present reports, make speeches, participate in debates, or do any other type of public speaking.

Go Figure. Use partner rehearsing to help students achieve automaticity in basic math facts, such as addition, subtraction, multiplication, and division. Have students drill one another (be sure listening partners mix up the order in which they present problems, so as to avoid memorizing the sequence of answers!), and follow up with frequent opportunities for students to solve problems with their math facts.

Bring It on Home. Partner rehearsing is a useful tool for helping students learn material to present at home: for example, a poem or song the class has been using that students would like to share with their families, or what they would like to say when showing their parents or family members their portfolios, and so on.

Make Meaning. Asking students to memorize lists of decontextualized words is a sure way to douse their interest in language, especially since children learn vocabulary primarily through hearing and using words in context. That said, there are still times when you will want to be sure students understand specific vocabulary—for example, important words they will encounter in partner reading or a unit of study. Be judicious and select just the key words for partners to rehearse—or better yet, let students identify and memorize words that they find interesting or important to their understanding of what they are reading. Partners needn't memorize the same words—in fact, they are likely to get twice the mileage by being "learner" and "listener" to two different sets of words. Vocabulary rehearsal also lends itself to creativity: Encourage students to use their imaginations to devise charade-like cues that help their partners learn and remember the meaning of words.

Spell It Out for Me. Have partners use the Rehearsing blueprint to learn spelling words—but instead of reciting out loud, students will "recite" in writing. Again, as with vocabulary rehearsals, partners needn't rehearse the same words; for example, each student might choose the words he or she will rehearse from among those that have been identified (in consultation with the teacher) as problematic in the student's writing. Have students give partners immediate feedback after each word, rather than waiting until the end of the list.

Rehearse on Request. After students have developed facility in memorizing and helping each other rehearse, encourage them to use partners spontaneously and informally to rehearse presentations or memorize information in math, language arts, and other academic disciplines. (You might even want to add "rehearser" to the categories of class helpers.)

≈ HINT ≈

Rehearsing with a younger buddy is a graceful way for older students to strengthen their understanding of remedial material they may not have had a firm handle on when they learned it at first. To deepen their learning and enjoyment of playing "listener," encourage older buddies to elaborate on the rehearsing format by devising a game or strategy to help their younger partner learn the material being memorized.

EXTENSIONS Rehearsing activities can be extended in any of the following ways.

✳ **What Did We Learn?** If students have memorized what they intended to memorize, then it will be pretty clear what they have "learned." Doing a presentation, however, can have more ambiguous results, and students will benefit from reflecting on how their presentations went and what they learned from their rehearsals. In either case, it's also a good idea to help students reflect on how they learned, how they worked together, what went well or didn't, what they might do the same or differently the next time they rehearse with a partner, and so on.

Dramatic Interpretation. Once students have committed poems or songs to memory, have them turn their attention to dramatic interpretation. Encourage partners to try different interpretations and agree on an approach; give students time to practice and then invite volunteers to perform their interpretations for the rest of the class.

Graphic Interpretation. Many poems and songs contain interesting visual images, and partners may enjoy illustrating such pieces that they have memorized. Have partners work together on drawings or paintings; you might also have partners contribute their creations to a whole-class mural. The art could also serve as interesting and colorful backdrops for a class recital of the songs and poems they have mastered. (See Graphic Arts on page 157 for further suggestions.)

Dance Interpretation. Have partners make up gestures, dance movements, and other theatrical touches to accompany pieces they have memorized. (See Dance and Movement on page 102 for further suggestions.)

Make a Problem of It. When students memorize math facts or other information or data, have them put this information to work to solve interesting problems. Students could also create their own word problems to illustrate the facts they've learned and then solve their partners' problems.

Editing

THE HARDEST PART about writing usually isn't getting the mechanics right—it's figuring out what to say, when to say it, and how to say it clearly. Sometimes just getting started can be the most torturous aspect of all! Students can help each other overcome these obstacles with peer editing, providing thoughtful responses to their classmates' work at the prewriting stage and throughout the work in progress. In prewriting activities, students "jump-start" each other's thinking by discussing possible topics and approaches; as their work progresses, they help each other reflect on the content and organization of their writing. The process benefits both writer and editor: Writers gain insight into the reader's point of view and how to communicate to readers, and editors becomes more analytical as they help writers reflect on content, style, and the fit between writers' ideas and presentation.

WHY TO USE

- to help student writers clarify and articulate their ideas
- to help student writers take the perspective of the reader
- to foster students' awareness of what makes writing effective
- to encourage student sharing of ideas

WHEN TO USE

- when students can exchange ideas and opinions respectfully
- before writing, to help students clarify what they want to write about
- after each draft of work in progress
- when a writer needs help with a specific writing problem
- whenever a writer will benefit from hearing another point of view
- when a piece of writing drafted by a small group is intended to represent the thinking of the whole class

HOW TO DO

The Editing blueprint asks students to

- listen carefully as the writer shares his or her prewriting ideas or reads aloud the work in progress
- ask the writer what he or she thinks works well in the piece, and discuss
- give their ideas about the strengths of the piece, and discuss
- ask the writer what he or she thinks isn't working well, and discuss what to do about it
- ask questions about anything else that seems problematic or unclear for the reader, and discuss
- talk with the writer about next steps

Developmental Considerations

Younger Students

For young children, the biggest challenge of writing is encoding the message rather than saying it well, and writers and editors alike will tend to focus on spelling and mechanics. So, even though you will want to repeatedly stress that editors should focus on the authors' ideas—not their spelling, punctuation, or capitalization—recognize that despite this admonishment younger students will likely find it easier to attend to these very things since they are still struggling with fundamental aspects of writing themselves. By the same token, don't expect young children's editing to result in profound changes in their partners' work—because they are so inexperienced, young children are more likely to suggest changing just a word here and a phrase there.

Older Students

≈HINT≈

Because prewriting conferences deal solely with ideas, they are important in helping students learn to focus on content.

Older students will also need frequent reminders that ideas, not technicalities, are the focus of peer editing. Even when they do attend to their partners' content, however, they may have difficulty responding honestly. Many older children have been socialized to compliment others—whether or not they really feel complimentary—and they may be reluctant to respond honestly if the truth is less than flattering. Remind them that an editor's job is both to encourage writers and to help them think critically about their work, and that a tactful question or suggestion can be a big help. (Social/Ethical Preparation, below, suggests role-plays you might do with students to help them learn to gracefully handle such editorial responsibilities.)

Grouping Considerations

Depending upon the product and its purpose, peer editing can be done in partnerships, in small groups, or even as a whole class. For example, students might work with

- a partner, responding to each other's work in partner writing conferences
- a small group whose members critique each other's independent work
- a small group whose members respond to individual pieces that will be compiled into a joint product

Whole-class editing may for the most part prove impractical, but it can be used when a few students draft something intended to speak for the whole class—invitations to guest speakers, thank-you letters to class helpers, inquiries to authors of books the class is reading, and so on—to give everyone a chance for input before the small group produces a final version.

Getting Students Ready

Academic Preparation

A good editor doesn't merely "fix" a writer's work, but offers the kind of questions and comments that prompt writers to think about their work, polish it in their own way, and perhaps gain some insights to apply to future writing. Use some of the suggestions below to foster the understandings and skills that will help students achieve this level of editing.

Come to terms. Help students understand their responsibilities as editors by introducing the terms *developmental editing* and *copyediting*. Explain that the kind of editing you want students to do is called developmental editing, in which they help writers develop the substance and organization of their piece of writing. Remind them that you really don't want them to worry about copyediting, which addresses mechanics such as spelling, punctuation, and capitalization (not that mechanics aren't important, but students have bigger fish to fry in helping each other shape the content of their work!). If possible, invite a developmental editor to visit the class and talk about her or his work.

Develop editors. Sometimes it can be just as difficult to get started editing as it is to get started writing, and your students will benefit from some guidance. The example of your own responses to student writing is an influential lesson in itself, of course, but you might also suggest a loose structure (such as suggested by the How to Do list on page 123) to help students get started and stay on task. And be sure to

≈HINT≈

After students have done their developmental edit, you might have them proceed to copyediting each other's work—but if so, you'll need to have a lot of confidence in students' mastery of writing mechanics or find some way to counter students' miscorrections.

Fly on the Wall

It is Writer's Workshop in Janet Ellman's fourth-grade class, and students are generating individual lists of possible story topics. A prewriting conference begins spontaneously when Jeffrey spies "Halloween Day" among Sharon's list of ideas. Seeing his interest, Sharon relinquishes the topic—and her attention to Jeffrey's initial attempts to relate Halloween memories helps him recall details and feelings that will contribute to an engaging story.

JEFFREY: *(Pointing to Sharon's topic list)* Was that this Halloween?

SHARON: No, when I was small and there was this bloody face on the porch and I was really scared because I thought it was real.

JEFFREY: When I was small, I thought all costumes were real. *(He adds "Halloween Night" to his list.)*

SHARON: Do you want to tell your story first?

JEFFREY: Which one of mine do you want to hear?

SHARON: "Halloween Night."

JEFFREY: When I was little, my mom fed me food. First I was early and then, after that, when I went outside, it was dark and scary.

SHARON: *(Surprised)* Did you have to go alone?

JEFFREY: No, everybody went. When I rang the bell at this one house, there was this guy, he was like this. *(He retracts his head into his sweater.)*

DANI: *(Who has been listening to the exchange between Sharon and Jeffrey)* Let me tell my story.

SHARON: No, let him finish. *(Turns to Jeffrey)* What happened?

Once students are familiar with the peer editing process, encourage them to initiate writing conferences with classmates of their choice on an as-needed basis—they will appreciate the autonomy, and they will benefit from receiving different perspectives on their work.

point out the how-to list's emphasis on *questions* and *discussion*—encourage students to go beyond stilted question-and-answer sessions to more probing and productive conversations.

Get specific. General responses such as "boring" or "great" don't tell writers anything about what works and what doesn't in their writing—but because many students experience a steady diet of "good," "excellent," "needs more detail" themselves, they may need help learning how to be more specific.

Offer examples of feedback that gives a writer some idea of where to go next—for instance, "I can't picture the meeting between Stacy and Jeremy—maybe it would help me if you told me something about where they are when they meet?" Equally important, encourage students to offer feedback that helps a writer recognize the effective aspects of his or her writing, such as "The way you described all the colors and sunshine and waves made me feel like I could reach out and touch the water."

Model the process. With a student or other adult, role-play a peer editing session and model how to focus on content rather than mechanics, how to ask questions and respond in ways that prompt a writer to think more deeply about her or his work, and how to give specific feedback.

Social/Ethical Preparation

A caring classroom is a prerequisite for peer editing—students need to value each other's perspectives and feelings enough to offer feedback kindly and to receive it graciously. The following are some social and ethical aspects of peer editing that you may want to help your students anticipate.

Responding kindly and honestly. Discuss with students the importance of being both honest and kind when responding to a writer's work, and ask them to think about the alternatives: What if their editorial comments were honest but delivered in a judgmental manner? What if their comments were kind and flattering but sidestepped telling the writer about problems in the piece? Help them think about ways to provide critiques in fair, nonjudgmental ways, such as placing the emphasis on what *they* as readers are having difficulty with, as opposed to pointing out what the *writer* "did wrong." For example, ask them to think about the difference in tone between saying "I didn't understand exactly what you were saying here" and "You didn't make this very clear." Have students role-play tactful responses to possible scenarios, such as the following:

- Your partner thinks he or she has written a really funny story, but it doesn't even make you smile.
- Your partner's story is boring.
- You can't keep track of which character is doing or saying what in your partner's story.
- Your partner's writing contains stereotypes or things that you know aren't true.

Being edited. Acknowledge that it's sometimes unpleasant to be edited, no matter how tactfully or sensitively a critique is delivered, and that students may resist, disagree with, or feel discouraged by their editor's comments. Discuss how students might handle such feelings and interact productively with editors.

WAYS TO USE *Editing*

ACTIVITIES

Every time students write, they can benefit from being edited—which means you can use peer editing throughout the curriculum to help students craft their narrative and expository writing skills. Below are some ideas for editing configurations, as well as some whole-class activities that both build community and give you a chance to model editing skills.

Prewriting Conferences. Having students talk about their writing before they write is a valuable first step for author and editor alike. Working in pairs or small groups, encourage students to discuss what they plan to write about—and encourage them to ask each other questions about their ideas and plans. For example, they may need to begin by coming up with a topic, in which case they can spark each other's imaginations; or they may need to choose one topic from many, and in explaining their choices to each other they will begin identifying important themes for their written pieces. Likewise, they might tell each other a brief version of the story they plan to write, and the editor's questions will help the writer anticipate what the reader needs to know. Meanwhile, editors also benefit from these conversations because they get an idea of the writer's intentions and meaning; later, when they read written drafts, this insight will help them assess whether the text meets the writer's objectives. Your students' age and experience will have a lot to do with the sophistication and impact of these discussions, of course, but even the most minimal of prewriting conferences will help young writers figure out what they want to say, and why!

Writing Conferences. Working with the same partner or small group with which they started in a prewriting conference, have students continue their collaboration throughout the writing of a piece. If your students are young or have little experience with peer editing, set aside scheduled time for peer editing sessions; more experienced students, however, may be practiced enough to set their own writing and editing schedule with their collaborators. Besides editing each draft of works in progress, also encourage students to consult with each other informally when confronted by specific problems (or writer's block!) in their writing. Keep in mind that it's always helpful to get another opinion—so even though continuity is important in a writer-editor relationship, you might also have writers show later drafts to a different editor just to get some fresh insights.

≈ HINT ≈

Students inevitably will compare each other's writing, especially when working in groups, but this needn't happen in a negative way. For example, encourage students to focus on interesting differences and similarities in the way group members approach an assignment, not on judging whose is "best."

Writers' Groups. Provide opportunities for students to form writers' groups based on shared interests, to give each other support and feedback on their writing in that area. For example, groups might be organized around a particular genre such as mystery, science fiction, biography, nature writing, or poetry, or topics such as dinosaurs, music, rocks, and so on. Invite a professional writer to talk to the class about how such groups help writers develop their craft and support each other's efforts.

Class Letter. Throughout the school year, your class may have occasion to send thank-you notes, invitations, requests for information, or other whole-class correspondence. In such cases, ask two or three students to write a first draft of the correspondence and then solicit their classmates' input before sending it. Editing the draft as a class gives you a good opportunity to model honest and kind editing, but you could also have students review the document individually or in small groups and submit their feedback to the writing group. Either way, including all students in the process not only heightens everyone's awareness of writing skills, but also builds community by keeping students connected to class business.

Class Record. Classroom record keeping is another vehicle for practicing editing skills and building classroom community. For example, have individuals, partners, or small groups create record sheets for math games, science experiments, book or ball sign-outs, and the like; then have the rest of the class respond to the suggested format before it is finalized. Students will have more investment in and commitment to systems that they have helped create—and you might end up with a better record sheet, too!

EXTENSIONS

Editing activities can be extended in the following ways.

What Did We Learn? After your class has finished a peer editing process, take time to reflect with students about ways in which it helped their writing. Discuss how things went—what worked, as well as any disagreements or problems that arose and how those were resolved. Also share your own observations; your insights will help students become more expert writers and responders. Help students build on these conversations by writing their ideas and observations on a posted class list of Editing Strategies from which students can draw in future writing conferences.

What's Next? Writing and editing are reciprocal processes: Every writing conference will produce new ideas to be incorporated into a next draft, which leads to another edit, and so on until a piece is finished. This is the essential "extension" of peer editing, but all sorts of extensions also derive from the finished product: Stories can be illustrated, reports read aloud, plays performed, material bound into a class book, and so on.

≈ HINT ≈

Most of us associate editing with written work, but students can also "edit" projects and presentations in other domains—visual and performing arts, for example. Use the Reviewing blueprint on page 129 to have your students respond to art, drama, music, and other unwritten material with the same spirit of encouragement and gentle challenge that characterizes peer editing.

≈ HINT ≈

When "publishing" students' writing, do a final copy edit so that student readers absorb correct rather than incorrect form and mechanics.

Reviewing

WE HAVE ALL been witness to the fact that children can hold strong opinions and even be their peers' harshest critics—so wouldn't it be great to put these very traits to work in positive and productive ways? As with peer editing, peer reviewing does just that, developing children's ability to helpfully critique each other's work—in this case, unwritten products such as artwork, performances, displays, and so on. (In fact, it's a great complement to the many activities in this book that involve "products," such as Graphic Arts, Readers Theater, Dance and Movement, etc.) In a cooperative classroom, reviewing someone's work isn't a matter of passing judgment—it's a process of asking questions and sharing ideas that help students "pass judgment" on their *own* efforts—recognizing what works, what doesn't, what to do next or differently. Reviewing each other's work, either in progress or when finished, students help each other get the most out of their own thinking and creativity—and see how much there is to enjoy and learn from the different ways people express themselves.

WHY TO USE

- to help students learn to articulate their ideas about their own and others' work
- to foster students' appreciation of different forms of unwritten self-expression and creativity
- to help students appreciate that taste and creativity are individual
- to help students appreciate that people's responses to others' efforts are individual

WHEN TO USE

- when students can exchange ideas respectfully
- after drafts or rehearsals of works in progress
- whenever a work in progress will benefit from other points of view
- when students have finished a project, to gain insight for future efforts
- when products created by individuals will be compiled into a group product
- after students have finished cooperative creative activities, to assess the resulting product
- *not* all the time

HOW TO DO

The Reviewing blueprint asks students to

- view the creator's work thoughtfully
- ask the creator what he or she thinks works well in the piece, and discuss
- give their ideas about the strengths of the piece, and discuss
- ask the creator what she or he thinks isn't working well, and discuss what to do about it
- ask questions about anything that they find problematic or unclear, and discuss
- talk with the creator about next steps

Developmental Considerations

Younger Students

Most young children are sophisticated neither in their knowledge of the arts nor in their ability to express reactions to others' creative efforts, and they may need help appreciating the wide range of comments that exist between "I like . . ." and "I hate . . ." Your own reactions to student work will help them develop the vocabulary they need to respond sensitively and specifically to classmates' work; you might also try some of the Getting Students Ready suggestions on pages 131–132.

Older Students

As with peer editing, older students may be especially reluctant to express negative, unpopular, or unusual ideas when reviewing their classmates' work. Try to help them understand that different perspectives are not only expected but also desirable—it is this variety of insights, after all, that can help creators think clearly and broadly about their current and future efforts.

≈ HINT ≈

Be sparing in the amount of reviewing you ask students to do—enough to get practiced, but not so much that every draft or product is critiqued.

In the same vein, help older students tap their capacity for understanding subtleties that elude younger students. For example, while younger students may respond to visual art solely in terms of what it does or doesn't look like, older students are better able to look at something in terms of what the artist *intended*. Encourage students to ask thoughtful questions that elicit the creator's intent and interpretation and to discuss the work from this perspective.

Grouping Considerations

Reviewing can be done in partnerships, in small groups, or as a class. Partner reviews can often be the most productive, as students can devote substantial attention to each other's work; also, the privacy of a partner review can be especially helpful in the very early stages of a project, when students simply want to bounce ideas off another person or feel shy or tentative about their work. Partner reviewing also allows for some flexibility and spontaneity in the reviewing process—partners can set aside time to exchange reviews, but each can also request feedback as needed, even when a partner isn't requesting help in return. (Understandably, it would be much more difficult to convene a small group or the whole class to solicit on-the-spot feedback!)

On the many occasions when students want or need to hear more than one point of view, reviewing can be done in small groups. For example, when members of a group are creating individual contributions to be compiled or integrated into a group product, the group should review each member's work together and agree on any changes that need to be made for the final version. Small-group reviewing can also be interesting when students are individually working on the same assignment; reviewing each other's efforts, group members broaden their perspective by seeing other students' approaches to the same project and by hearing a variety of responses to their own work.

Try beginning whole-class review sessions with a graffiti board activity: Post four or five graffiti boards with headers such as "I was interested in . . .," "I am curious about . . .," "I was surprised by . . .," "It made me think of . . .," or the like. Have students move around the room, anonymously writing their responses and reading their classmates', and then use the comments as a springboard for the whole-class discussion.

Whole-class reviewing also offers the benefit of multiple perspectives and is particularly useful in preparing for a presentation to a broader audience. For example, the class can help a student refine a speech to be delivered at a school board meeting, provide feedback to classmates dancing in a school assembly, or review a dress rehearsal of a play to be performed for parents.

When students, partners, or groups have all done the same assignment, you might use a modified version of the blueprint as a class: While it would be impracticable to have the whole class use the how-to steps listed above to critique *every* piece of work, you could have informal class discussions about the different pieces. Encourage children to ask questions of each other and compare and contrast the different works—emphasizing, of course, that the point is not to judge which is "best" but to give everyone a chance to learn from and about one another, to recognize the many talents of their community of learners, and to appreciate differences and similarities in how classmates approach the same topic or problem.

Getting Students Ready

Academic Preparation

To do cooperative reviews, students need questioning and analytical skills that will help them prompt the creator's own reflection. Use some of the suggestions below to foster students' ability to do thoughtful, helpful reviews.

Define reviewing. If students have little experience with peer reviewing, they may only associate the term *review* with popular examples such as *Siskel and Ebert,* in which the reviewers deliver opinions *to the public,* to help the public make decisions about what's worth viewing. Make sure students understand the somewhat different objective in peer reviewing—that is, to have a helpful conversation *with the creator* about strengths and weaknesses of his or her work.

Review reviewing. Even when students understand the nature of peer reviewing, they may still need guidance and practice in holding such conversations. Suggest some "steps" for a peer review—for example, you might turn How to Do (on page 129) into a brief list of directions for students, posted where they can refer to it as necessary. Also point out that the steps emphasize questions *and discussion*—encourage students to have conversations with each other about their work, not just question-and-answer exchanges.

Refine reviewing. A helpful review uncovers specific information about a piece's strengths and limitations, but students may need some help pinpointing and expressing the underlying causes of their likes and dislikes.

To help students move beyond general opinions ("I like . . ." and "I hate . . .") to specific comments, suggest prompts such as

- I was interested in . . .
- I am curious about . . .

Students will benefit from collaboration with others outside their partnership or group—have partners or groups occasionally team up with another set of students to get fresh feedback about their work.

- I was surprised by . . .
- I was moved by . . .
- It made me think about . . .
- My first impression was . . ., but then I thought about . . .
- What stands out for me is . . .

Model the process. Revealing your own thinking about what you see in a piece can demonstrate key concepts (for example, the importance of being specific) and establish important guidelines for students' own reviewing. For example, review a "real life" piece of art (not the work of one of your students) and demonstrate the prompts suggested above and other such language that gives a creator information and insight (for example, "the painting really *feels* angry because the artist used brush strokes that look like angry slashes"). Give the students some practice, too—invite their reactions and ask follow-up questions that will help them recognize and articulate the range of thoughts and feelings that art can evoke. (It might also be interesting to read or show an interview with the artist, to give students a sense of the artist's perspective and compare it to their own impressions.)

Social|Ethical Preparation

Just as with peer editing, students need to feel part of a caring and respectful classroom community if they are to successfully give and receive reviews. The following are some social and ethical aspects of reviewing that you may want to help your students anticipate.

Responding kindly and honestly. Discuss with students the importance of being both honest and kind when responding to another student's work, and ask them to discuss ways they can carry out their responsibilities as reviewers without hurting or badly discouraging the creator. Remind students to speak in terms of what *they* are thinking about rather than in terms of what the creator "did"—for example, saying "I am curious about why you used green for the color of the sky" instead of "Whatever possessed you to paint the sky green?" (The point is nicely made in Miriam Cohen's *No Good in Art,* which young children might enjoy hearing you read aloud: In this story, a kindergarten art teacher insensitively points out what is wrong with a boy's picture and "fixes" it for him, without consulting him or considering his feelings.)

Being reviewed. Just as the reviewer is responsible for offering respectful and appropriate feedback, so is the creator responsible for accepting feedback in a fair and reasonable manner. This isn't always easy, however, no matter how considered and helpful a reviewer's comments are—and especially when they aren't! Discuss with students how they might respond to reviews that are discouraging, off the mark, or even unkind.

WAYS TO USE *Reviewing*

Reviewing can be used any time students create a product—art projects, historical illustrations, science displays, math games, musical or dramatic performances, and so on. Below are a few suggestions for using reviewing at various stages of creating a piece.

Encourage reviewers to take a few minutes to think about and jot down two or three initial responses to what they have seen before sharing their ideas with the creator. This will give reviewers a chance to clarify their thinking, deter any unfortunate impetuous remarks, and provide a bit of a framework to get the conversation going.

Under Way. When students review project plans and designs prior to execution, they can encourage and perhaps further inspire each other. For example, the whole class could review the mock-up of a class mural, small groups might review another group's plan for a model city, partners can review each other's sketches of posters publicizing their favorite books, and so on—any time students can enrich each other's thinking and final results!

After the Fact. Gentle and thoughtful peer reviews of finished pieces can inform students' future work—both the creator and reviewer will gain new insights. Given that the pieces being reviewed are finished, however, remind reviewers to refrain from comments about what the creator could or should do about the piece; instead encourage them to emphasize what works (and could be applied other efforts) and what doesn't (and could be done differently in the future).

Creative Collaboratives. Encourage students with the same creative interests—drawing, painting, dance, drama, music, etc.—to form a group whose members can offer each other support, feedback, and information. Besides reviewing one another's work, the group might also invite guest artists to share their work, methods, inspiration, and ideas. They might even extend membership beyond their classroom and peers—to all interested students in the school as well as interested parents, teachers, and community members.

EXTENSIONS

Reviewing activities can be extended in any of the following ways.

✱ **What Did We Learn?** Take some time to help students reflect on how their reviewing activity went—in other words, help them review their reviewing! Discuss what students think went well, any problems that arose, and how problems were resolved. Ask for examples of changes they made in their thinking or their work as a result of the review process, and any ideas students have about what they might do differently next time. Share your own observations, too—your insights will help students become more thoughtful reviewers.

Do not let reviews turn into competitions—when students are responding to the work of more than one student or group, their focus should be on the strengths and problems associated with each piece and similarities and differences in the way the artistic problem was handled—never on judging or comparing worthiness.

Write It Up. If the piece students are reviewing is a favorite or particularly important project, preserve the reviews in writing. For example, you might have all partners or small groups write out their reviews and compile them in a class book, or a subset of students might write a review that captures the ideas of everyone involved (remember to include the creator's responses as well!), or individuals might record their own responses on graffiti boards or in a class book, and so on.

One-Way Review. While reviewing has been described in these pages as a cooperative activity—essentially a thoughtful, productive conversation between classmates—students might also practice their skills in one-way reviews of art exhibits, plays, films, television shows, and so on. After the class has seen a film, for example, have students brainstorm the questions they would ask the filmmaker if they could, as well as their comments and suggestions. Have a small group of students use these ideas to draft a review; then mail it to the filmmaker—you may even receive an answer, in which case the review won't be one-way any longer!

JOINT PRODUCTS

Poetry

OETRY accounts for some of the best-loved and most evocative literature in the world's cultures, yet people are often intimidated by it, as well. Fortunately, since most children begin enjoying poetry quite young (think of Dr. Seuss or Mother Goose), ignorant of any "accessibility" issues, the regular reading and writing of poetry in elementary school can lead to a lifelong comfort with and appreciation of the genre.

In fact, writing poetry appeals to many students, even those who otherwise do not enjoy writing, because it allows them to break conventions (for example, poets don't have to write in complete sentences) and because it stresses distilling ideas by using few rather than many words. And writing poetry with a group demonstrates the genre's flexibility even further: Each group member contributes a line or section of the poem, and the whole group makes decisions about line order and form. As group members discuss their contributions, arrange and rearrange the lines, and help each other with language use and mechanics, they experience poetry (and language in general) as a powerful, malleable tool of communication.

WHY TO USE

- to help students appreciate and enjoy poetry
- to demystify poetry
- to encourage appreciation for different ways of seeing and saying things
- to encourage students to play with syntax, vocabulary, and sounds of language
- to give students a flexible, creative mode of self-expression
- to provide students who have limited writing skills the opportunity to create a longer, more complex product

WHEN TO USE

- in response to an evocative issue, topic, story, or event
- as a follow-up to reading poetry that speaks to students
- when students have the skill to respond respectfully to one another's work

HOW TO DO

The Poetry blueprint asks students to

- brainstorm and/or discuss ideas for the poem
- write their part of the poem
- read aloud their part of the poem to the rest of the group
- suggest, discuss, and agree on revisions to each other's writing
- with the group, decide on how to arrange the parts of the poem

Developmental Considerations

Jay birds land on wires very quickly.

I see lands of trees ahead of me
when I look.

> —*A five-year-old's composition after looking through a pair of binoculars*

Young children have a knack for seeing and describing their world in unusual ways—ways that often move the rest of us to see things with new eyes. This ability to tweak our assumptions and help us look at the world differently makes young children natural poets, since this quality is also a hallmark of poetry.

Simply give children an engaging, immediate subject about which to write; whereas older students can respond to more abstract topics, such as social issues or other people's experiences, younger children will do better with things they can see, touch, or personally relate to. For example, provide them with interesting experiences—observing an insect or animal, examining a rock or shell, gazing at the stars, or looking at the ordinary through a different lens, such as binoculars or a microscope—as the basis for writing poetry. Or tap into their feelings about important aspects of their lives—hopes, wishes, relationships with pets and people, and so on.

As for the actual writing of a group poem, emphasize ideas over form with young children—their group poems can simply be a mosaic of individual responses with minimal editing of each other's work. Encourage them to ask each other for help while working on their lines but emphasize that the focus of cooperative poetry writing is expressing their thoughts, not the mechanics of writing. To that end, free verse poetry is ideal for young writers: Lines can be of any length, they can be repeated, "sentences" can be incomplete, and syntax can be unconventional. Also to that end, beginning writers might write or dictate their lines, and students should feel free to use temporary spelling and punctuation on their first drafts.

I'll climb the highest tree and bring you back
an apple.

I'll go on the biggest stage and I will sing
the song you love.

I'll fly in the sky and bring you back the
shiniest star.

If you want, I'll read a book for you.

> —*Second-graders respond to the spirit of the book* Chicken Sunday

Ziggy

Ziggy feels like a velvet teddy bear,

He looks like pancakes with syrup,

He smells like nature,

He sounds like he's interested,

Ziggy tastes like a steak fresh off
the grill.

—*Fifth-graders describe their pet rat*

≈ HINT ≈

Because poetry is about feelings, you'll always want students to write about topics they genuinely care about. However, if a topic is likely to be intensely personal, it is probably best left for individual writing rather than a group effort.

Older students are more thoughtful about language and can experiment with different approaches to writing poetry, looking for the best way to convey their ideas. Encourage this exploration—unfettered by prose conventions, they may come up with some unique imagery (and as a reader, allow yourself to be unfettered, too, and enjoy their creations!). Likewise, as students work together, encourage their experimentation by suggesting that they strive for interesting relationships between ideas or sounds when putting together the individual parts of their group poems.

Grouping Considerations

Once you have introduced the class to cooperative poetry by doing some whole-class poems, you will probably find that small groups are the best configuration for poetry activities—enough mix and variety of ideas to keep things interesting, but not so many as to make the task unwieldy. There are projects, of course, for which partner poems are suitable.

Getting Students Ready

Academic Preparation

The best preparation for writing poetry is being exposed to a variety of good poetry—hearing it, reading it, and reading about it. Use the suggestions below to introduce your students to the many sounds of, and ideas about, poetry.

Read poetry. Read a variety of good poetry with the class—not just to introduce cooperative poetry activities, but all the time and throughout the curriculum. (Ways to Use Poetry, below, includes some suggested sources of poetry and related activities.)

Read about poetry. Sometimes hearing *about* poetry can inspire (and reassure) students. The introduction and appendix to *Talking to the Sun: An Illustrated Anthology of Poems for Young People* offer wonderfully practical and inspiring comments about poetry—for example:

"Different poems mean different things to different people at different times, but that isn't something you need to think about when you read a poem. In fact, worrying about finding the 'right' meaning can get in the way of your liking and understanding poetry. Just as you don't have to understand everything about your friends in order to enjoy them and learn things from them, so you don't have to understand everything about a poem to like it and get something from it." (This anthology, edited by Kenneth Koch and Kate Farrell and illustrated with works from New York's Metropolitan Museum of Art, is also a good source of poetry to read *to* students.)

Talk about poetry. Introduce poetry activities by reading an adult poem and talking with students about a significant idea in it—an idea that will inspire their own poems. For example, in his book about teaching poetry to children (listed in Ways to Use Poetry, below), Kenneth Koch describes how after reading William Blake's "The Tyger" he has his students write a poem "in which you are talking to a beautiful and mysterious creature and you can ask it anything you want—anything. You have the power to do this because you can speak its secret language." Koch points out that "what matters for the present is not that the children admire Blake and his achievement, but that each child be able to find a tyger of his own."

Read and talk about poetry with a poet. Invite a poet to the class to read her or his work and talk with students about writing poetry. (Many schools participate in Poets in the Schools programs, which can help you find a guest poet; get information about such programs from your principal or local or state arts council.)

Model the process. Do some whole-class poetry writing to give students a foundation for their small-group work. Choose a topic, such as "Surprise is . . ." (or "Red is . . .," "Friendship is . . .," etc.) and write it on the board. Ask students to think about a time when they were surprised and how they could describe that experience in a phrase that begins "Surprise is." Encourage them to think of many kinds of surprises: happy, silly, scary, and so on. Record students' responses on strips of paper, and with students' help arrange the strips into a poem. If students' descriptions lack detail, ask questions to help enliven their images; model ways to respectfully ask for clarification, make suggestions, and incorporate different people's ideas into one poem.

≈ HINT ≈

Use a pocket chart and sentence strips to make it easier for students to play with different line arrangements during whole-class and small-group poetry writing activities.

Social/Ethical Preparation

When creating a poem from their individual contributions, group members must be able to cooperate on several levels—in making and accepting constructive suggestions about each other's work and in agreeing on the final composition of the poem. The following are some social and ethical aspects of poetry activities you may want to help students anticipate.

Responding respectfully. Help students appreciate that poets enable people to see things in new ways by saying things in new ways—and that perhaps they'll learn from each other's new way of saying things, too. Encourage them to think about how they could respond to a group member whose ideas they find difficult to understand. How would they like someone to respond to them if *their* ideas were found difficult to understand? What kinds of questions or comments might make groupmates feel defensive or insecure about their work? What kinds of approaches would help them discuss and clarify their ideas?

Editing respectfully. In group poetry writing, groupmates suggest edits to each other's work—but even the most objective or minor suggestion, delivered tactlessly, can feel difficult to accept. Discuss the benefits and burdens of group editing, and ask students to consider how to make editing suggestions. What are some considerate ways to make editing suggestions? How would they like someone to approach them with an editing suggestion? Why can it be difficult to accept editing suggestions, no matter how helpful? How can students handle such difficulties?

WAYS TO USE *Poetry*

ACTIVITIES

There are many excellent guides available for using poetry with young people, such as *Let's Do a Poem: Introducing Poetry to Children* by Nancy Larrick (which is especially helpful for introducing poetry to young students). Another excellent resource is Kenneth Koch's *Rose, Where Did You Get That Red?*, which contains great poetry, student poetry inspired by great poetry, and lessons that served as a bridge between the two; although Koch does not ask children to write cooperatively, many of his "poetry ideas" can easily be adapted for group poetry writing. You might also try *Knock at a Star: A Child's Introduction to Poetry,* edited by X. J. Kennedy and Dorothy M. Kennedy, which includes dozens of poems categorized in ways that help children appreciate the many ways a poem "works"; the book also has concise, useful suggestions about using poetry with children. Or, try some of the ideas below!

Feelings. Have group members talk about a single "feeling" word, such as *surprise,* and what that word means to them. Encourage students to ask one another questions about their ideas and help each other express their thoughts. After some conversation, have group members each compose a line beginning with the theme word ("Surprise is . . .") that describes a favorite or meaningful association; the group then decides on a line order and makes editing suggestions. Keep in mind that people can feel vulnerable revealing feelings—especially negative ones—so it is best to start with words that evoke happy feelings (such as *surprise, curious, excited)* until you see that students are accustomed to working kindly and respectfully with each other. As you continue using this activity, increase the challenge by introducing more complex theme words, such as *ambivalent* or *devoted,* or words that might have more sensitive connotations, such as *alone* or *afraid.* (The versatile *C Is for Curious: An ABC of Feelings* by Woodleigh Hubbard is a good source of words for this activity.)

In Character. Adapt the activity above to help students gain insight into stories the class is reading. Choose a feeling that is a central element of a story (for example, Jimmy Jo's shyness in Katherine Paterson's *Come Sing, Jimmy Jo*) or have group members themselves identify a feeling theme. Ask students to put themselves in the character's place and write their feelings poem from the character's perspective.

Use Your Senses! In this activity, students work in small groups to explore how all the senses apply to an object, place, event, or concept—which can add thought-provoking dimensions to science, history, literature, and other curriculum areas. Have students observe and handle an interesting object and, focusing on one sense at a time, ask themselves such questions about the object as If this had a taste, what might it taste like? What does the sound of this remind me of? What smells do I associate with this? What words would I use to describe what I see and feel? Encourage students to search for associations that linger just beyond literal descriptions. Each group member then composes a descriptive line based on one of the senses, and the group agrees on how to arrange the lines to create the poem. After students have experience writing about tangible objects, invite them to apply the senses to more abstract ideas (such as *friendship, guilt, green, success),* historical incidents, and so on.

Art Poetry. Students are often asked to illustrate stories or poems— but the process is reversed for this activity, in which students write a poem inspired by a piece of art. Have small groups select an art print or photograph and create a poem about the picture; if possible, have available a wide variety of art from which students can choose (better yet, visit your local art museum and have students work from the real thing). To introduce the activity, show students an example of poetry translated to art in *Talking to the Sun:* On page 90, William Carlos Williams's "The Great Figure" is accompanied by a Charles Demuth painting inspired by the poem.

Story Poetry. As a variation on Art Poetry, have partners or small groups use a favorite illustration or scene in a book as the basis for a poem about the story. For example, have each group member take a different character's perspective to write a line or verse about an illustration or passage. Or do a variation of Use Your Senses! and have group members write about a different sense—what a person or animal in the illustration might be seeing, hearing, tasting, smelling, and feeling.

EXTENSIONS

Poetry activities can be extended in any of the following ways.

❋ **What Did We Learn?** Give students a chance to talk about the group writing process. Based on your observations of group interactions, ask about a topic (or topics) most likely to yield an interesting discussion: for example, How did group members show consideration and respect for different ways of seeing or saying things? What kinds of suggestions did groupmates make about each other's work that proved helpful? Did any group have difficulty making decisions about line order? How did groups resolve such difficulties? What did students like about writing poetry with a group? What didn't they like? What might they do differently next time?

Poetry Reading. Have a poetry reading so that groups can share their work with each other. Give students time to plan and practice their presentations (for example, groups might choose a single reader or perform a choral reading), and discuss with the whole class the atmosphere they would like to create for the reading (Do they want to present from a stage? Serve refreshments? Invite guests? Have the option of playing recorded music to accompany their readings? and so on). If students seem inclined toward ambitious ideas for this event, hold a class meeting to discuss plans and assign responsibilities.

Poetry Art. Have groups illustrate their own or another group's poem and compile a class book or bulletin board of these poetry-art partnerships.

Narrative

WE USUALLY think of writing as a solo endeavor—we may even have images of writers sequestering themselves to write in isolation—but that's not always the case. Much writing is collaborated on by two or more people sharing ideas, information, expertise, and even the writing itself, and it's a type of collaboration well worth exploring with students. Narrative writing poses particular challenges and rewards for collaborators, of course—the challenge of melding different people's ideas of what to tell and how to tell it, and the rewards of working with a richer mix of ideas than individual writers might have on their own. Working in pairs or small groups, students also have the opportunity to combine, balance, and benefit from each other's talents—one may be particularly imaginative, another able to organize ideas, someone else a skillful writer, and so on. Writing together, students learn to appreciate each other's contributions, different approaches to the writing process, and the fun of group improvisation as they create their collaborative narratives.

WHY TO USE

- to help students appreciate and enjoy writing from their imaginations
- to encourage students' appreciation for different ways of seeing and saying things
- to experience the pleasures of group improvisation
- to foster students' oral and written language
- to foster students' understanding of storytelling conventions
- to provide students with the opportunity to create written products that are more complex and elaborate than they can produce on their own

WHEN TO USE

- when students have the skill to respond respectfully to one another's work
- when literature, history, or social studies curriculum poses interesting storytelling possibilities
- when students' shared experiences pose interesting storytelling possibilities

HOW TO DO

The Narrative blueprint asks students to

- brainstorm and discuss ideas for the narrative
- agree on what to include in the narrative
- divide the writing into sections and decide who will do each
- write their sections
- review each other's drafts and discuss revisions
- combine the revised sections

Developmental Considerations

Younger Students

As anybody knows who has ever listened to a preschooler's seemingly never-ending story, very young children can be eager storytellers—but writing the story down might pose some difficulties. Even the most experienced writer can find the sight of a blank page intimidating, and beginning writers may find it easier to work "backward"—first illustrating their part of a narrative and then adding captions to their illustrations (give students the choice of approaching the task from either direction). To encourage their developing writing skills—and their enjoyment of them—have beginning writers dictate their narratives or use temporary spelling if they are able; if possible, also set up a writing center in the classroom (stocked with lined and unlined paper, writing and drawing tools, staples, hole punches, envelopes, dictionaries, etc.) so that children have lots of informal opportunities to practice their literacy. Since students using the center at the same time will invariably share ideas and writing, a writing center has the benefit of giving students some spontaneous practice in collaborative writing, as well.

In fact, the collaborative aspect of group writing might take quite a bit of practice, and you may want to start off with projects that allow group members to work independently and then fit their independent products together. Group members might each contribute an illustrated page to the story, for example, or write sentences on strips of paper and paste them on a page with other group members' contributed sentences. Many topics lend themselves to such an arrangement—for example, groups might write about a field trip, with each group member contributing a favorite memory and then working together to arrange the memories to tell a story, or group members might write about how they get ready for school in the morning and then put their writing together to create a story, and so on.

As students progress, a good first step toward more collaborative work is partner dialogues, in which partners write a dialogue between two characters, each filling in the words for one of the characters. These dialogues require students to pay attention to a partner's ideas, but the writing resembles spoken language and can be relatively short; in fact, you might have children write their dialogues in cartoon form, with characters speaking in thought bubbles—a format that is both familiar and engaging to most young children.

Older Students

Older students can tackle more ambitious writing tasks and work more collaboratively than younger children, who are still struggling with encoding skills. (If, however, your students are unused to writing collaboratively, you might start off with projects that allow group members to work independently and then fit their independent products together.) Older students have also been exposed to, and will enjoy experimenting with, a wider range of genres—everything from historical fiction that synthesizes what they have learned in social studies, to fantasy and science fiction that incorporates their growing scientific knowledge, to adventure and romance that reflects their maturing ideas and dreams of the world around them.

With more collaboration, however, comes the possibility of more disagreement among group members, and students may need some help achieving an even-handed, nonjudgmental approach to group narrative writing. Often this comes down to their recognizing, valuing, and respecting that different people contribute to group products in different ways—and that they themselves are capable of finding ways to settle disagreements fairly. While it is important for all group members to contribute to a product, for example, equity does not require each group member to take a turn as scribe, contribute the same number of pages, think up the same number of ideas, and so on. With your help, older students will be able to develop more sophisticated understandings of what it means to divide work fairly, appreciation for different kinds of contributions, and problem-solving skills.

Grouping Considerations

Cooperative narrative writing can be done in partners or small groups, depending upon the nature and scope of the task at hand. For example, working in pairs is particularly effective when students are writing dialogues between two characters; small groups, in contrast, are a better configuration for large projects that can be divided into more manageable elements. Many of the activities below suggest that small groups divide the writing task and then all together agree on what to revise and how to combine the sections, which makes the writing more manageable while still challenging students to collaborate on the overall product; as your students collaborative skills mature, they can initiate more sophisticated approaches to defining and appreciating each other's contributions.

Getting Students Ready

Academic Preparation

Make a connection. If students feel invested in a topic, they will rarely have trouble knowing what to write—and even when they are writing about a preassigned topic (rather than one they have chosen themselves), you can help them feel connected to it. The surest way to connect students to a topic is to invite their personal experiences, worries, memories, or opinions about it; you might engage students in a number of other ways, as well: Read a poem or story excerpt that will pique their interest in the subject, read something you have written that helps them understand its relevance to you, or have students role-play some aspect of it.

Promote prewriting. Much of the benefit of group writing is derived from the discussion that happens *before* students actually put pen to paper. Some students may have little experience of (and patience for) these preliminaries, however, and you might need to emphasize the importance of prewriting conversations. Encourage students to take time to think and talk together, and suggest different prewriting strategies groups might use to get started—brainstorming and talking, drawing, outlining or mapping ideas, role-playing, and so on.

Emphasize ideas. Stressing the importance of prewriting conversations will also help convey that you value the *ideas* students express in their writing, not just their ability to use the correct spelling and punctuation to express those ideas. Don't discourage group members from helping each other with the mechanics of writing, of course, but first and foremost encourage students to concentrate on content.

Teach some technique. Then again, depending upon the kind of narrative students will be writing, it may sometimes behoove you to give brief minilessons (not longer than three to ten minutes) on specific, relevant writing strategies and mechanical skills. A good source of ideas for such minilessons is Lucy M. Calkins's *The Art of Teaching Writing* (Heinemann Educational Books, 1986).

Model the process. Go over directions for student groups, modeling or discussing any areas that may cause difficulties. You won't be able to model an entire writing process, of course, but you might role-play or discuss aspects of the process that are unfamiliar to students (or ones with which you have observed they need help). If students are new to collaborative or narrative writing, you might also model the process by starting with some whole-class narratives: Brainstorm the narrative together, have each student contribute a line, and review and revise the results together.

Social/Ethical Preparation

When incorporating different people's ideas into one narrative, group members can be faced with some interesting challenges—agreeing on what narrative to tell or what to include in it, dividing the work, accepting each other's ideas and constructive suggestions, agreeing on the final composition, and so on. The following are some social and ethical aspects of narrative-writing activities you may want to help students anticipate.

Recognizing contributions. When students have a clearly "defined" task, such as writing, they may too narrowly define what it means to contribute to the task and fail to recognize all the different ways people may be helping: suggesting interesting ideas, setting ideas in effective language, doing the actual writing or acting as scribe, helping resolve disagreements that arise in the group, and so on. Help students appreciate their own and others' ways of contributing with a brief whole-class discussion about such questions as What are different ways people can contribute to the group's work? How can it be helpful for different group members to have different strengths and interests? How can that be challenging?

Sharing the work. Even when they appreciate that people contribute to a task in different ways, children may still be ruled by their keen sense of fairness about people pulling their own weight. Anticipate decisions groups will have to make about dividing the work fairly (such as sharing the writing) and invite students to brainstorm solutions.

Responding respectfully. Group members will be fielding each other's ideas throughout the narrative-writing process—ideas about what to write, how to manage the work, how to put the piece together, and so on. Whether artistic or logistical, practical or outlandish, "right" or "wrong," these ideas should be respectfully received and thoughtfully considered. Ask students to take the perspective of the person offering an idea: How would they feel if their ideas were dismissed out of hand or ridiculed? What kinds of questions or comments might make group-mates feel defensive or insecure about their ideas and work? What kinds of approaches would be helpful? Ask students concrete questions to help them think of ways that people might disagree with one another and show respect at the same time, such as What if Arta suggests an idea that doesn't make sense to Joseph? What could Joseph do?

Editing and being edited. In group narrative writing, groupmates will have comments and suggestions about each other's work—but it's not always easy to accept these suggestions. Ask for students' ideas about how to make the editing process as constructive (and easy to swallow) as possible; turn to Editing on page 123 for further ideas.

WAYS TO USE *Narrative*

ACTIVITIES   Cooperative narrative writing can be most successful when students write from a shared experience or a prompt, such as a photo. Below are a few suggestions.

What Happened Next? Have students read the beginning of a story and then write their own ending for it, applying whatever is relevant from the story and inventing the rest. For example, folktales are ideal prompts because they generally present a character in some dilemma, so you can give students just the part of the story that presents the dilemma but doesn't hint at the resolution. (Avoid stories where it might be within character for antagonists to simply kill each other off, though.) Another good prompt is a historical context, which enables students to write creatively using their knowledge of history—just be sure students understand there's no particular right or wrong or by-the-history-book story ending expected of them. Initiate such activities by reading the beginning of the story aloud to the class; then have students re-read the beginning with their group, discuss what they know about the characters and the situation, and brainstorm different possible endings before deciding what to write.

Worth a Thousand Words. According to the old adage, a photograph or art print should be good for at least a thousand words of

prose from students! Have students write about the story they see in an interesting, evocative picture—photos you've brought from home, art prints, pictures clipped from magazines, or anything else that has some narrative quality. Usually, but not always, pictures that show some interaction between people work best—the best test of whether a picture will work for the activity is to try to think up a story for it yourself (if you can't, chances are your students won't be able to, either). If possible, have each group work with a different picture, both for the sake of variety and to avoid competition to tell the "best" story about the same picture. Suggest that groups take a few minutes to quietly study and think about the picture before brainstorming, and suggest that they discuss what may have occurred before *and* after the photo was taken. Display students' stories with their corresponding pictures.

If It Could Speak to You. Bring in objects that could suggest a story—an antique doll, a head of lettuce, an old basket, a hammer, a well-worn baseball, a potted plant, or the like—and ask students to think about what story the object might tell if it could speak to them. Suggest some questions to get their thinking started—for example, Where did it come from? To whom does (or did) it belong? What is (or was) it used for? What is the happiest thing it ever saw? What is the saddest thing it ever saw? Ask students what other questions occur to them when they look at the object(s), too.

If I Could Speak to You. Although writing letters isn't specifically an exercise in narrative writing, it *is* a great way for students to respond to a narrative. Students often make emotional connections to story characters and their situations, and expressing that connection deepens both their understanding of a story and their appreciation of reading. After the class has read and discussed a story, have small groups talk about what they would like to say to a character in the story—different groups may decide to address different characters—and agree on how to present that in a letter to the character. A variation on this activity would be to write a letter from one story character to another or a letter to a historical figure. (You may need to make sure, however, that younger children understand that the story characters will not actually receive or be able to respond to their letters!)

True to Life. Students may be accustomed to reading fictional narratives, but of course some of the best stories in the world are those based on real people and events. Challenge students to find a story in an everyday shared experience—a game of softball, lunch, recess, a science experiment, a field trip, a class meeting, an assembly, or the school day in general. What happened that was especially exciting? Silly? Weird? Surprising? Funny? Sad? Scary? Have a few whole-class informal conversations about such topics (for example, a review of a day or a week) before introducing this as a writing activity, and help students think about ways to write about classmates and other real people in ways that are both engaging and respectful. In fact, be sure to emphasize this last point and help students understand the importance of not writing about their classmates in embarrassing or hurtful ways when depicting them in a narrative.

≈ HINT ≈

While students should be encouraged to do plenty of peer editing, you may want to serve as final copyeditor for any "published" pieces of writing.

Without a Word. Wordless books demonstrate the essence of narrative and help children learn important conventions of storytelling—and not only are they the first texts children can read independently, they are also the first narratives children can "write" independently. Once students have had some exposure to wordless books, have them work in small groups to create their own, using any of the ideas suggested in the activities above. Afterward, compile a class library of the books so that classmates can read each other's creations.

EXTENSIONS

Narrative writing activities can be extended in any of the following ways.

✳ **What Did We Learn?** Give students a chance to talk about the group writing process, and help get the discussion going by asking questions such as How did group work go? What went well? What difficulties did you have? How is group writing helpful? How is it difficult? What did you learn about how to tell a story? Also ask questions to highlight successes and problems you observed during student work: How did you solve any disagreements that arose in your groups? Can anyone suggest another way they might have solved their problem? What did someone in your group do to help you? How did group members show respect for one another? and so on.

Second Opinion. Have groups read their stories (or sections of their stories) aloud to the class and solicit feedback. For example, groups might read aloud from a work in progress specifically to get help with some particular aspect of the narrative—"We were wondering if this part makes sense," "Can you get a picture of what this character looks like?" and so on. You might also have groups exchange drafts for a more formal peer editing effort (see Editing on page 123 for further ideas).

If I Could Speak to You, Too. When students write letters to a story character, an interesting follow-up would be to have groups exchange letters and respond in character.

Go Public. Since writing is an act of communication, it is important that students have an audience for their completed work—their classmates, members of the school community, their family, or other audiences outside of the classroom. For example, partners or groups could host a read-aloud night to share their narratives with their families, produce a class anthology to take home or place in the school library, create a hallway display of story excerpts and illustrations, read their stories to a buddy class, and so on.

Expository

EXPOSITORY WRITING, just like narrative writing, can provide a rich collaborative experience for students, but to a different end: Instead of combining their imaginations or memories to tell a story, students combine their ideas to inform or persuade an audience about a topic. As with narrative writing, partners or group members must work together to decide what to include in their prose and how to divide the work; then, after each student has written her or his part, they work together again to decide how best to combine the individual pieces into a coherent whole. The challenge, of course, is for students to discuss, compare, and contrast their ideas to arrive at a successful melding of their contributions—and the reward is their opportunity to enrich their thinking, expand their ideas, and enliven their writing.

WHY TO USE

- to foster students' oral and written language
- to increase pleasure and facility in expository writing
- to foster appreciation for the knowledge, interests, and abilities of different classmates
- to encourage students' appreciation for different ways of seeing and saying things
- to encourage students to deeply explore an aspect of an issue, event, etc., in the context of the whole

WHEN TO USE

- when students have the skill to respond respectfully to one another's work
- when a project will benefit from different points of view, skills, and knowledge
- when literature or content areas pose interesting expository possibilities
- when class discussions highlight interesting expository possibilities
- when a project is large and can be better executed by students working together

HOW TO DO

The Expository blueprint asks students to

- brainstorm and discuss ideas for the piece
- agree on the content of the piece
- divide the writing into sections and decide who will do each
- write their sections
- review each other's drafts and discuss revisions
- combine the revised sections

Developmental Considerations

Younger Students

Although many of us associate expository text with mature, even learned writing, much of children's early writing is expository in nature, too: a child composing a birthday list, labeling a box "Special Things," or making a "Do Not Enter!" sign for a bedroom door is writing to convey information. What these examples have in common is that the child sees the purpose of the writing—understands the reason, knows the audience, even initiates the process.

Likewise, collaborative expository writing projects should be connected to real things and real audiences so that young children see the purpose of their writing. Think, for example, of students writing the instructions for cleaning the hamster cage, making a poster of classroom norms, composing a list for a substitute teacher, and labeling storage cubbies: These are purposeful activities that not only allow students to use their emerging writing skills, but also actively connect children to the life of the classroom and build their sense of the classroom community. In fact, children can compose and write many of the classroom charts, signs, and labels traditionally made by the teacher— and because beginning readers are more likely to understand text that they construct themselves, such writing also becomes an important impetus for learning to read.

As always, the emphasis should be on content rather than on writing mechanics. For example, beginning writers can dictate or copy text, can combine writing and drawing to express their ideas, and can use invented spelling to get their ideas into print. Also encourage group members to share writing strategies, skills, and knowledge with each other as they work.

Older Students

Group expository writing on a topic of mutual interest is an effective way to increase older children's pleasure and facility in writing as well as their appreciation for the knowledge, interests, and abilities of different classmates. Older students can also be exposed to, and try their hand at, lots of different kinds of expository writing—reports, instructions, persuasive essays, exhibit notes, and so on.

Collaboration also allows older students to tackle larger and more sophisticated projects than any individual group member could accomplish alone—publications such as yearbooks or newsletters, for example. You'll want to help inexperienced students gauge what they can accomplish with the available time, skills, and resources, however—watch groups as they are planning their projects, and keep an eye out for those who need help narrowing their focus as well as for others who need help expanding their thinking.

Grouping Considerations

Expository writing is well suited to small-group work, as many expository writing projects (producing a magazine, newsletter, or yearbook, for example) are ambitious undertakings whose success depends on many heads and hands. It is usually easiest to coordinate such projects by having group members write individually or in pairs, with the writing stimulated, reviewed, and compiled by the whole group. Similarly, a whole-class project could be divided into discrete small-group tasks.

Students can also write in partnerships, of course—for example, when an activity requires students to reach consensus on a single piece (such as a book or movie review), it is often more effective to have students work in pairs.

Getting Students Ready

Academic Preparation

Make a connection. For students to write interestingly and well about a topic, it helps for them to *find* the topic interesting—after all, would you want to go to the effort of conveying information about a topic you find boring or persuade an audience of something other than your own convictions? Likewise, students need to feel some connection to the subject of their expository writing: Give them as much leeway as possible in choosing the topic about which they will write, help them understand why you consider an assignment important and relevant to their lives, connect it to students' prior knowledge or familiarity with the subject, spur their interest with related reading or class discussions, or otherwise try to engage them in the purpose or significance of a topic before they tackle it.

Promote prewriting. The thinking and talking that students do before they start writing are just as important as the writing itself—not only do they drum up ideas during their prewriting discussions, but they also learn from and about each other. Explain why it's time well spent to have such conversations, no matter how eager students are to get started on their writing, and suggest different prewriting strategies groups might use—brainstorming and talking, drawing, outlining or mapping ideas, role-playing, and so on. Also encourage students to probe each other's thinking during their conversations—emphasizing the need for thoughtful prewriting conversations will convey that good writing is about ideas, not just mechanics.

Teach some technique. If, however, you have noticed particular mechanical aspects of students' writing that *do* warrant some attention, provide brief minilessons (not longer than three to ten minutes) on those skills. For some minilesson ideas, consult Lucy M. Calkins's *The Art of Teaching Writing* (Heinemann Educational Books, 1986).

Provide opportunities for practice. Informal collaboration around a shared interest is good preparation for more formal group work, and a classroom writing center is an ideal way to prompt such "practice" collaboration. Depending upon your students' literacy development, stock the writing center with magnetic letters, word banks, word charts, dictionaries, paper of all sorts, small blank books, writing and drawing implements, and related supplies (stamps, hole punches, staplers, stickers, and the like); add some informational books to inspire students, and see what interesting conversations and efforts result.

Model the process. Go over directions for student groups and model or discuss any areas that may cause difficulties or are unfamiliar to students. Or show them a work of your own—perhaps you and a colleague wrote a grant proposal together, or a small group of teachers wrote a parent handbook or a visitors' guide to the school, or the like—and explain some of the thinking processes you went through to produce it.

Social/Ethical Preparation

As with all collaborative writing activities, students doing expository writing together will have to negotiate content, style, and execution. The following are some social and ethical aspects of expository writing activities you may want to help students anticipate.

Recognizing contributions. Doing a writing project together encompasses myriad tasks and aptitudes, but students may not always recognize the many different ways that group members have contributed: suggesting interesting ideas, setting ideas in effective language, doing the actual writing or acting as scribe, helping resolve disagreements that arise in the group, and so on. Help students appreciate their own and others' ways of contributing with a brief whole-class discussion about such questions as What are different ways people can contribute to the group's work? How can it be helpful for different group members to have different strengths and interests? How can that be challenging?

Sharing the work. As you help students appreciate different kinds of contributions, tangible and otherwise, also help them take this into consideration when deciding how to divide their work fairly. Anticipate decisions groups will have to make (for example, what to do when every group member wants to write the same article for their magazine), and invite students to brainstorm solutions in a whole-class discussion.

Responding respectfully. Like any group endeavor, group expository writing necessarily involves the exchange of ideas on all sorts of matters—what to write, how to divide the work, how to combine individual contributions, and so on. Lead the class in a brief discussion about how to give each other a fair hearing, and suggest that students take the perspective of the person offering an idea: How would they feel if their ideas were dismissed out of hand or ridiculed? What kinds of questions or comments might make groupmates feel defensive or insecure about their ideas and work? What kinds of approaches would be helpful? Invite volunteers to role-play their suggestions.

Editing and being edited. Being respectful doesn't preclude disagreement, and students will be critiquing each other's ideas and work throughout the group expository writing process. But no matter how well tendered these critiques may be, it's not always easy to be the recipient. Invite students' ideas about how to make the editing process as constructive, kind, and productive as possible (turn to Editing on page 123 for further ideas).

WAYS TO USE *Expository*

ACTIVITIES   Opportunities for cooperative expository writing abound throughout the academic and social life of the classroom. Below are just a few suggestions.

Word Collage. Information can be conveyed with discrete words and images, not just sentences and paragraphs, so this activity is ideal for students who are just beginning to write letters or words. Have students work in groups of four, and start them off by asking them to think of words they associate with the topic at hand—grandparents, volcanoes, courage, the ocean—any topic related to a story or subject the class is studying. Have group members discuss each other's suggestions and then each write and illustrate (or decorate) their words, each on a separate piece of paper. Finally, have the groups decide how to arrange the individual words on a background. Children adjust the task to their own skill, knowledge, and interests by focusing on letters, words, or drawing; using more or less sophisticated words; and including words in the different languages of group members.

Post It! Have small groups assume responsibility for designing and making the many signs, charts, and labels that help organize the classroom and help students learn—for example, lists of class norms, cubbyhole labels, instructions for doing "housecleaning" or academic tasks, and so on. Create groups to make signs as needs arise, rotating the responsibility so everyone gets a turn. Or add "sign makers" to the list of classroom helpers, with two or three students collaborating on the job at a time. (A fun way to introduce the role and responsibilities of sign making would be to read aloud Tedd Arnold's *The Signmaker's Assistant,* a humorous story about the power of the written word.)

How-Do-You-Do's. One way to build students' writing skills and sense of classroom community is to have them create how-to manuals that explain the norms, values, and day-to-day operations of the classroom. Such manuals can be tailored to any newcomer to the class: a "How to Sub This Class" manual for substitute teachers, a "Learn about Your New Class" booklet for new students, an orientation manual for parent volunteers, and so on. Students could also create "internal" manuals that describe how to do different classroom jobs, such as "How to Be the Class Zookeeper," "How to Be the Class Gardener," or "How to Be the Ball Monitor." Introduce the activity with a class meeting to brainstorm and discuss what the new person needs to know about the class; help students anticipate the specific needs of different kinds of newcomers and the specific demands of different kinds of jobs. Also discuss the tone of the manual with the class—how the use of language, humor, and art might make a newcomer feel welcome, for example, or might prevent instructions from sounding bossy. After the class agrees on what to include in the manual, have each group write a section.

Field Notes. When students record their observations of the natural world, they stimulate both their curiosity about and knowledge of their environment. Begin with a "field experience" such as a visit to a garden, field, or wooded area; a close look at a square foot of school playground; an observation of a classroom pet, insect, or other animal; daily observations of a plant or other life form in the classroom; and so on. Have a discussion ahead of time to help students anticipate what they might see, why it might be significant, and how they might record their observations—for example, students could make lists; take measurements; or make other notes to help them remember what they see, hear, and feel (or they might just take it all in and record it later). After their field work, have group members discuss their observations; decide what they want to include in their notes; divide the work of writing and illustrating different sections; and then review, revise, and compile the sections.

Get the Word Out. Have groups create an advertising brochure or flyer to publicize an event such as Back-to-School Night, Family Math Night, Open House, or the like. Begin with a whole-class brainstorm about necessary information (time, date, location, and so on) and perhaps some "selling points," and then leave it to the groups to come up with inviting presentations. This activity can be adjusted to suit your students' cooperative skills, writing ability, conceptual complexity, and attention span: For example, younger or inexperienced students might construct a brochure consisting of three or four independent sentences and illustrations, while older students might take a few class periods to produce a brochure that includes headlines, several paragraphs rewritten for style and coherence, and photographs or illustrations carefully chosen to coordinate with the text.

. . . That's Fit to Print. A student-produced newsletter about class goings-on is an important link between school and home, keeping parents informed and inviting students to reflect on their accomplishments, as well. Have groups rotate responsibility for producing a weekly or monthly class newsletter; begin with a class meeting to give all students a chance to offer suggestions about what to include in the issue, and then have the responsible group produce a draft (group members needn't do all the writing—they could also solicit articles from other classmates). Have the whole class look over the draft (see Editing on page 123) before the group produces the final version.

In Circulation. Producing a magazine together encourages students to explore a topic from a variety of angles and allows them to pool their talents, interests, and knowledge to create a product larger and richer than they could probably produce on their own. Introduce the activity by inviting students to share their favorite magazines and explain what makes them appealing; also show magazines you find especially effective (and be sure to point out the large staffs involved in producing a magazine!). If possible, use as your models magazines or journals devoted to a single subject, as students will be producing single-topic publications. To give students some insight into how to construct an article, have them read a published article related to the magazine topic and then discuss it. Then have groups begin their magazines by brainstorming what they know about their magazine topic, what articles they might write about the topic, and how to organize these articles in their magazine; group members will then have to decide how to divide the work, write their respective articles, review each other's first drafts and make revisions, and finally combine the finished articles in the agreed-upon manner. Afterward, have the groups circulate their magazines—in class or beyond.

Taking Stock. As school draws to a close, creating a yearbook helps students recognize their accomplishments and appreciate their classroom community. Give students a couple of days to think of the important events and learnings of the school year, and then hold a class meeting to list and categorize their ideas (see Sorting and Classifying on page 32). Have each group choose a category and brainstorm how to chronicle that aspect of their class history and divide the work; group members will edit each other's work, of course, but you might also have groups swap their sections for group peer editing. Decide with the class whether they would like to add anything else—favorite jokes, for example, or small self-portraits akin to the photo portraits of students found in most yearbooks; also involve the whole class in decisions about the overall layout of the book. If possible, make a copy of the book for each student and give students time to exchange autographs and phone numbers in their yearbooks, or place the yearbook in the school library.

Class Correspondence. As the need arises, have partners or groups assume responsibility for writing letters for the classroom community—for example, to ask for information related to a topic of study or a prospective field trip destination; to tell an author what the class thought of her or his book; to thank a parent helper, substitute, special guest, or others who have enriched the class in some way; and so on. Before the group begins writing, have a class meeting to discuss what should be included in the letter—background information, the specifics of the request, how the recipient's response will contribute to classroom activities, and so on. Have students edit the first draft as a class, being sure to review kind and helpful ways of responding to others' work beforehand (see Editing on page 123). Also encourage students to collaborate on such letters for partner or small-group projects.

EXTENSIONS Expository writing activities can be extended in any of the following ways.

✳ **What Did We Learn?** Many of the expository writing activities suggested here are directed to a real audience—classmates, parents, or people in the community—and much of the satisfaction students derive from their writing depends on whether it accomplishes its goal: Did the brochure draw people to an event? Did the guest speaker accept the invitation? Did the yearbook capture the feelings students have about their class? Spend some time helping students reflect on such outcomes as well as on the collaborative writing process itself. Discuss what students thought went well, the advantages and disadvantages of writing as a group, how they solved disagreements (and whether there were other alternatives), and so on. Be sure to focus on successes as well as shortcomings, including your own observations that might help students think about their work together.

What Do You Think? Have groups read their writing aloud to the class and solicit feedback. For example, groups might read aloud from a work in progress to address a concern with some particular aspect of the narrative: Would you be able to follow these directions? Is there enough explanation there to understand why this is important? and so on.

Finishing Touches. In most cases, expository writing is "for publication," in which case students may need several class sessions for peer editing and revisions. While the emphasis should be on helping each other with content, students can also edit mechanical errors as they are able, with the final copyediting left to you (see Editing on page 123 for further ideas about peer editing).

Follow-Up. When students' expository writing projects have involved writing letters asking for information or the like, make sure students follow up on any response they receive. For example, if an author responds to a query about her or his book, have students write again to tell the author how that information helped them think about the book or complete a related activity; if they wrote to request information about a field trip destination, have them follow up with a letter describing their experience there; and so on.

Graphic Arts

IN COOPERATIVE graphic arts activities, groups create a drawing, painting, or collage that incorporates the ideas of all group members. These projects can help students organize, clarify, and express their thoughts on a wide range of experiences—social studies or science topics, fields trips or assemblies, stories or poems, even recess and other such everyday events. Working together, students learn from each other's contributions, see possibilities besides what they had imagined, and inspire each other's creativity. Group graphic arts projects also bring out the skills of different kinds of learners, giving students who communicate more adeptly visually than verbally a chance to shine—and perhaps expanding students' ideas of the talents and abilities that make a person a "good student."

WHY TO USE

- to consolidate and represent shared knowledge or experience

- to help students recognize how art can communicate knowledge and ideas

- to help students learn elements and principles of design and composition

- to add variety to the ways that students convey academic learning

- to broaden students' opportunities as learners and contributors in classroom life

WHEN TO USE

- when knowledge or experience about a topic can be graphically represented

- when the focus of the art work is shared knowledge or experience rather than individual self-expression

- when all students have something to contribute to the product

- after a unit of study or shared experience, to summarize, categorize, and reflect on what was learned

HOW TO DO

The Graphic Arts blueprint asks students to

- brainstorm and discuss what they know about the topic

- decide what to include in their product

- decide how to divide the work

- decide on the composition or arrangement

- leave themselves open to changing their minds and incorporating new ideas as they go along

Developmental Considerations

Younger Students

Group murals, drawings, and collages are adaptable to a wide range of collaborative abilities and can be structured to develop young children's group work skills. Introduce cooperative graphic arts with activities in which students contribute individual pieces to a whole-class product (for example, quilt squares to a class quilt, cut-out animal drawings pasted on a mural background, and so on). Even though such projects entail a lot of individual work, there will be plenty of informal collaboration among students as they talk with and help each other during their work. With early projects you will need to help them organize their pieces into a coherent whole and model the reasoning involved; as their collaborative skills develop, students can take on more responsibility for planning and compiling joint products, and they can move from whole-class products into partner or small-group efforts.

Older Students

Although older students typically use writing and speaking to consolidate or convey their knowledge, group graphic arts activities add creative variety to their academic program and help develop their aesthetic understanding and appreciation. While students may still need "coaching" on their collaborative skills, they are more capable than younger children of coordinating their actions and negotiating decisions about the content and design of their work. They can also be granted increasing autonomy in choosing subjects, how to represent their ideas, the medium to use, how to divide the work, and so on.

Grouping Considerations

Graphic arts projects can be done in partnerships, in small groups, or as a class. Whole-class art projects for which students create individual contributions give them a sense of accomplishment and belonging that connects them to the group and fosters class unity; these are useful in the beginning of the year not only for building community, but also for giving students a chance to practice their group artwork skills under your guidance before graduating to more independent partner or small-group projects.

Students will also enjoy and learn from partner and small-group projects, either creating their own stand-alone products or components of whole-class products. Working in pairs or small groups, students have more opportunity to contribute to the product and exercise "creative control," and the whole class benefits from seeing the variety of results—different approaches to the same subject, choices of different subjects, the range of creative expression, and so on.

Getting Students Ready

Academic Preparation

To do group graphic arts projects, students need a rich, shared database from which to draw and some understanding of the techniques and skills involved. Depending upon your students' experience, use one or more of the following suggestions to lay the foundation for their work.

Cover the topic. Really immerse students in a topic before they do a graphic arts project on it, especially if the subject is a different culture or historical context. For example, to prepare for the Ohlone village mural activity described in the Fly on the Wall vignette, students read and discussed several texts about Ohlone life and watched a film about an Ohlone village. An added benefit was that this preliminary work consisted of various other cooperative learning formats involving brainstorming and discussion, partner work, and collaborative academic problem solving.

Appreciate art. Discuss with students the meaning of "a picture is worth a thousand words" or "every picture tells a story." What would be advantageous about using a picture to express ideas? What might be difficult? Show students lots of examples of drawings, paintings, murals, and the like from different cultures and help them think about the many ways people have expressed their ideas through pictures.

Talk technique. As students take more responsibility for the form of their products, help them think about the benefits and burdens of different media—paint, pens, pencils, charcoal, torn paper, glue and glitter, found objects, and so on. Introduce issues related to design and composition, perhaps highlighting one or two such decisions groups will have to make (for example, whether to use color, how to balance two subjects on one page, and the like).

≈ HINT ≈

Circumvent potential messes and disappointments by giving students (especially young ones) a chance to "mess about" with and learn how to use unfamiliar materials before they start their projects. For example, if children will be using glue and glitter, let them experiment with those materials a bit to get a feel for how much glue to use, to find out that glitter sticks only where there is glue, and so on.

Fly on the Wall

Fourth-graders Cullen, Fahim, Marea, and Shonta are working together on a mural of an Ohlone Indian village. The following brief exchange shows the rich interpretation of Ohlone village life that group members have developed, as well as their comfortable exchange of opinions (solicited and otherwise) and informal negotiation of content and style.

CULLEN: *(Speaking in the voice of a figure he's drawing)* "Deer! Deer!" *(He writes the words in a speech bubble.)*

MAREA: *(Adding musical notes to her drawing of a woman singing)* Don't make them talking.

CULLEN: It looks good. *(To Marea, who is now drawing a male figure)* Make him talking—"I got a fish!"

MAREA: No—he's saying, "Mmmm, yum." *(She writes this in a speech bubble.)* But don't make everybody talking, Cullen. *(Continuing to work)* Are we going to color this?

CULLEN: You want to color?

MAREA: It looks better like this. We'll have a vote. Fahim, do you want it colored or black and white?

FAHIM: *(Answering while he draws)* Colored.

SHONTA: Coloring is better. *(Pointing at a neighboring group)* They colored theirs.

MAREA: They're them. Let's make a guy with a flute.

SHONTA: Should we color if we're finished?

CULLEN & MAREA: *(Still drawing)* No.

MAREA: *(Still negotiating)* Remember that book we were reading in the library today? It was black and white. It looked pretty cool, didn't it?

Begin together. Whether students are creating whole-class, partner, or small-group projects, help get their thinking started by doing a whole-class brainstorm about ideas they could include in the product. Emphasize that this is just a starting point, however—more ideas are sure to come up as they work, and they have the flexibility to change course or agree on new directions as their product evolves.

Review the process. When students will be working in partnerships or small groups, remind them of the various collaborative steps involved in producing their joint work of art: brainstorming and discussing what they know about the topic (which, as noted above, you may decide to do as a whole class), deciding what to include, deciding who will make different parts, making the different parts, and deciding on the arrangement. Talk about why it's useful to start out with a fairly good idea of what the product will be—hence the importance of the initial brainstorm and discussions about what to include—but why it's also useful to consider and incorporate new ideas that emerge as students work.

Social/Ethical Preparation

The following are some social and ethical aspects of cooperative graphic arts activities that you may want to help your students anticipate.

Including everyone's ideas. Talk with students about why it is important to listen to everyone's ideas when conceptualizing and executing their project. If a group member feels his or her ideas haven't been listened to, how will that person feel about working on the project? If someone's ideas are ignored, how might that affect the nature or quality of the product? Ask for students' suggestions about how to be sure everyone has a chance to share her or his ideas, and discuss how people might respond respectfully to ideas with which they don't agree.

Making decisions as a group. Ask students to identify what decisions will have to be agreed upon by the group, such as what to include in the piece, how to share the work, how to include everyone's contributions, and so on. Talk about how these decisions can be made fairly and, depending upon students' experience with reaching consensus, review some consensus-building strategies.

≈ HINT ≈

Cooperative graphic arts activities focus on students' shared knowledge or experience—so in considering topics for group art activities, avoid those that would tend to elicit students' unique experiences or individualistic self-expression.

Offering help and encouragement. Acknowledge that some students are more confident about doing artwork than others and invite students' suggestions for how they might either offer or ask for help during the activity. What are some ways to gauge if someone would welcome assistance if the person hasn't asked for it? What would make someone feel comfortable asking for help? What kinds of responses or comments would make someone feel bad about his or her work? Students might enjoy role-playing "good" and "bad" ways to handle such situations.

ACTIVITIES

MURALS

Murals can be wonderful whole-class cooperative projects to which students contribute individually or in groups. Below are some ideas for mural topics, all of which involve some common steps for students: discussing and agreeing on what to include, how to divide the work, and the composition of the mural.

Long Ago and Far Away. Murals such as the Ohlone village mural project described in the Fly on the Wall vignette are a way to help students realize a time and place that they can't experience—a distant civilization or era they have been studying in social studies or history, for example. Begin by having students discuss and list their ideas about what was important to the society and why that should be included in the mural; as students plan the piece and how to divide the work, also be sure they understand that they can modify the plan as other interesting ideas come up during their work.

Narrative Mural. Students can create murals to chronicle important incidents from a story, a shared experience, a historical episode, or other events. Begin by having students discuss and agree upon the aspects of the story to include; if necessary, allow time for students' additional research to double-check the sequence of events or fill in gaps in their knowledge. You might also bring in examples of narrative murals to show them, such as the work of Mexican muralists José Clemente Orozco, Diego Rivera, and David Siqueiros—or even comics, in which each panel portrays a different event. (Panel treatments are also useful for involving students who are less skilled in collaboration, giving them a chance to work individually but still contribute to a group collaboration.)

Sum of the Parts. Students can refine their understanding of science, social studies, and other multifaceted subjects by creating a mural that shows the relationships between different aspects of a topic—for example, integrating knowledge of ocean flora, fauna, geology, and physics in an oceanography mural. Have students begin by listing the different parts of the system they want to include and discussing how to show the relationships between these parts. For example, how would a mural about the food chain show predator-prey relationships? How would it show the cyclical nature of the chain? Students might also enjoy seeing an entertaining example from Joanna Cole's *The Magic Schoolbus* series—for example, when Ms. Frizzle has her class create a mural showing what they learned about water in *The Magic School Bus at the Waterworks*.

Public Art. Have students design and paint a mural that enlivens a public place—a school corridor, cafeteria wall, public building, or the like. You might introduce the project by reading a picture book such as Patricia Markun's *The Little Painter of Sabana Grande* and lead a class conversation about how and why people try to make their communities more beautiful. Finding a venue and obtaining permission for the project will be necessary first steps for students, as well as a great

≈HINT≈

Depending upon the interests and sophistication of your students, successful murals can range from simple or fanciful works with little or no attempt at precision to precise scale models carefully researched for authentic detail.

lesson in community activism! Getting a local artist to help supervise the mural would be an interesting way to help manage and add interest to the project, as well as involve the community; contact your state or local arts council for information and suggestions.

Sidewalk Art. Have students use colorful chalk to create murals on a sidewalk or school blacktop—again, like the public art described above, finding a suitable location and obtaining permission will be great skill-building first steps for students. This activity also accommodates a wide range of collaborative abilities—younger or inexperienced students could informally collaborate, talk, and share ideas while drawing on adjacent sidewalk squares, while more sophisticated groups could plan and execute a whole piece together. And because sidewalk art is appealing to students of all ages, this project also makes a great buddies activity for older and younger students.

COLLAGES

Collage activities can range from the simple to the sophisticated: individual drawings pasted on a common background, pieces that incorporate text as well as pictures, or elaborate compositions made from a variety of materials and objects. In any case, groups working on a collage will have to agree on what to include, how to divide the work, and how to arrange the various elements on a background; at the same time, students have room for plenty of individual expression in choosing or creating the pieces of the collage.

Introduce any of the following collage activities by showing students examples of collages done by artists, such as Picasso, who use materials in surprising and fanciful ways. Arresting collages can be constructed simply from colored paper or magazines; or you might make available a wide range of materials for students to use in their collages—magazines, newspapers, fabric, textured and patterned papers, found objects such as bottle caps and string, natural materials such as acorns and leaves, and so on—and give them free rein in choosing how to use or combine the materials. You could also have students collect materials as an introductory activity to their collage making.

What We Like. At the beginning of the year, as a way to help students get to know each other and build classroom community, have students work in small groups to create collages about things they like. The activity could be very open-ended, or it could focus on such specifics as Things We Like to Do in the Summer, Things We'd Like to Learn This Year, and so on. Be sure students understand that they don't all have to like the same things—part of the fun of the collage is seeing how everyone is alike *and* different.

Story Illustration. Have students work in small groups to make a collage that illustrates a scene from a story they have read in class, each group member drawing and cutting out part of the scene and pasting it on a background. Encourage older students to negotiate how to divide the work (for example, which student draws which part of the scene) and to plan a coherent scene or sequence of events. With younger students, however, you might just have them draw their own versions of the scene and cut out the parts they want to contribute to

In many cases, students will need several sessions to complete their projects—one for planning, several for doing. Periodically bring the class together to check on how things are going, to give groups a chance to share problems, progress, and ideas and perhaps to renegotiate how much time students need to complete their work.

the collage; a satisfactory product can result even if they all end up choosing to paste the same character on the collage or are only capable of random placement of the story elements on the common background.

A Picture of Our Learning. At the end of a unit of study, have students reflect on and celebrate their learning by constructing a collage that illustrates important things they have learned. Choosing and discussing what to include will give students opportunities to practice the skills of summarizing, categorizing, evaluating, and justifying their choices—and the end result will help them all appreciate what they have accomplished both in the unit of study and in creating the collage!

Remember When. Students' shared experiences—field trips, class plays, buddy activities, and the like—build class unity that can be enhanced by sharing memories. Remember When collages can be used simply to reminisce, to thank those who made the experience possible, to show appreciation for a buddy class that shared the experience, and so on.

Our Patchwork Quilt. Students can make group or class "quilts" on any number of subjects—themselves, math concepts, historical events, science topics, some of the collage ideas described above, and so on. Begin the year with a whole-class quilt as a community-building activity: Have students each write their names on a six-inch unlined square of paper and decorate their patches with drawings, patterns, cut-outs, or the like (if possible, bring in materials such as fabric remnants, magazines, colored paper, stickers, ribbons, glitter, etc.). Assemble the individual squares, including one for yourself, into a quilt (you may need to fill in some spaces with solid squares), and make a two-inch border of dark construction paper. Quilts on other topics can follow the same basic process, except that students can graduate to working in groups and taking responsibility for a portion of the quilt (or for making small "crib quilts" of six or eight squares), making their own content, design, and composition decisions.

POSTERS

Creating group posters gives students an engaging and even dramatic way to demonstrate knowledge, express their beliefs, and persuade an audience (for example, parents, the student body, teachers, the community). Introduce these activities by showing students examples of posters that display information or express opinions; your local library may have an illustrated history of poster art that shows the power and artistry of the genre in many cultures. Ask for students' ideas about the design and composition elements that contribute to the effectiveness of some of the examples—in fact, you might ask students to bring in posters they like and explain to the class what they think makes those posters effective, too. For an alternative introductory activity, invite a local graphic artist to share his or her poster work with the class (and vice versa, after students have created their own posters).

Poster activities can vary greatly in complexity and length, using materials and inspiration at hand or requiring time for research and materials collection. Generally, however, you will want to ask groups to brainstorm and agree on the content of their poster, make rough drafts, and then critique each other's drafts (see Editing on page 123 for suggestions on how groups might give respectful and constructive feedback). Check groups' revised drafts for spelling and writing mechanics before they produce their finished version.

Class Norms Poster. After students have agreed on norms for their class (see the Ways We Want Our Class to Be activity in Brainstorming, page 17), have them create posters to formalize the adoption of these norms. Allow groups to choose which norm they want to illustrate, but make sure that none of the norms is left unillustrated (or simply have students group themselves according to the norms they are interested in illustrating). Ask groups to brainstorm ways to illustrate the importance or impact of their norm—for example, by showing behaviors that are and aren't consistent with it. Display the posters in the classroom throughout the year, as reminders of important and abiding decisions students have made for themselves; the posters would also be a great way to communicate students' norms for classroom behavior to parents at Back-to-School Night.

Informational Poster. Have groups make posters to publicize upcoming events, such as a class performance, bake sale, open house, student art exhibit, or the like. Students could also make information posters reminding them of classroom routines and responsibilities, such as how to care for the class pet.

Commemorative Poster. Have partners or groups make posters to commemorate an important occasion, such as Martin Luther King Day, Women's History Month, the anniversary of the United Nations, or Banned Book Week. In the same vein, students can also make posters to commemorate historical injustices (such as the internment of Japanese Americans during World War II) and historical breakthroughs (such as the Underground Railroad or the invention of the polio vaccine).

Book Poster. Have partners or small groups make posters about a favorite book or story. Ask your local bookstore for examples of promotional book posters to show your students, and discuss with them what elements of the posters might make someone interested in reading the book. During their brainstorming, encourage students to consider what characters, scenes, moods, and words would best convey the spirit of the book they have chosen to "promote."

Social Issues Poster. Have groups make posters to display information or opinions about a social problem, current event, or community issue. Introduce the activity by showing the class examples of such posters (again, an illustrated history of posters will be a good source) and discuss what purpose such posters perform, and how.

BANNERS, FLAGS, AND SHIELDS

Emblematic art such as banners, flags, and shields can both brighten a classroom and help build students' sense of teamwork and community.

Group Shields. Partners, buddies, or small groups can practice their interviewing, brainstorming, and decision-making skills when creating group shields bearing their "coat of arms"—emblems that represent the whole group but also show how the group is made up of members with individual interests and abilities. Introduce the activity by showing the class examples of heraldic coats of arms (if possible, displayed on a shield) and explain that the purpose of such a decoration was to both identify a person and illustrate the qualities and history of his or her family. Ask groups (preferably not larger than four members) to create shields that tell something about who they are as a group. First, pairs of group members interview each other about qualities that describe them (see Interviewing on page 19); then the whole group reviews these lists and selects one or two characteristics of each group member to symbolize on the shield. Encourage students to think about how to represent qualities symbolically—for example, in the way that heraldic shields often used animals as symbols. Then have interview partners draw each other's quadrant of the shield and paste the finished parts together on a background sheet in the shape of a shield.

Announcement Banner. Decorative banners can festoon classroom or schoolwide activities, such as Back-to-School Night, science or art fairs, family reading or math nights, and Open House, or they can emblazon a classroom with its name or motto. Help students discuss what they want to communicate about their class, school, or event and how they can do so simply on a banner. The banners can be made of fabric or butcher paper, depending upon the availability of resources, the number of banners to be made and the space they have to cover, and how long the banner has to last.

ILLUSTRATION

Cooperative graphic arts activities need not be major projects—for example, simply drawing a picture with a partner can evoke the same thoughtfulness and good feelings as reading a book with a friend. Have students do partner illustrations when they would benefit from close collaboration; subjects for such projects include almost anything partners can talk or write about (and sometimes more than they can talk or write about), such as the following:

- things they have learned, done, or seen
- places they have been
- objects they have found
- people or animals they know (or wish they knew)
- solutions to math problems
- a problem they are having
- a favorite character or scene from a story
- responses to poetry or music
- a set or costumes for a play
- ways of being safe, kind, and responsible
- hopes, fears, and dreams

EXTENSIONS Graphic arts activities can be extended in any of the following ways to help students reflect on their learning and share their artwork with their classmates.

✳ **What Did We Learn?** Invite students' comments about their experience of creating a piece of art together. How did they handle group members' different creative ideas or opinions on what the piece should be like? How did they divide the work? What worked well? What might they do differently next time? What did they particularly like about the project?

Show and Tell. Have a series of whole-class interviews in which groups show and explain their work (see Interviewing on page 19). Encourage students to take an active role in the interview, asking questions and sharing observations about the artwork.

Look and Tell. Another way to share and think about groups' work would be to display their artwork around the classroom (or at each group's work station) and have students spend some time moving around the room to look at the work. Afterward, give students a chance to tell what they think about any or all of the pieces, either orally or in writing.

Art Exhibition. Have a committee of student "curators" (consisting of at least one representative from each student work group) set up an exhibition of the groups' artwork. Discuss with students where they would like to have the exhibition—for example, in their classroom, a school corridor, the school library, the district office, or the public library—and help the curators with any necessary arrangements to use the chosen location. Have the class create an exhibition catalogue: Bring in some museum exhibition catalogues for students to use as models and ask each group to write an explanation of its work for the catalogue (they might also write this description on a small placard to hang beside the work of art). Finally, have the curators write an introduction that describes the groups' task, important differences and similarities among the ways groups approached the task, highlights of the exhibition, lessons learned, and so on.

Readers Theater

WHEN CHILDREN discover the delights of reading aloud a favorite or familiar text, they discover an important way to enjoy literature. Readers Theater provides such opportunities: Broadly defined, it encompasses any experience of expressively reading aloud (not reciting from memory) a text—from a class doing a choral reading of a familiar poem to students taking roles and reading a script they have written from a story. Unlike a full-blown dramatic production, however, students don't have to worry about memorizing lines or their acting skills. Instead, the drama derives from students' *reading* dramatically—and the benefit derives from students having concentrated on the text and its meaning well enough to be *able* to read it aloud well. Further benefits result, of course, from the collaboration inherent in Readers Theater—students helping each other understand and read text, negotiate role assignments, rehearse, and polish their scripts and performances—the many aspects of working together on a reading that inspire mutual insights, support, and appreciation.

WHY TO USE

- to foster students' enjoyment of reading and literature
- to deepen students' understanding of literature
- to provide a supportive context for young children to learn to read aloud with meaning and expression
- to develop speaking and listening skills
- to encourage students to use their imaginations
- to encourage students' self-expression

WHEN TO USE

- when doing a choral reading of a familiar poem, text, or speech can help students practice inflection and syntax
- when a story lends itself to a read-aloud with students assuming different roles
- when students can deepen their understanding of historical or current events by translating them into dramatic read-aloud scripts

HOW TO DO

The Readers Theater blueprint asks students to

- read the text silently
- discuss their ideas about what the speakers or characters in the story, text, poem, or speech are thinking and feeling
- decide who takes what part
- rehearse
- discuss changes they would like to make
- rehearse the revised version ▶

HOW TO DO

If students are creating their own script, the Readers Theater blueprint asks students to

- discuss their ideas about what the characters are thinking and feeling
- write the script
- decide who takes what part
- rehearse
- discuss changes they would like to make
- rehearse the revised version

Developmental Considerations

Younger Students

Readers Theater is ideal for beginning readers: Reading aloud a familiar text helps students see relationships between spoken language and print (the foundation for reading) and improves phrasing (an important comprehension skill). But most importantly, the playful and informal nature of Readers Theater helps young children enjoy and gain confidence in reading.

You can use the Readers Theater blueprint throughout the day to read a variety of texts—big books, language experience stories, nursery rhymes, poems, and songs. It's best and most practical, however, to introduce Readers Theater to beginning readers with choral readings, especially using familiar pieces with repetitive phrases or verses. Since students have a good idea of what the text says, decoding challenges are few. Instead, children can focus on the connections between the spoken and written word, and they have the help of all the readers around them to get through any difficulties.

Another important way to assist early readers is to read aloud the text to the class first and then read it all together. To facilitate students' recognition of the word they are reading, write the text on chart or butcher paper and point to the words as the class reads together. Then, when students have practiced reading the text a few times, invite volunteers to read lines or sections in their own style; also invite several students to read the same section, to help students see that text can be interpreted in many different ways—*their* ways.

As students become more comfortable reading aloud, have them begin taking different parts; for example, use songs or poems that have clearly defined roles or divide the class into two or more groups and have groups read alternating lines or verses—you might even ask students to suggest their own choral arrangements for songs or poems. (A great resource for suitable material is Jill Bennet's *Roger Was a Razor Fish and Other Poems,* an anthology of poems that are nearly all question-and-answer, echo, or other pieces in two or more voices; Nancy Larrick's *Let's Do a Poem!* is another useful resource and includes ideas specifically for use as Readers Theater.)

≈ HINT ≈

Repetitive songs such as "Old MacDonald," "The Wheels on the Bus," and "Down by the Bay," in which children make up new verses to familiar songs, make great introductions to whole-class Readers Theater for young students—the melody and rhythm give children a structure for learning material and "reading" in unison.

You may find that your young students are only ready to take on whole-class Readers Theater, albeit with divided parts, which is fine. If, however, you feel your students are ready to do more independent reading in partnerships or small groups, again begin by using familiar poems or picture books as scripts, so that even students who aren't independent readers can perform with confidence and success. (See the fuller description of Readers Theater scripts, below; depending upon your students prowess, you might even have beginning readers write their own Readers Theater scripts with the help of a scribe— performing can be easier when students are reading their own words.)

Older Students

Intermediate students can perform a broad range of whole-class, partner, and small-group Readers Theater activities, but again it is often best to start them off with some whole-class choral readings such as those suggested for younger students. Whole-class activities give you the opportunity to introduce some guiding ideas about how to read aloud effectively and give students the opportunity to become comfortable doing so.

When students are ready to try scripted Readers Theater activities, begin with the most obvious and easily managed "scripts"—that is, storybooks that have a fair amount of dialogue: One student plays each character, reading only the dialogue spoken by her or his character, while one more student takes the role of narrator and reads the connecting text. In lieu of storybooks, of course, students could read play scripts or scripts written specifically for Readers Theater activities.

≈ HINT ≈

Without the need for sets or physical acting, Readers Theater actors generally sit or stand in a row and read to the audience. While they primarily must rely on their voices and delivery to create different characters, of course, students could also use simple props such as a hat or a shawl to differentiate their roles.

If your students readily take to these activities and find themselves able to read aloud effectively, you might move them on to creating their own scripts. For example, have them take a book they have already read aloud for Readers Theater but, instead of having all of the connecting narrative read aloud by a student in the narrator role, challenge students to turn narrative into dialogue where possible (see Academic Preparation for suggestions about helping students take on this task). Keep in mind, though, that such tasks challenge not only students' creative and writing abilities, but also their collaborative skills—there's another whole level of negotiation involved when students are deciding which portions of narrative should be turned into narrative, how their new dialogue should read, and so on, and you may need to prepare them to manage that transition.

Grouping Considerations

As indicated above, Readers Theater can be performed by the whole class, small groups, and partnerships—the deciding variables being your students' reading level and experience. Of course, once students are ready to work more independently, group size may well be dictated by the number of roles available in the script at hand. Continue to intersperse small-group work with some whole-class activities, though, which are excellent community builders and give you ongoing opportunities to model Readers Theater skills and develop students' abilities.

Getting Students Ready

Academic Preparation

Much of the academic preparation for Readers Theater involves helping students understand the genre and the skills involved, both through example and practice, such as the following.

Hark back. If students are new to Readers Theater, they may have very little notion of how to communicate a story with only their voices. Remind them that before the era of televisions and VCRs, people *listened* to their entertainment—to storytellers, to books read aloud, to radio dramas. Ask them what they think might be the difference between watching a show on television and listening to one on the radio: What might be different for the audience? What might be different for the actors? What do they think are the advantages of one medium over the other? Invite students to model the difference—first acting out a suitably histrionic line or scene and then trying to achieve the same dramatic effect just using their voices. If possible, play an audio recording of an old radio play and invite any new insights about dramatic reading students might have.

Say it like you mean it! Students can make their voices express different feelings by changing the rate, stress, pitch, volume, and pauses of their reading—and they could probably benefit from practicing some of these variables before tackling a script. Help students practice by asking them to use different emotions to say simple sentences—for example, saying "I closed the door" first angrily, then amusedly, then nervously, then sadly, and so on will demonstrate just how evocative an instrument their voices can be.

Write it as you mean it. When your students are ready to move on to writing their own scripts, help them think about some of the considerations involved. Have them take a look at a published script (a Readers Theater script they have performed is a good choice), and ask them what they notice about how it is written. Students may offer observations about mechanics (such as "You start a line with the name of the character who is saying it") or more stylistic observations (such as "The speeches are short—one character usually talks only a little before the next person says something"). Encourage this range of comments and help students think through the reasons for what they see (for example, that it helps move the story along when characters have fairly brief sections of dialogue). As necessary, guide students' attention to other factors, such as the use of sound effects and stage directions—even the most obvious elements, such as the fact that characters use direct speech. List students' observations and have the class help you categorize them, and post these Playwrights' Pointers for students to refer to when writing and editing their scripts (and encourage students to add to the list as they experience and learn from their script writing, too).

Model the process. Every time you read aloud a story to your class, you will be demonstrating how Readers Theater can make literature come to life. In fact, when students are new to the genre, you might model Readers Theater by reading aloud a story they have heard you present before—but this time, ask them to pay particular attention to how you use your voice for effect. Invite students' comments (even critiques!) and try out any suggestions they may have for how you could read the story differently. Similarly, you might play an audio recording of Readers Theater performed by professional actors and ask for students' observations. Also model the script-writing process, when students are at that stage: Create a short script as a whole class, using their Playwrights' Pointers as a guide.

Social/Ethical Preparation

When collaborating on Readers Theater activities, students could find themselves negotiating everything from what to say, to who will say it, to how they'll say it—it's a creative endeavor, and students are bound to have some different ideas about how to approach it. The following are some social and ethical aspects of Readers Theater activities you may want to help students anticipate.

Dividing roles. Talk with students about fair and kind ways to figure out who gets what role—for example, how a group might reach a fair decision if more than one person wants the same role or nobody in the group wants a particular role. Ask students how they have resolved such issues before, and invite any new ideas that may have occurred to them in the meantime.

Respecting everyone's contribution. Help students think about the many ways they can contribute to the success of a Readers Theater activity—and help them think beyond the writing or reading aloud of text. For example, some students may be particularly good at helping others decode and become comfortable with the text; others may be skillful playwrights. Some may be able to coach another's bravura performance, while others still may have a natural dramatic flair. And in all these realms there is, of course, room for disagreement about what someone's contribution should "look like." Discuss how students might respond respectfully to other's ideas and find ways to include all contributions in one way or another. Give examples from previous Readers Theater activities and invite students' suggestions.

Helping everyone contribute. In some ways Readers Theater is simultaneously the simplest and most challenging form of theater: Sure, actors don't have to "act" in the fullest sense of the word, but they also don't have props and movement to help convey the drama (or mask nervousness). Some students may find doing Readers Theater intimidating at first, but they can help each other master the form. Ask students to think about how they can help each other contribute to and benefit from Readers Theater: How might they encourage shy students to participate? What kinds of responses would have just the opposite

≈ HINT ≈

Be sure Readers Theater material is accessible to all group members—through either their familiarity with the text or their ability to read it with relative ease. Group members will of course have different reading abilities and should help one another through difficult parts, but you'll want to avoid situations in which the group depends on one or two members' ability to decipher the text.

effect? What makes it easy for group members to ask each other for help? What are some respectful ways to offer help, unsolicited or otherwise? Invite examples from other "helping" situations, such as peer editing or role-plays.

WAYS TO USE *Readers Theater*

ACTIVITIES

The following are just a few general suggestions for using Readers Theater—be sure to check your library or bookstore for the many available titles that provide Readers Theater scripts and offer even more detailed suggestions.

Poetry Theater. As mentioned above, reading poetry aloud is an excellent way to start students in Readers Theater. Some characteristics of poetry, such as rhyme and repetition, help students master and enjoy reading aloud, and you can use poetry as an informal way of practicing Readers Theater without undue emphasis on polished performances. For example, use spare minutes between cleanup and recess, or at the start or end of the day, for whole-class poetry reading—students will welcome the change of pace, become comfortable with reading aloud, and also become comfortable with poetry! Also invite students to do their own choral arrangements of poems and lead the class in readings of some favorite poetry.

Story Theater. Many picture books and favorite stories are easily usable for Readers Theater, whether you use them verbatim or turn some of the narrative into dialogue (see Developmental Considerations on pages 168–169). The most promising possibilities are those that have dramatic excitement and lots of dialogue (or potential for dialogue from narrative, if your students can write their own scripts); for younger children and whole-class readings, ideal candidates also have repetitive structures, rhymes, and refrains. Start off with familiar stories, and as students become comfortable with the genre, encourage them to choose their own titles to use for Readers Theater.

History Theater. There is no reason to restrict Readers Theater to fiction, of course—historical events also provide wonderful subjects for dramatic readings. For example, students might enjoy doing a choral reading or a moving speech by a historical figure; they might weave together pieces of diaries, letters, background information, and sound effects to present an episode in a person's life; they might base a script on oral histories; and so on.

Real-Life Theater. Students can also capture the drama of real life in Readers Theater scripts—current events, classroom episodes, or personal stories. To give students an example of such possibilities, read a book such as *Storm in the Night* or *The Stories Julian Tells,* in which characters transform everyday events and relationships into engaging stories. (In fact, students might want to write Readers Theater scripts of such books before venturing into original subject matter.)

EXTENSIONS

Readers Theater activities can be extended in any of the following ways.

✳ **What Did We Learn?** Help students think about their experience of Readers Theater: How did it feel to try to express something just with their voices? What did they find challenging about doing Readers Theater? What did they most enjoy? What new ideas did they have? Also encourage them to reflect on their collaborations: How did group members help each other? What was helpful about working with a group? What was difficult? What might they do differently next time?

Showcase. When partners or small groups all work on the same piece, have them perform their versions for the whole class so that students can enjoy and learn from the range of interpretations their classmates come up with. Ask students to comment on differences and similarities they see between different performances, what they learned from each other's interpretations, or any other observations. Likewise, when they work on different pieces, have them perform for the rest of the class and discuss each other's efforts.

Tableaux. At various points during a Readers Theater performance, freeze the action and invite the audience to question the various "characters"; the performers will answer in character. This is a good way to deepen students' understanding of characters' motivation and to introduce unstated but implicit background information.

Join In. When partners or small groups have done Readers Theater of different poems or songs, have them perform for the class and then lead their classmates in the piece they performed—in no time, the class will share an impressive repertoire!

Variety Show. Because Readers Theater pieces can be quite short (even a comic strip can be turned into effective Readers Theater!), students could mount several pieces in a production for parents, a buddy class, senior citizens, or other audience. For example, the class could decide on a selection of favorite pieces they have done over the school year or choose new pieces around a common theme; for the sake of variety, you might want to encourage a mix of genres, such as stories, poems, nonfiction, and some pieces in which the audience can join. Have the class agree on the selections, the order they are to be presented, casting for each—maybe even invitations, playbills, and other such trappings.

Puppet Theater. Puppetry is a natural extension of Readers Theater, as the effectiveness of both depends in large part on the performers' voices. Have students design and make their own puppets—anything from simple paper and Popsicle stick constructions to more elaborate fabric concoctions (spark students' imaginations by showing them pictures of puppets from different cultures). For the production, some students will manipulate the puppets to act out the drama while others read aloud the puppets' dialogue and narrative.

≈ HINT ≈

Except in the case of guided choral reading with very young children, it is best for students to have personal copies of the script, with their respective parts highlighted.

Role-Playing

PLAYACTING is intrinsically interesting to children—from a very young age they demonstrate great skill and verve at it—and it can also contribute to important academic and ethical understandings. When students take the role of a story character, historical figure, or peer, they are learning to take other perspectives and thereby deepening their understanding of the world around them; they also must apply (and extend) what they know and believe to new situations—abilities central to thoughtful and principled decision making. What's more, role-playing is inherently cooperative: Children not only inhabit their own character but must also learn to communicate and empathize with their coplayers to create a coherent presentation. In the classroom, such "presentations" can run the gamut from simplicity to sophistication—from the informality of rehearsing a telephone conversation to get information about a class field trip to the formality of performing a theatrical piece complete with scenery and costumes. Regardless of the circumstance or sophistication, role-playing activities tap into children's natural affinity for play while also building their lifelong collaborative skills.

WHY TO USE

- to give students a chance to walk in someone else's shoes
- to have students apply what they know and believe to new contexts
- to help students make a personal connection to literature, history, and other subjects
- to deepen students' understanding of a story or situation
- to let students consider alternative ways to consider and solve problems without fear of losing face
- to foster self-expression

WHEN TO USE

- when students will benefit from seeing a situation from different points of view
- when students know a character or event well enough to play with it in new contexts
- when it can help students consolidate what they know about a complex character or topic
- before group work, to model ways to approach a task
- when students need to resolve a classroom or playground problem and can try out different solutions with a role-play
- when students will benefit from rehearsing a new academic, social, or ethical task

HOW TO DO

The Role-Playing blueprint asks students to

- agree on how to distribute the roles to be played
- improvise the role-play on the spot, or write and rehearse a script for it
- talk about how it went and agree on any changes
- perform the final version, either for themselves or for an audience

Developmental Considerations

Younger Students

For young children, playacting can seem more real—and certainly more compelling—than life itself, which makes role-playing a very useful tool for problem solving and decision making in the classroom. Stepping into a role can help a young child see a point of view he or she failed to grasp just seconds before, despite a teacher's or classmate's best attempts at persuasion; role-playing can also reduce the emotional entanglement children feel when dealing with a loaded situation, allowing them to explore and accept alternative solutions without fear of losing face.

Children need lots of informal dramatic play experience prior to performing structured role-plays, though; then, whether for academic or decision-making purposes, they will be able to employ drama more successfully in structured activities and more challenging situations. Create a drama station for children's free-play time, a place where they can spontaneously and informally choose their own "dramas" and situations to act out. Introduce structured role-playing in conjunction with familiar tales that have strong story lines and dialogue—fairy tales; scenes from favorite picture books; even nursery rhymes, songs, or poems. Children immensely enjoy acting out stories as they are read aloud.

As you move into more structured role-plays, keep the activities' scope and instructions clear, simple, and explicit. You may need to explain even the most obvious steps—for example, that when students are doing a partner role-play, the first thing they have to do is decide who will be which character. With young children you will also want to minimize the use of scripted plays, to avoid having the content of their role-play upstaged by the challenge of following the script and stage directions.

≈ HINT ≈

When students are young or new to doing role-plays, they may have trouble focusing on the activity because it involves an intangible "product." If possible, try to have an extra pair of hands about to help groups get started and keep them on task—for example, parent volunteers or older buddies who can help you monitor and gently guide partner and small-group work.

Young children's involvement in their role-plays can also be enhanced with simple costumes or props to help them step into character (just a hat, for example, or an object that is central to the situation being role-played); such devices also provide a cover that encourages even very shy children to take the stage. It's a good idea, however, to give students plenty of time to use costumes and props in free-play situations prior to using them for structured role-playing activities—otherwise, the props themselves, rather than the role-play, will likely be the focus of children's attention. Again, a classroom drama center stocked with props is a great way to get students accustomed to both the accessories *and* the content of doing role-plays together.

Finally, be prepared to deal with conflicts between children who have equally firm ideas about exactly how a role-play should go. Part of learning to do and benefiting from role-plays is learning to listen to and respect each other's ideas—but many children will have to practice that tolerance, just as they learn to practice the role-plays themselves.

Older Students

Drama is a wonderful way for older students to experiment with different identities—an inevitable aspect of growing up—without going to all the trouble (or even risk) of actually changing their lives or personalities! Another inevitability, however, is that older students might be quite self-conscious about "playacting" with or for their peers, and some may need quite a bit of encouragement to do so. Role-playing can be a powerful cognitive and emotional tool, though, even when a student's performance appears nervous or lackluster, and you will want to cultivate a receptive and respectful environment in which students can experience such activities—both within their collaborative group and in front of their classroom audience. While older students may not be as blunt and dogmatic in their opinions as younger children, their ways of expressing ridicule or disdain can be more hurtful; spend some time raising students' consciousness about how to encourage each other's best efforts.

As they work on such skills and become comfortable with role-playing, older students can also engage in more sophisticated activities than can their younger counterparts; they might even extend their experience to writing their own scenarios and dramas, independent of any extant story inspiration or play script. Finally, encourage older students to take advantage of their role-playing skills on their own, to solve problems and try on other people's perspectives.

Grouping Considerations

In many cases, the optimal number of students for a role-play or play will be dictated by the activity itself—rehearsing for a telephone conversation requires two students, for example, while four students would be required to model a lesson in which students work cooperatively in groups of four; a scene from a story might involve three characters, and so on.

As usual, however, it's probably best to start small and work up to more ambitious projects, allowing your students the time and practice necessary to become accustomed to doing role-plays. For example, activities that extend a familiar story, such as having partners role-play a conversation between characters, are good ways to introduce role-playing—cautious partners can simply retell the story, while others might venture into unfamiliar territory and create original dialogues. When you move to larger groups, begin with activities that have fairly prescribed roles so that students can concentrate on coordinating the actions of several players; as students gain experience with the format, encourage more improvisation.

Getting Students Ready

Academic Preparation

Imagine the possibilities. If students are new to doing role-plays—and especially if they are reluctant to do them—you might want to help them think about the value (not to mention possible fun) of these activities by reading aloud a related story. For example, *Amazing Grace* by Mary Hoffman tells the story of an imaginative little girl who loves to act out stories so that she "can be anyone she wants to be." Invite students to share their responses to the book and talk about role-playing and

TWO KINDS OF ROLE-PLAYS *In two different classrooms, children demonstrate the power of perspective taking to deepen their understanding of themselves and others.*

PROBLEM-PLAY

Before her kindergarteners resume work on a project they had begun the day before, Michele Frisch takes a few moments to help students reflect on how they might help things go a bit more smoothly today. Pointing out that some children had been upset and had their feelings hurt, Michele asks for students' ideas about how they might treat each other better when working together—and her students, accustomed to using role-plays to think through such dilemmas, enthusiastically and productively adopt that tool in this discussion.

MS. FRISCH: Today we need to practice two things—not shouting at each other and being kind. Who has some ideas about what to do when we disagree on sharing things?

VALERIA: We can tell them to please stop it.

AMY: Like this coconut. *(She holds up a walnut.)* When she wants it, she can just say, "Can I have this coconut back?"

MS. FRISCH: Do you guys want to stand up and show us? Your nut is called a walnut.

LISA: *(Standing with Amy to role-play for the class)* Can I please have my walnut back? *(Amy gives it to Lisa, and then Shelby asks for a turn at role-playing.)*

SHELBY: *(To Lisa)* Can I please have it back? *(Lisa gives it to him.)*

MS. FRISCH: What if someone won't give it back? Hannah?

HANNAH: *(Role-playing with Ms. Frisch)* Can I please have the coconut back?

MS. FRISCH: No. I like it. *(To the class)* What's Hannah going to do? Alex?

ALEX: You could get another one.

MS. FRISCH: Okay—like if you ask for the scissors and someone won't give them to you, you can get another pair?

SHELBY: What if they're all gone?

IAN: Say, "Please can I share them?"

STORY-PLAY

After reading a chapter from Barbara Brenner's *Wagon Wheels*, Laura Ecken asks students in her combined second- and third-grade class to consider why the father in the story left his three boys behind when he went in search of new land to homestead. After the class discusses these reasons, Laura asks each partnership to write a dialogue between the two oldest boys, Johnny and Willie, showing how they felt on their first night home alone. Discussing their dialogue, Jonathan solicits Larry's ideas while also gently keeping things focused.

JONATHAN: How can we put this?

LARRY: When the dad left, he cried.

JONATHAN: No, we're talking about what Johnny and Willie said when their dad's gone. Like, what would—

LARRY: "I'm going to miss him"?

JONATHAN: Yeah, but who's going to say it, which one? Me or you?

LARRY: You?

JONATHAN: Okay, but we still need to talk it over. What're you going to say?

LARRY: "We got to hunt for food." I mean, "You gotta help me hunt for food."

JONATHAN: How 'bout we kind of put that later on in the story? Right now we're talking how we feel.

LARRY: "I hope he comes back."

pretending: Why is it nice to pretend to be someone or something different than you are? Why might someone want to do so? Why is it important for people to have a chance to pretend to be someone or something else? Have students share something about which they like (or would like) to pretend.

Cover the context. To assume a role, students need to be familiar with the character and with the context of the role-play. So, for example, students will need to have thoroughly read (or have had read to them) and discussed a story whose characters' perspectives they must assume, they will need to have learned about and discussed the historical episode they will enact, they will need to know the nature of the problem to be solved, and so on. Before having students embark on their role-plays, help them explore its topic from different angles—both to give them enough content to go on and to expose them to different ideas and opinions that might influence their role-playing and understanding of the subject at hand.

Talk technique. Lead students in a discussion about how they might best project the ideas and tone of their role-play. For example, what clues in the story might give them some ideas about a character's gestures or facial expressions? How would they feel if they were in the midst of the historical episode they will be portraying? How could they get these ideas and feelings across? Show them a play script and point out how a playwright indicates emotions and gestures with brief parenthetical references; encourage students to discuss these elements, not just the words they will be saying, when working on their role-plays together.

Show an example. If groups will be performing role-plays based on literature, show them a videotape of professional actors acting out a familiar story. Ask students what they notice about the translation from word to action—expressions and gestures that might not have been spelled out in the story, for example, but are used to good effect in the enactment. (A good source is *Faerie Tale Theater*'s sixty-minute productions of familiar tales, which feature a variety of well-known actors.)

Attend an example. Better yet, take the class to see a play performed by professional actors or older students—how about inviting the local high school drama class to stage a performance for your class? Arrange for students to interact with the actors following the performance.

Model the process. If students are new to role-playing and drama, then role-play how to do a role-play. Explain your thinking and invite students' comments about what they might have done differently—not only to get them thinking, but also to make explicit that you value and encourage their varying approaches.

Social/Ethical Preparation

The following are some social and ethical aspects of role-playing activities you may want to help students anticipate—and of course, role-playing some of these considerations is an excellent way to help students think about them!

Dividing roles. Have students consider role assignment issues—for example, how a group might reach a fair decision if more than one person wants the same role or if nobody in the group wants a particular role.

Respecting everyone's contribution. Students can contribute to role-plays in a number of ways—some may have lots of ideas about what to include in the role-play, for example, while others may be particularly creative about how to act it. Likewise, there are many opportunities to disagree about each other's contributions! Discuss how students might respond respectfully to others' ideas and find ways to include all contributions. Give examples from previous role-plays and invite students' suggestions.

Helping everyone contribute. Some students may take easily to role-playing, while others might find it a bit scary. Help students think about how they can help each other contribute to and benefit from role-plays: What might they do to help each other remember their parts? How might they encourage shy students to participate? What kinds of responses would have just the opposite effect? What makes it easy for group members to ask each other for help? What are some respectful ways to offer help, unsolicited or otherwise?

Being the audience. Role-playing is challenging enough in itself, in that it stretches students' perspective-taking skills and imagination—but then to have to perform in front of your peers, on top of that! This prospect will seem a lot less daunting in a caring and respectful classroom, where students know they can take the risks associated with learning without risking ridicule. Discuss with your students what they think it means to be a good audience and why this might be important; ask them how they feel when they are performing, what helps or discourages them, and so on.

WAYS TO USE *Role-Playing*

ACTIVITIES

Free-Play. As mentioned above, a great way to introduce children to role-playing and dramatic games is to set up a drama center they can use during their free-play time. Stock it with any variety of props and story suggestions, including props that are related to subjects students are studying in class.

Poem-Play. Very young children especially enjoy role-playing familiar nursery rhymes and story songs, such as "Little Miss Muffet." This is a particularly useful introduction to role-playing because children needn't be able to read the words to act them out; they will know them quite well already, and you can have students role-play with partners or small groups while you recite the rhyme or song aloud.

Problem-Play. Role-playing helps students explore alternative solutions to conflicts that arise in the classroom or on the playground, and it can also help them anticipate the academic, social, and ethical challenges of group work. After identifying and discussing with students the issue at hand, invite volunteers to model approaches to the task or problem and encourage students to act out the variety of different approaches that occur to them.

Story-Play. Have students assume the identity of story characters to explore situations from the story—a scene as it happened, what they might have done differently, alternative endings, or any other setup that will deepen students' understanding of a story and of themselves. Similarly, you might have students role-play interactions between characters from different stories, which gives them interesting insights into common themes and ideas. For younger children, wordless books provide great opportunities for role-plays.

History-Play. As with literature, history provides plenty of "stories" for students to bring to life with role-playing—anything from a conversation between two historical characters to a full-fledged reenactment of an event, such as the debate over the Bill of Rights or the Emancipation Proclamation. An interesting variation would be to have students role-play meetings between historical figures from different eras.

Improvisation-Play. A fun improvisational variation of either Story-Play or History-Play is to write various characters' names and scenario ideas on different slips of paper, put these in a hat, and have students draw from the hat and improvise being those characters in that situation. Some wonderful and thought-provoking variations on the story or scene can result!

Vocabulary-Play. Drama can help children learn new vocabulary in ways that are both fun and memorable (as long as the vocabulary being learned is derived from a meaningful context, such as a story being read or a topic of study). To "role-play" vocabulary, have partners or small groups pantomime the words in a game of vocabulary charades. Or, have them role-play If Someone Were . . ., another improvisational vocabulary activity. (For example, if the word *dangling* is being introduced, partners would define it in a sentence—"If something were *dangling*, it would be hanging and swinging loosely"—and then act it out.)

Art-Play. Give small groups an interesting photograph or print of a painting, drawing, or sculpture of human or animal subjects. Have groups study the picture, discuss what might be happening in it, and then create a role-play of it. For an added challenge, have the group begin or end their role-plays by striking the pose of the subjects in the work of art.

Simulation-Play. A simulation is a particular kind of role-play, usually involving more extensive assumptions of entire experiences and therefore focusing more on context than characterizations. For example, students might simulate a distant time or place to deepen their understanding of and empathy for individuals and ways of life outside their own experience: When students "live," even temporarily, in the cramped quarters of slaves on the middle passage, they are likely to understand those inhumane conditions better than they would by simply reading about them in a book. Or students might simulate a situation that fosters greater understanding of human interaction and decision making: Small groups planning to colonize another planet because of an impending disaster on Earth must grapple with selection and survival issues, as well as any other number of social, ethical, and practical considerations. Simulations can also help students understand relationships between parts of a system, such as the solar system or the court system, in science, social studies, or other disciplines. (If the class is planning an elaborate simulation—in which students will spend a day or week becoming members of the society you are studying in social studies, for example—have small groups assume responsibility for different aspects of the role-play: One group might plan food, another furnishings or shelter, a third recreation and entertainment, and so on.)

≈ HINT ≈

Students can use puppets to do many of these role-play activities, a fun variation that also offers very shy children a vehicle for playing more active verbal roles. Students can make puppets from paper bags or socks, or use commercial puppets, and perhaps even make a puppet stage.

EXTENSIONS

Role-playing activities can be extended in any of the following ways.

✳ **What Did We Learn?** Ask students to reflect on their role-plays, prompting their thinking with such questions as What did you learn about the character, historical figure, story, or event from doing the role-play? How did other group members help you understand the person or situation better? What did you like best about your group's role-play? What might you change? Also invite students' comments about how the activity went—how they divided roles, how they helped each other, what didn't work so well and might be done differently next time, and so on.

Break a Leg. Have partnerships or small groups perform their role-plays for the whole class, so that students can appreciate and learn each other's interpretations of the situation or characters. Invite students' comments on differences and similarities between different role-plays, what they learned from each other's role-plays, or any other insights. (Of course, when your students' role-play is a bona fide theatrical production, they will want to perform it for buddies, parents, or other classes.)

Just a Moment. To encourage students to go even further in personalizing history or understanding the interior lives of characters, have them do tableaux of their story and history role-plays. Invite volunteers to do their role-plays for the class and, at any given moment, ask the actors to freeze the action and describe their characters' unspoken thoughts or feelings at that moment. Also encourage students in the audience to ask questions of or respond to the characters.

3-2-1 Action! Students might enjoy having you videotape their role-plays for a class "portfolio"; older students could videotape each other's role-plays, which would challenge them with another whole level of collaboration—dividing the tasks involved in filming, acting, and editing the piece, for example. In either case, the videos can provide a record for students to use throughout the year—to chart their progress, to compare and contrast different role-plays that overlap in interesting ways, and so on.

Model Building

T HE CREATION of representational structures—that is, models—is a regular part of children's play. The block structure that represents what a child knows about buildings, the Lego vehicle that represents what a child knows about cars, the flour-and-salt representation of a volcano—all these are creations that demonstrate children's understanding and exploration of the world around them. In the classroom, model building is the original integrated curriculum: Students apply principles and understandings from different disciplines to build representations of something they have learned—geography, historical sites, scientific systems, and so on. And because model building requires a range of knowledge and skills, children benefit from collaborating on models—sharing and appreciating each others' strengths, abilities, and aptitudes to achieve a common goal.

WHY TO USE

- to make abstract ideas more concrete

- to integrate learnings across disciplines

- to allow students with different interests, abilities, and skills to contribute to a joint product

WHEN TO USE

- when learning can be represented by concrete objects

- as the culmination of a unit of study

- when working with students of different abilities, skills, and interests

HOW TO DO

The Model Building blueprint asks students to

- brainstorm and agree on what to include in the model

- design the model

- gather materials needed to construct the model

- construct the model

Developmental Considerations

Younger Students

Making materials do what you *want* them to do can be a challenge for anyone constructing a model—but especially for young children, whose fine motor skills and knowledge of how things work are still developing. Have children use materials that are large and easy to manipulate—materials they can use independently without serious frustration (such as building blocks rather than toothpicks, Styrofoam forms rather than spools, and so on). And because young children are learning how things work, you may have to spend considerable time emphasizing process rather than the final product—what makes things stick together, where to put the glue or tape (and how much to use), using scissors, and so on.

Older Students

HINT

Graham crackers and icing are wonderful construction materials for young children (although older students find them irresistible, too). Add other bits and pieces—edible or otherwise—to create structures, from whimsical gingerbread houses to miniature pueblo villages.

As children get older, their curriculum deals increasingly with abstract ideas and provides few opportunities to apply learning to concrete situations. But older students love to create, and building models often helps them internalize and remember abstract ideas. (In fact, next to taking field trips, model building is often one of the few experiences adults recall from their elementary school days!) Older students can manage more challenging materials than younger children, but they also benefit from using tried-and-true materials in sophisticated ways (in fact, they often enjoy revisiting materials, such as building blocks or Legos, that they used when they were younger).

Because older students are able to attempt more challenging materials and models, however, they may also end up investing considerable time and effort in their projects and become quite attached to what they produce. For example, the class that built an Ohlone village in the Fly on the Wall vignette thereafter made regular visits to their model (and were thrilled when the structures they built survived a heavy rainstorm). Especially in the case of long-term projects, creating a venue for displaying and explaining finished models is important—both academically and affectively.

Grouping Considerations

Model building is enhanced by collaboration between students with different abilities, skills, and perspectives, and working in pairs or small groups allows students to actively participate in the project while also benefiting from others' various strengths and skills. Models can also be whole-class projects, such as the Ohlone village, in which partners or groups create different parts of the whole; not only does this contribute to classroom unity, but also the pooling of talents and abilities can be impressive—and the amount of time spent creating the model is reduced without diminishing the learning benefits derivable from creating the whole model.

Getting Students Ready

Academic Preparation

Develop their database. Be sure students have sufficient knowledge of the subject of their model, whether by covering the material as a class or, especially with older students, by having them research the topic. For example, the students who constructed the Ohlone village did a lot of preparation beforehand: Through text, film, and hands-on activities, they studied Ohlone technology, economy, and social relations. In fact, having learned that Ohlone houses were made from available materials, they were inspired to use pine needles found in the school courtyard as construction materials—thereby integrating and applying concrete information and abstract concepts in their model building.

Fly on the Wall

Janet Ellman's fourth-grade class has transformed an empty school courtyard into an intricate Ohlone Indian village. Small groups of students cluster around diminutive conical houses they are building from willow branches, tule grass (provided by Janet), and the pine needles that litter the school courtyard. Some groups carefully landscape areas adjacent to their domes to conform to what they know about Ohlone life; others, such as the group below, struggle with engineering problems—how to achieve symmetry, how to get the pine needle cover to adhere to the willow frame, how to lash willow branches together, and so on—and experience the dilemmas and decision making of the people they're studying.

HEATHER: *(Surveying the partially built hut wall)* Maybe what we should do is put more ties here.

DANI: Yeah, like move this pole in the middle and move this one out so the wall's not skinny here, but it's like, out.

HEATHER: This thing has to be sort of—

DANI: Why's it fat on this side?

HEATHER: Well, let's put more stuff over here. *(To Vishaal)* Okay, give me—*(Indicates strands of shredded willow)*.

DANI: How are we going to weave them in and out?

HEATHER: Let's see. These start in. In, out . . .

VISHAAL: In and out. I'm trying my best to try and keep them—I'm trying to put the sticks so we'll be able to weave it. So when there's an empty space, put more of the willow stuff there.

DANI: Where're we going to make the door?

HEATHER: We'll leave a hole for the door when we add the pine needles, okay?

Later that day, Janet talks with her class about the activity—and helps them see how they not only built an Ohlone village model, but also followed the Ohlone model of collaboration and sharing knowledge.

MS. ELLMAN: So, can anyone tell me something else they decided about how to build their house?

JEFFREY: We put a lot of grass because it looks like it was going to rain, so we put a lot to protect it.

DERRICK: I showed them how to put the pine needles on it, starting from the bottom.

MS. ELLMAN: Like we were talking about yesterday: When the Ohlone people found a way to use things in their environment, they didn't have books to write down this knowledge—they had to pass it from person to person. So, in many ways, we went through the same process as we figured out how to build the huts.

Consult about construction. Children are natural engineers, intrinsically interested in making, shaping, fashioning, designing, and planning, and they can generate many interesting and unusual ideas for model building if given the opportunity. Invite students to share ideas about materials and approaches that might be used in the model-building activity and, as a class, consider the benefits and burdens of each (thereby offering your own model for students to use in their partner or group decision making!).

Comment on construction. Introduce any special engineering issues or problems students will encounter—or you would like students to consider—before they run up against them.

Mess about. When students will be using unfamiliar materials to build their models, consider allowing them some "messing about" time to get accustomed to the materials before starting the project (see Messing About on page 63).

Plan ahead. If the project is an elaborate one that will be spread over several sessions, help students develop a realistic work plan—in fact, you may want to devote the first group session entirely to planning and encourage groups to revise their work plans periodically during group work.

Model the process. While you can't model the entire model-building process, you may want to demonstrate particular aspects—how to handle materials, how to sketch out an idea, how to reach important decisions about planning and production, and so on.

Social/Ethical Preparation

The following are some social and ethical aspects of model-building activities you may want to help students anticipate.

Respecting ideas. As with any collaborative creation, model building will inspire many different ideas—and students won't always agree on the merit of each idea! Discuss with students ways they might entertain each other's ideas respectfully, without acting dismissive or judgmental, and invite students to role-play their suggestions.

Resolving differences. While students may *receive* each other's ideas respectfully, that's no guarantee they'll *accept* them—and students may benefit from some conversation about how to negotiate and agree on which ideas to pursue. Review consensus-building strategies with students, and invite students' comments on strategies that have worked for them in other such situations.

Making the most of everyone's abilities. Model building can provide students with very rich collaborative experiences because such projects encompass a range of conceptual, communication, and mechanical skills. Encourage students not only to appreciate the different and individual ways that their classmates contribute, but also to actively elicit and acknowledge each other's strengths and contributions.

WAYS TO USE *Model Building*

ACTIVITIES

Geography and Topography. Three-dimensional maps—those time-honored creations of flour and salt—help students understand the relationship between conventional maps and the landscapes they represent. Don't limit these maps to geography lessons, though—students enjoy making them and retain the information involved in their creation, so use them throughout the curriculum. In addition to geography maps of states or countries, have students make history maps of explorers' expedition routes or the migration routes of peoples or animals, social studies maps of the community and environs, science maps of tectonic plates and seismological features, and so on.

Ecology and Technology. Model building is an interesting way to help students understand an important ecological principle: that people can use available materials and technologies to make what they need. Working in small groups, have students use materials they find around them to make utilitarian objects—an item of clothing, an umbrella, something in which to carry things, a toy, a musical instrument, a hairbrush, or the like. The students who built the Ohlone village, for example, had studied the diverse materials and styles used by different groups of Native Americans to build shelters and boats, and they followed this up by making their own boats from household materials—living the lesson that any community's technology depends on available materials.

Systems. Models help students see relationships between parts of a system as well as important principles and characteristics of systems. For example, relationships between the sun and earth, day and night, summer and winter, and so on become real when students construct a model solar system. Have students work in small groups to construct models of any of the many systems they encounter in their curriculum—the solar system, the food chain, systems of the human body, molecules, and so on. Use stuffed paper, papier-mâché, clay, Styrofoam, pipe cleaners, and other appropriate materials—in many instances, students might even combine model building and drama to create "living" models in which group members role-play different parts of the system!

Communities. Building a model community, such as the Ohlone village, can help students integrate what they know of the social, economic, and technological aspects of a community or culture. Have students build such models as the culmination of a unit of study, to make the most of (and further reinforce) learning they have acquired.

Games. Just as commercial games such as Life, Stratamatic Baseball, and The Oregon Trail are models of real or imaginary events, so might students enjoy creating their own games that incorporate their knowledge of social studies, science, math, PE, or literature. Depending upon your students' age and experience, they could venture into creating board, computer, card, or playground games. For example, students might invent a playground game about the food chain, in which some players are primary producers, some primary consumers, some secondary consumers, and some decomposers; a board game

≈ HINT ≈

For many students, games are synonymous with competition—so you may need to challenge groups to create games in which players cooperate to achieve their goal. Show students examples, such as Deep Sea Diving, one of the engaging cooperative board games created by Family Pastimes (29 Ingram Dr., Toronto, Ontario M6M 2L7).

might model the legislative process, in which players encounter obstacles and receive assistance while trying to get a bill through Congress; or another board game might position players as animals threatened with extinction, encountering both threats and assistance to their survival. Have groups teach their game to the rest of the class, and keep the games available during free-play times.

EXTENSIONS

Model-building activities can be extended in any of the following ways.

✱ **What Did We Learn?** Give students an opportunity to reflect on what they learned about the subject and about planning, designing, and constructing models. Ask open-ended questions such as What important ideas or information did you try to include in your model? How adequate was your original plan? What changes did you make? What problems did you encounter in constructing your model? What solutions did you try? What did you learn? Also let your observations of group work guide discussion of how students worked together, and elicit their observations about what went well and what problems and solutions groups experienced.

Trial Runs. If groups have created functional objects, bring the class together to test and discuss them: Are boats seaworthy? Do airplanes fly? Are toys engaging? Do bridges support weight? Focus the class discussions on what students can learn from each design—successful or not—rather than on competition between designs.

Game Day. After groups have created games that incorporate what they have been learning, hold a Game Day in which students teach their games to each other and to guests, such as buddies or parents—it will make an engaging and educational finale to a social studies or science unit.

Exposit. Have students write explanatory pieces to accompany their models—for example, to highlight important features of its design, explain how it works, describe the group planning and construction process, and so on (see the Expository blueprint on page 149).

Teacher Support Materials from Developmental Studies Center

Among Friends: Classrooms Where Caring and Learning Prevail

In classroom vignettes and conversations with teachers across the country, this 202-page book provides concrete ideas for building caring learning communities in elementary school classrooms. With a focus on how the ideas of the research-based Child Development Project (CDP) play out in practice, Australian educator Joan Dalton and CDP Program Director Marilyn Watson take us into classrooms where teachers make explicit how they promote children's intellectual, social, and ethical development simultaneously throughout the day and across the curriculum. A chapter on theory and research provides a coherent rationale for the approach teachers demonstrate.

At Home in Our Schools

The 136-page book focuses on schoolwide activities that help educators and parents create caring school communities. It includes ideas about leadership, step-by-step guidelines for 15 activities, and reproducible planning resources and suggestions for teachers. The 12-minute overview video is designed for use in staff meetings and PTO/parent gatherings to create support for a program of whole-school activities. The 48-page study guide structures a series of organizing meetings for teachers, parents, and administrators.

The Collegial Study Package includes the book, the overview video, and the study guide. (Also available separately.)

Blueprints for a Collaborative Classroom

This 192-page "how-to" collection of partner and small-group activities is organized into 25 categories that cover the waterfront—from a quick partner interview to a complex research project. Over 250 activity suggestions are included for all elementary grades, in such categories as Mind Mapping, Deciding, Partner Reading, Editing, and Investigating. In addition, Fly on the Wall vignettes offer insights from real classrooms.

Choosing Community: Classroom Strategies for Learning and Caring

In 9 videotaped presentations, author and lecturer Alfie Kohn describes pivotal choices that promote community and avoid coercion and competition in classrooms. A 64-page facilitator's guide for use in staff development accompanies the presentations, which include such topics as "The Case Against Competition," "The Consequences of 'Consequences,'" "The Trouble with Rewards," and "Beyond Praise and Grades." The package also includes Kohn's influential book *Punished by Rewards: The Trouble with Gold Stars, Incentive Plans, A's, Praise and Other Bribes.*

Homeside Activities (K–5)

Six separate collections of activities by grade level help teachers, parents, and children communicate. Each 128-page collection has an introductory overview, 18 reproducible take-home activities in both English and Spanish, and suggestions for teachers on integrating the activities into the life of the classroom. The 12-minute overview video is designed for use at parent gatherings and staff meetings as an introduction to a program of Homeside activities. The 48-page study guide structures a series of teacher meetings for collegial study.

The Collegial Study Package includes six books (one each grades K–5), the overview video, the study guide, and a 31-minute video visiting 3 classrooms and parents working at home with their children. (Also available separately.)

Number Power (Grades K–6)

Each 192-page teacher resource book offers 3 replacement units (8–12 lessons per unit) that foster students' mathematical and social development. Students collaboratively investigate problems, develop their number sense, enhance their mathematical reasoning and communication skills, and learn to work together effectively.

Reading, Thinking & Caring: Literature-Based Reading (Grades K–3)

A children's literature program to help students love to read, think deeply and critically, and care about how they treat themselves and others. Teaching units are available for over 80 classic, contemporary, and multicultural titles. Each 3- to 10-day unit includes a take-home activity in both English and Spanish to involve parents in their children's life at school. Also available are grade-level sets and accompanying trade books.

Reading for Real: Literature-Based Reading (Grades 4–8)

A literature-based program to engage the student's conscience while providing interesting and important reading, writing, speaking, and listening experiences. Teaching units are available for over 100 classic, contemporary, and multicultural titles, and each 1- to 3-week unit includes a take-home activity to involve parents in children's life at school. Also available are grade-level sets and accompanying trade books.

Reading for Real Collegial Study

Videotaped classroom vignettes illustrate key concepts and common stumbling blocks in facilitating literature-based classroom discussion. A 64-page study guide structures a series of 5 collegial study meetings that cover the following topics: "Reflecting and Setting Goals," "Responding to Students," "Handling Offensive Comments and Sensitive Topics," "Guiding Students' Partner Discussions," and "Assessing Student Progress."

That's My Buddy! Friendship and Learning across the Grades

The 140-page book is a practical guide for two buddy teachers or a whole staff. It draws on the experiences of teachers from DSC's Child Development Project schools across the country. The 12-minute overview video is designed for use at staff meetings to build interest in a schoolwide buddies program. The 48-page study guide structures a series of teacher meetings for collegial study and support once a buddies program is launched.

The Collegial Study Package includes the book, the overview video, and the study guide. (Also available separately.)

Ways We Want Our Class to Be: Class Meetings That Build Commitment to Kindness and Learning

The 116-page book describes how to use class meetings to build a caring classroom community and address the academic and social issues that arise in the daily life of the elementary school classroom. In addition to tips on getting started, ground rules, and facilitating the meetings, 14 guidelines for specific class meetings are included. The 20-minute overview video introduces 3 kinds of class meetings and visits a variety of classrooms in grades K–5/6. The 48-page study guide helps structure a series of teacher meetings for collegial study. In-depth video documentation shows 7 classrooms where students are involved in planning and decision making, checking in on learning and behavior, and problem solving.

The Collegial Study Package includes the book, the overview video, the study guide, and 99 minutes of video documenting 7 classrooms. (Also available separately.)